PROJECTIONS

PROJECTIONS

A Forum for Film-makers

edited by
John Boorman and
Walter Donohue

faber and faber
LONDON · BOSTON

First published in 1992
by Faber and Faber Limited
3 Queen Square London WC1N 3AU

Photoset by Intype, London
Printed in England by Clays Ltd, St Ives Plc

This collection © John Boorman and Walter Donohue, 1992
Copyright in individual chapters remains with the contributors

A CIP record for this book is available from the British Library
ISBN 0-571-16729-2

10 9 8 7 6 5 4 3

Contents

List of Illustrations

Acknowledgements

The editors and publishers thank the BBC for permission to reproduce the material used in 'Demme on Demme'. 'Losing Touch' was first published in *London Magazine* and then printed privately for Peter Jolliffe and Bob Castle. The lines from 'Luggala' by John Montague from *New Selected Poems*, ed. Peter Fallon and Dillon Johnston, Bloodaxe Books, are reprinted by permission.

Stills and other photographs appears by courtesy of BFI Stills, Posters and Designs; BBC London; BBC Scotland; New Line Cinema Corp.; New World Pictures; Paramount Pictures; United Artists; Universal Pictures; Orion Pictures; MGM; True Fiction Pictures. Photograph of John Boorman by Steve Pyke; of Gus Van Sant by Enzo Savino; of Hal Hartley by Rick Ludwig; of Michael Mann by Mike Connor; stills from *My Own Private Idaho* by Abigayle Tarsches; stills from *Surviving Desire* by Richard Ludwig; stills from *Last of the Mohicans* by Mike Connor are copyright of Twentieth-Century Fox Film Corporation. Thanks are also due to Bob Aaronson at Clein & White Marketing and Public Relations.

Fade In . . .
John Boorman

What is happening to the movies? As Hollywood crushes indigenous film cultures across the world, the major studios themselves are suffering from ruinous costs that threaten the very survival of the system. Hundred-million-dollar budgets abound, but hundred-million-dollar grosses do not. The majority of American movies are callously manipulative. They are contrived by marketing men using the mighty armoury of modern movie technique to arouse the baser emotions of a mass audience.

The state-supported cinemas of the former Communist bloc have collapsed. British film, which is in perpetual crisis, has sunk to new lows. Yet interest in seeing movies and hearing about them has seldom been greater. Despite all the problems and against all odds, some good films get made each year and keep alive our hopes for what could be.

As film approaches its centenary, what are its prospects? In the first twenty-five years, a new art, a universal language, sprang up fully formed. By the end of the First World War, the silent era had given us a flowering of great works – in Russia, America, Germany, France, even Britain. Such was cinema's penetration that within three years of starting to work in film, Chaplin was the most famous man the world had ever known. Motion pictures had taken the world by storm. *Citizen Kane*, now fifty years old, came at the halfway point. Where do we go from here?

Images proliferate. TV ads and music videos have plagiarized cinema; like marauding barbarians they have conquered classicism, overthrowing all rules and theory. Television and VCRs have miniaturized movies, diminishing their magic. New mega-systems like IMAX and Show-Scan have brought the magic back, but achieved no more than a toehold in the public imagination. So far, they are only the penny arcades of hyper-reality.

Film magazines are obsessed with budgets, grosses and gossip. The business of movies has become 'business'. Film people talk about the 'Business', the 'Industry'. A script is a 'property'. My contracts with the studios give them the right to 'exploit' my films in perpetuity. And we film-makers, when we talk to journalists and critics, are mostly promoting our 'product'. We lie a lot. Mendacity and marketing are like love and marriage.

Projections has come about so that film-makers may reflect on their concerns with as much honesty as they can muster and speak directly to fellow practitioners – as in the unguarded and penetrating interview between River Phoenix and Gus Van Sant during the shoot of their film *My Own Private Idaho*.

We plan to publish annually, making a series of snapshots of the year, reports from the war zone, but also speculating on and dreaming of what is to come. The spine of it will be a personal film journal kept over the year by a director or screenwriter or designer. This task has fallen to me in the first issue of *Projections*. I have written about films seen, colleagues talked to, a stillborn movie I failed to make, and another I hope to shoot soon. In next year's issue, Bertrand Tavernier will be the diarist.

My fellow editor, Walter Donohue, inspires many of the film books at Faber and Faber. His antennae reach out to the far corners of the world and he manages to identify exceptional work wherever it occurs. He introduced me to the brilliant work of the independent American Hal Hartley, and we print Hartley's new script, *Surviving Desire*, because its verbal felicities and wry, mordant humour give it a literary life and express the unique vision of its author.

Jonathan Demme is quite different – a movie buff who has tiptoed through the minefield of mainstream Hollywood with several movies exploding in his face, and yet maintaining a bemused good humour, before finally reaching the safe haven of a mega-hit with *Silence of the Lambs*. Each year *Projections* will include a substantial auto-cineography like 'Demme on Demme'. In contrast, the Michael Mann piece, instead of concentrating on the whole scope of a director's career, is an intensive study of a single film – in this case, *Last of the Mohicans*.

The celebrated cinematographer Nestor Almendros takes us on a journey through the landscape of the human face. I hope a cameraman will cast his light on us every year.

After the death of Emeric Pressburger, his grandson Kevin McDonald discovered a journal he had written of his time as a starving, aspiring screenwriter in the Berlin of the 1920s. It takes us back to the beginnings of movies once again. Also, as a way of acknowledging, and celebrating, our cinematic past, we have included Tony Harrison's tribute to the veteran Hollywood director George Cukor.

We sent out a questionnaire to directors throughout the world. We all struggle for the freedom to make our movies the way we want to. Yet how many of us could cope with absolute freedom, without the constraints of money, time and the need to sell tickets? Orson Welles, who once had it, said, 'The enemy of art is the absence of limitations.' The responses to this burning question are surprising and intriguing.

I started out by asking, 'What is happening to the movies?' I hope *Projections*, over the years, will help us find out.

John Boorman

1   Bright Dreams, Hard Knocks: A Journal for 1991
John Boorman

1 January

This journal is meant to record my observations about film in the coming year. Had I written it in 1990, it would have been something of a horror story.

In February 1990, my film *Where the Heart Is* opened disastrously in the States and, throughout the year, in other territories without much more success. I wrote a screenplay of Lindsay Clarke's novel, *The Chymical Wedding*, which so far has failed to find a taker among the Hollywood studios. My agent and other friends in Hollywood urged me to do a 'studio' picture, to get back in the mainstream, to make a hit, rather than go on trying to finance my own quirky projects. Sheepishly, I pointed out that *Where the Heart Is* had been my attempt to make a contemporary American movie. Somehow it mutated into a creature that was not quite mine and not quite theirs. As Disney chief Jeffrey Katzenberg put it when our horns were locked over the script, 'The trouble is, it's still a Boorman film. It's not a Disney film.' Afterwards, he thanked me for trying to accommodate their wishes and lamented, 'I guess, if you ask Hockney to paint a Renoir, however hard he tries, it will still come out looking like a Hockney.' I had to agree with him.

As 1990 wore on and *Chymical Wedding* looked more and more shaky, the pressure mounted. Richard Gere was making a picture for Warners called *Final Analysis*. He wanted me to direct it, and Warners were happy if he was.

I read the script. It was about a psychiatrist who falls in love with the sister of a patient. It turns out that the two sisters are conniving in a convoluted plot to involve the gullible doctor in providing a medical alibi for the older sister to get away with murdering her brutal husband. The script was a sly sleight of hand written by Wesley Strick. If you picked a hole in it, the whole thing unravelled, but it was intriguing. I set out to work on the script and wrote a new treatment in which I tried to make some sense of the plot and characters. I set the story in the context of a New York seen as an insane asylum.

Gere and Warners enthusiastically embraced my approach and a deal was struck. I went over to New York and visited some mental institutions in the amusing company of Dr Bob Berger, who was the model for the Gere character. These places were havens of tranquillity in the paranoia of Manhattan, partly because of the drugs dispensed, and partly because the inmates were safely out of the battle field.

In Los Angeles, Wesley Strick and I locked ourselves in a bungalow at the Beverly Hills Hotel and plotted out a new script. It began to feel good: a man caught in a nightmare, in a nightmare city.

I went back to my home in Ireland while Wesley wrote it up. We had worked it out in such detail that it took him only ten days. Warners read the script, and made a few comments, but their reaction was positive and enthusiastic.

Richard Gere had gone off to Japan to act for Kurosawa. The script was waiting for him when he got back. He hated it. Wesley and I asked him to be specific; maybe we could modify it. But he said, 'No, it's the whole tone of the piece that's wrong.' Gere was very pleasant about it. He said, 'You know exactly the film you want to make. Go ahead and do it with another actor. I'll step away.'

Warners, of course, given the success of *Pretty Woman*, wanted a Richard Gere movie. I went to LA and became marooned in a hotel room. Nobody at Warners would take my calls while they tried to make up their minds about what to do. As I languished there, my only sustenance was gossip coming from old friends at Warners. I discovered that Harold Becker had been engaged to direct *Final Analysis* before me, but Gere had not liked his version either, and he was canned.

Finally, I had a painful meeting with the head of Warners, Terry Semel, a man I have known for twenty years, going back to *Deliverance*. He agreed with Gere. My script was much too dark. He wanted it to be light and entertaining. They were aiming for the *Fatal Attraction* audience. Well, the two pictures shared the same initials. That was a start.

I went home. They engaged Phil Joanou to direct *Final Analysis* and poor Wesley Strick had to start all over again. I understand they now have a script that pleases Mr Gere. That more or less concluded my year.

26 January

The Academy voting papers arrived today. They list around 350 English-language films released in the United States in 1990 which are eligible for Oscars. I've ticked off the ones I've seen. About forty. Another 100 titles were familiar; I had been aware of their existence. So more than half the films released in the United States failed to impinge on my consciousness. Sadly, I expect my own contribution, *Where the Heart Is*, aroused only vague stirrings or sorrowful headshakes from Academy members: 'I didn't know Boorman made a picture last year,' or, 'Boorman really fell on his face this time.' So I join the phantom ranks of films that fail, our dismal shuffle to oblivion recorded in that list. Like the names on a war memorial, the Academy immortalizes our anonymity. When I recall the anguish and hopes poured into my film and then multiply it by, what?, 180 – what a deluge of disappointment. Yet a business that is obsessed with success needs failure to feed on. The Oscar ceremony, that annual blood-sport, deems that all but one shall fail. *Hope and Glory*, my previous effort, swept critics' awards in Britain and America, won a Golden Globe and sundry other trophies and was nominated for five Oscars; 100 million people witnessed my failure to win one.

At the dinner afterwards the bravest approached me with the awkward long faces people wear when they struggle to console the bereaved. Most of them shunned me in case failure was contagious.

That was failure at the summit. *Where the Heart Is* was a failure from the outset. It is dispiriting when your movie is both reviled by critics and spurned by the public. It did pick up a few passionate advocates along the way among both critics and public, and I was both delighted and astonished when it found its way into a few 'ten best' lists in the States and won the US National Critics award for best cinematography. However, its abject showing in the box office has dented my credit rating at the studios.

The rejection of my screenplay of *The Chymical Wedding* by all the likely studios in the States is not unconnected to that débâcle. British Screen has offered money and enthusiasm and Canale Plus is ready to put in some investment, although somewhat reluctantly. Perhaps I can find a way of financing it without the Americans.

I plan to shoot it in Ireland rather than England (where the novel is set), since here we can get tax-shelter investment which can contribute up to 15 per cent of the budget. While the British film industry suffers one of its worst declines, Ireland flourishes. You fall over film units here, and all because of this modest incentive. The net gain to the Irish Exchequer is prodigious.

European investors often make their involvement conditional on getting US distribution. Having done the rounds, my last hope was Orion, for whom, ten years ago, I made *Excalibur*. Last night I talked with Bill Bernstein, who now runs the company. He had read the script carefully and was able to quote scenes and discuss characters. He claimed to like it and understand it, yet feared that its themes were too removed from the American movie-goer's experience for it to find an audience. He was expressing politely what other studios had put more crudely – this is not an American movie. Americans are interested only in Americans. Go away. Yet we are so dependent on the American distributors that we cannot go away. We have to go back cap in hand and try again. Perhaps this will be different.

So far, the money I can raise falls just short of the very minimum I need to make the movie. It is so frustrating to be almost there, yet not quite. That last 10 per cent is always so elusive.

My interests and themes seem to get further away from those of the mass audience as I get older. For most of my career I have managed, by the skin of my teeth, to stay in the mainstream, usually by taking genre material and subverting it. *Point Blank*, for instance, was based on a pulp thriller that I tortured into an existential dreamscape. They are getting wary of me. Last year, Warners caught me at it with *Final Analysis*. They probably remembered ruefully how I had turned a sequel to *The Exorcist* into a metaphysical thriller that baffled its audience.

I feel at odds with the films that do succeed at present – *Pretty Woman* and *Home Alone* being the latest. These studio pictures have the unmistakable mark of the committee about them: schematic, contrived and manipulative.

In the 1970s, the studios believed in directors. They left it to us. When Michael Eisner and Jeffrey Katzenberg took over the flaccid and ailing Disney Studio they applied the methods they had learnt in television and had not been quite free to apply so ferociously in their earlier stint at Paramount. They set up stringent controls at all stages of film-making, particularly the scripting and casting. I experienced their rigorous regimen when I made *Where the Heart Is* for them. All the major studios have now adopted their methods, wresting control back from the film-makers. Now studios all have 'Creative Groups' which make detailed notes on each draft of the script so that anything illogical or quirky or irrational is rooted out at an early stage. The victim of this system is originality. Elements that cannot be recognized as familiar from past successful films are ruthlessly eliminated. The New Disney understood that audiences are bottle-fed and weaned on television. They determined to make movies which were enlarged versions of TV drama. They correctly concluded that movie audiences would respond to films that follow the rigid formulae so insistently applied by the networks.

The American movies I've seen recently that stay in mind are all genre films that in various ways transcend their familiar limitations. *Goodfellas* is a gangster movie. The script is relentless in demonstrating that the characters are without redeeming virtue – cruel, ruthless, unforgiving, brutal. It is Scorsese at his virtuoso best. The script may deplore these people but Marty's camera caresses them, celebrates them, dances attendance on them like the most sycophantic fan. This sets up an uneasy tension in the audience. When a movie is as well made as this, we are seduced. Our moral judgement collapses. We identify. But in *Goodfellas* it goes further, we 'become' these characters and commit their crimes. Marty makes us all gangsters.

Pauline Kael said *Goodfellas* was not a great film, it was a great documentary. Perhaps I am saying the same thing. It was not about what happens to gangster characters, it was about what it is like to be a gangster. Kael also said it was about 'getting high on being a guy'. Marty certainly gets high on making movies, and takes us up there with him. But he shamelessly lacks moral responsibility for what he does. Paul Schrader provided a stern Protestant conscience in the scripts he did for Scorsese. Marty, left to his own devices, treats plot, characters, moral issues as colours, as paint he slaps on his canvas with ebullient skill. That is why *The Last Temptation of Christ* faltered fatally. Marty just went limp when confronted with thorny theological issues. He got going only when he could hammer nails into hands and so forth. Conversely, his segment of *New York Stories* was some of his best work ever. Significantly, it was about a painter who frenetically slapped paint on to canvas: the irrational artist, paranoid, passionate, frantic and brilliant. Just like Marty, except he is not paranoid.

The profound unease we feel in identifying with an evil character in a movie is the recognition that we may be capable of such evil. Conversely, identifying with a hero elevates us, leads us to believe ourselves capable of sacrifice, honour and courage. So many actors when required to play bad guys cannot resist some coded plea to the audience for sympathy. My dear friend Lee Marvin never did, which is why his villains were so shocking. Lee knew from his war experiences the depth of our capacity for cruelty and evil. He had committed such deeds, had plumbed the depths and was prepared to recount what he had seen down there. What characterized his performances was an unflinching truth that was sometimes almost unbearable. He knew this stuff was hard to take. Also he had to live in the world, the Hollywood world. Just as alcohol offered him an escape from unbearable reality, so his other acting persona, the bumbling drunk, released him from his obligations to truth-telling. The two manifestations are perfectly paired in *Cat Ballou*, where he played the dual roles of deadly killer and hopeless drunk.

Point Blank became an inner portrait of Lee Marvin, a set of variations on his relationship with violence. We continued this journey into his psyche in *Hell in the Pacific*, which took him back into the Pacific War that he had fought (I always liked the contradiction in that phrase, Pacific War, and wish I had been allowed to use it as the film's title). It was to be a redemptive experience for him, finding his way towards an accommodation with Toshiro Mifune, the enemy. Yet it was an outcome he devoutly desired, rather than deeply felt.

Marvin was driven by the American *Zeitgeist*, so, although he came to love Mifune, he still wanted to kill him, which is how I should have ended the film. Lee's widow Pam is, at my insistent promptings, writing his biography. On my desk are her latest chapters. A fascinating picture emerges. He was a young boy when he witnessed and perpetrated the atrocities of war. His wounds never healed. They left him raw, and all life was salt that rubbed into

Lee Marvin in *Hell in the Pacific*

them. Here is a brief extract from Pam's book, an account of his wounding in his own words:

Phase 1
Saipan, Mariana Islands, June 1944

Fourth Day – Called up to replace K Company of 3rd Battalion, 24th Marines, as they had received heavy fire and casualties and had fallen back to their original cover. The assault platoon, 1st Plt., and 4th Plt. of I Co., 3rd Bt., 24th Marines would jump off from the same position, only in flanking positions, 1st to the left, 4th to the right. All positions are looking north. Meanwhile the 2nd and 3rd Platoons would push straight forward. At the signal we moved out. Mike Cairns and I were the 'point' of the assault platoon. Moving at a slow walk, we bore to the left and forward. There was nothing to be seen, the ground cover was thin and high, high brush with an occasional tree. The terrain was flat and slightly dish-shaped. All was quiet. We had just passed an abandoned thatched hut approaching a slight mound with three palm trees on it about thirty yards in front of us when suddenly there was a shot and a loud slap to the immediate left of me. It was Mike and he was down. He said a quiet 'Oh,' and then, 'Corpsman,' just as quietly. There was blood on his dungaree blouse. I went down to him and tore open his jacket, and there, just one inch below his left nipple, was a small dark hole. The blood was pink and bubbly, a lung shot. I tried to put my finger in the hole, but it would not fit. His eyes were closed and he said 'Corpsman' twice more in a whisper and was dead.

The high-sounding Jap machine-gun and rifle fire, then I heard Mac's voice, our platoon leader, shouting for all BAR men to stand and fire magazine. Mike's BAR was next to me. I picked it up and put twenty rounds into the brush at the base of the palm trees, but didn't see anything. Mac was shouting for me to pull over to the right and join the rest of the platoon. There was no way that I could get Mike's ammunition belt off him as it had shoulder straps, so I pulled the trigger group off his BAR and threw it away and, grabbing my MI, headed off low and fast where I thought the rest of the platoon were.

All was chaotic, shouting voices, the heavy sound of our weapons and the high, shrill, fast sound of theirs. I still could not see the Japs! They were close, for I could feel the blast of their weapons. Then I could see the 1st Platoon, they were all down, some firing forward, some on their backs and sides. 'Oh my God! They got us!' As I was running, the twigs and small branches were flying through the air as their machine guns were cutting everything down. I figured I had better get down too. And just in time. All the brush around me knee-high just disappeared. I looked forward and my leg flew to one side. I couldn't feel anything. 'This is getting bad.' Looking down my side, I saw that the heel had been shot off. Looking up again to see where it had come from, there was another crack and my face was numb and eyes full of dirt. It had a set-up of rhythm. I knew. Burying my face in the ground and gritting my teeth in anticipation, SLAPPP!!! The impact caused a reflex that lifted me off the ground. I lay still for a long time. I knew that I was hit. I shouted, 'I'm hit!', and a voice nearby said, very calmly, 'Shut up – we're all hit.' I was slowly tensing my various muscles. By the process of elimination, I figured it was somewhere below the chest. By then, Schidt and Pedagrew crawled up and told me I was hit in the ass and proceeded to dump some sulfa in the wound and said they would try to get me out of there and to follow them.

I disassembled my MI; my cartridge belt had already been cut off, so we began to crawl to the right. I could not believe the number of dead marines. I would recognize certain personal touches of equipment my friends had and there they were, lifeless. We got over to the 2nd Platoon area and they were as bad off as us. We started back towards our line. Now most of the fire was Jap. Where were our mortars and tanks? All at once we were stopped by an opening, completely with no cover, a fire lane about 20 feet wide. There was no way to get through there crawling. Schidt said, 'If we can get you up, can you run?' They did get me up and shoved me out into the cover on the other side, then crawled to a large-trunked tree, about 4 feet thick. Rose was sitting there with his back to the fire. He asked me if I wanted a cigarette and gave me one; he also offered me water. On returning the canteen to him, he leaned out a bit to put it away in its cover on his cartridge belt. He was hit immediately and fell over on me and died without a word. I could not get him off me. Then somebody stepped on my wound. I shouted. Fortunately, they were stretcher-bearers. Then Callelo was brought in; he had been hit in the head and was screaming that he could not see. They loaded him on the stretcher and at the same time they got hit again, killing one of the bearers. He was out of his head now. They got him out of there fast. I shouted, 'What about me?' They said I was next.

What frightened me now was that I would be lying face down on the stretcher about 1½ feet above the ground. Just the height their machine guns usually were set at. There was nothing I could do. I had to get out. The bearers were running as fast as they could, the fire was all around, then one of the front bearers went down, only a stumble, they got me back to Battalion aid, still under heavy fire. At Battalion, a guy, stripped to the waist with two nambu pistols stuck in his belt, asked me if I needed plasma but I didn't know. He gave me a surrette of morphine and had me put behind a long stack of 81mm morter HE shells. They were still in their clover leaves and I could hear the strays hitting them. All at once I noticed Schidt squatting by me and he was asking me for my .45 automatic, which I had in my shoulder holster. I had to give it to him, he had gotten me out of there. I told him it was my father's pistol and not to lose it. He thanked me and took off.

Just then somebody in the distance started shouting, 'Counter-attack, counter-attack,' and the panic of trying to get the wounded out of there began. I didn't even have my .45 any more. And by now my leg was totally useless. Then a terrific explosion, a big ammo dump about 100 yards away had gone up and I could see people floating through the air. A lot of confusion and I found myself in a stretcher jeep, two of us and two ambulatory, but we were going the wrong way, back to the fire fight. I shouted at the driver a number of times and finally he swung around and headed for the beach. I don't remember too much of the trip; we were about three or four miles in on the fourth day.

When the haze cleared, a corpsman was filling out a tag and attaching it to me with its wire. Then he took a red crayon and made a mark on my forehead saying that he had given me morphine. There was a lot of heavy stuff going off around us. I was under a torn canvas fly on the beach: equipment was stacked everywhere and it was getting dark. I asked him if there was any chance of getting off tonight and he said, 'No!' My heart sank. The Japs had the beach zeroed in and were pounding it. We would never make it through the night. Above all the noise, a voice from the water shouted, 'Anybody going out?' The corpsman hollered, 'How much room you got?'

The next time I awoke, I was listening to a diesel-engine throb. I knew we were passing ships but didn't much care. I was face down on a stretcher and was aware of much light, then a pair of shiny black shoes with white trousers. A lot of shouting, then I was in a bright companionway painted yellow with Glenn Miller's 'Moonlight Serenade' playing from somewhere. A nurse in white was reading my tag and asking if I wanted some ice water or ice-cream. I didn't know what to say. Some man's voice said, 'GU' and they took me away. Still on the stretcher, I was next to a low bunk with a thick mattress and white sheets on it. A voice asked if I could climb on to the bed. I said I'd get the sheets dirty, and the voice said, 'That's OK, we got more.' They cut the dog tag off my shoe and put it in my hand. I asked them not to take my helmet, and please turn off the lights. 'Don't worry.' In and out of focus for a while, then I heard it: from the island, the fire-fight was still going on. My company, what was left of it, was still there and I was safe on a hospital ship. Ice-cream, water, clean sheets, Glenn Miller, nurses. I was a coward! And cried.

Phase 2
Oahu, Hawaiian Territory, November 1944

Out on the south-west beaches of this beautiful island they had it all set up for us. Plenty of beer, good chow and even things like inner-tubes so that we could play in the surf if the fancy caught us. There was no schedule, except for eating and lights-out. A real rest camp. We were told that we would probably be here for three or four weeks, so enjoy it. After this, the doctors would examine us again and it would be back to duty or Stateside. There was a general uneasiness among all the men.

I had a lot of time to think about things, starting with the hospital ship, *Solace*, then three months at fleet 108 on Guadalcanal, Espirito Santos, New Caledonia, and finally Navy no. 10 at Aiea Heights. I had long ago arrived at the decision that I could not go back.

The days drifted by. But I was starting to have a recurring half-dream and half-fantasy. As 'taps' would sound each night, we would climb into our bunks and pull the mosquito netting down. There were eight of us to a paramedical tent with the sides rolled up as the nights were so balmy. Each evening, as I was drifting off to sleep, I would see figures slipping from one palm tree to the next. Very quietly and with caution, coming towards me. They were Japs! I would sit bolt up and stare at them and they would disappear. I would look around in the tent – all seemed secure – and peer under my bunk. My MI was there, but we had no ammo. We were in a rest camp in a rear area. It was 3,000 miles to the action, but we had slipped in on them at night. Why couldn't they do the same thing? By now I was fully awake and realized how foolish I had been, so I would change the subject of my thinking and fall off to sleep.

I got very comfortable with this fantasy, even anticipating it as I would go to bed. After all, how secure can a guy be? 'I will wake up and they will all disappear.' Then one night as I sat up to look at them, the loudest siren I have ever heard turned on. What?! Then the 90mms started up. It sounded as if the air-raid siren and the anti-aircraft guns were right in my tent. I leapt out of bed grabbing my rifle at the same time, landing on my knees on the plywood floor. There was a lot of shouting and screaming, lights were flashing and the 90s kept blasting away. I had my rifle clutched in my hands, but no ammunition! Caught again – I tried to stand up but my legs would not respond. Just immobile panic. I stayed like this for I don't know how long and then things began to slow down. The guns ceased firing and the siren wound down. I could see and hear men running and shouting, 'It's all right – it's all right – just a test – just a test.' The lights went on in the camp and in our tent. We were all in strange positions and just looked at each other. I don't think much was said. Slowly, we all crawled back into our cots and the lights went out again. I don't know. I don't know.

A lot of that experience found its way into *Point Blank*. Lee was hypersensitive to everything going on around him. He could walk into a room of people and feel all the pain. His mind was still on combat alert. Drink desensitized him, but he always carried America's guilt in his heart. He felt America was doomed because it was founded on the genocide of the Indian nations. He believed, therefore, that America could only express itself through violence. America was war, and he was a conscripted warrior. My camera held Lee at arm's length in *Point Blank*. It framed him in stark compositions. He was beyond human help, beyond redemption. The audience could feel compassion for his isolation, for a condemned man, but at a distance. A man, a nation, in violent and hopeless pursuit of their destiny.

I wonder if Marty Scorsese's obsession with American violence is connected with the same guilt that Lee bore? The same dread and love of it? Marty's camera flirts with his gangsters, sways around them like a nightclub stripper. He seduces us into falling in love with them. I was disgusted with myself for having such feelings. After half an hour I managed to pull myself together and from then on watched in detached admiration, rather than with emotional involvement. I saw *Goodfellas* at Mann's Chinese in Hollywood. The audience whooped and cheered at the violent moments, sharing the camera's exhilaration. But they also grew quieter as the movie progressed, perhaps affected as I was.

Miller's Crossing gave us a town comprised solely of gangsters, crooked cops, whores, treacherous bookmakers, cynical barmen. The gangsters smash each other's faces and blow each other's heads off after cheating and betraying one another. The dialogue is Damon Runyan out of Dashiel Hammett. The lighting and staging is elegiac, the acting is John Ford Irish. It is a potent mix. The Coen brothers have a genuine vision. They bring us a cinema which is distinctly their own. *Blood Simple, Raising Arizona* and *Miller's Crossing* are brilliant pastiches which have their origins in popular American culture. Through high style they rocket these simple stories into giddy orbit. They seem to be saying that only by keeping your feet in the mire of America can you dare poke your head in the sky.

David Lynch takes it further still. *Wild at Heart* and *Twin Peaks* both use high style to celebrate trash. Trash is all that is left, he seems to be saying, the last thing we are comfortable with. Trash seems to be the only meeting place of intellectual and public. We are steeped in garbage and only art can lift our snouts out of it. Hockney's obsession with the banality of Los Angeles is all about making art out of trash. Andy Warhol was perhaps the first to recognize the supremacy, the sovereignty of trash. And now trash art reigns.

The high style of Lynch and the Coens keeps us at a slight distance, while Scorsese's style sucks us in. Some movies draw us in, others keep us out. Hollywood wisdom is that the audience must have someone they can root for, but identification in the movies is more mysterious than that. We know it is safe to step inside Clint Eastwood and fire his gun. We have been there before. He is a pal. He will take care of us. Marvin, however, was always unpredictable, always taking us to the dangerous edge of truth.

Shortly before Michael Powell died, I dined with him and his wife Thelma Schoonmacher in Marty Scorsese's apartment on the seventieth-something floor of his building in Manhattan. Michael was wise and mischievous, as ever. Marty and I had, for some two years, been jointly prepared to produce a film that Michael was to direct. It transpired that the next day Michael was to speak to the film students at Columbia University. As it turned out it was to be his last public appearance. The students had earlier screened *Peeping Tom*.

'You've just seen the movie that ended my career,' he told them. The head of the film school made a long rambling introduction during which Michael stood patiently on the stage, his arms drooping at his side. His face was puffy, giving his skin a smooth baby-like look. He beamed his moon-smile over the students like a benediction while the Dean went on and on about how etched in his memory certain scenes from Powell's movies were: he asked Michael if he recalled the details of a particular review of one of his films. Michael paused in the disconcertingly blank way he had that made you fear that he had not understood, or that senility had finally claimed him. 'No, but I remember the film.' The students roared approval.

As he spoke of *Peeping Tom*, it became apparent that he was still perplexed and wounded by the brutal mauling he had received from the critics. Why had it aroused such anger, indeed fury? He looked over the upturned admiring faces. 'Can any of you tell me?' None could, or would. 'John, what do you think?' He called me to task and all eyes turned upon me.

I ventured an explanation. I said that in listening to Michael speak we had witnessed the way he could draw us instantly into an intimate relationship with him. He did this in his films. We identified with his characters in the deepest and easiest of manners. They quickly became our good friends. In *Peeping Tom* the central character was a brutal murderer played by a creepy, unsympathetic actor. Yet Michael's skill was such that he obliged us to identify with that character. I suggested that the critics who reviled the film were probably horrified to find themselves projected inside that character and killing those girls themselves. Since they could not accept that they were capable of such deeds, they transferred their guilt to Michael and blamed him for what they felt. What made it worse is that the camera becomes the murder weapon so that you feel it is the film-maker himself who is doing the killing. What did Eliot say? 'Every man wants, once in his life, to do a girl in.' Michael paid a heavy price for impaling those girls on his camera.

We want the movies to take us into forbidden places, and through the hero we wish to experience the unknowable, but it must still be make-believe, for, as Michael found, a terrible vengeance awaits the director whose skill and innocence takes us through the mirror and puts the movie into us, into our dark secret places where our dragons lurk, waiting to devour us.

31 January

As *Chymical Wedding* appears doomed, I am trying to detach myself from it. A decent period of mourning is necessary. I feel a sense of shame towards these characters left stranded on the page. The light falling on those scenes, so luminous in my mind's eye, is now extinguished. A 'chymical wedding' is the alchemical coming together of disparate, conflicting elements into a con-dition of harmony, be it the traditional opposites of sulphur and quicksilver, sun and moon or, at the highest level, man and woman. The novel is a fevered *tour de force*, a passionate plea for peace. Is there an accountant somewhere totting up the sum of human misery back to the beginning of time? The suffering inflicted on man by man seems to accumulate. It passes down the generations, lying dormant then erupting to seek redress and vengeance for past ills. This last year, which saw the end of the cold war and the unification of Germany, left a vacuum. Hostility and vengeance had lost their focus. They searched for a new home and landed in the Gulf. The Americans have unleashed their weapons of destruction with, not exactly glee, but a kind of relief, as though having them, with no prospect of using them, built up a massive craving, such as an addict might feel. The release of all those bombs and missiles was morphine to our psychic ache. Is war the natural condition of man? The whiff of war was in the air as I circulated *Chymical Wedding*. Sanctions were being applied against Iraq. The script was out of joint with the times.

How uncannily similar are the war scenes we watch on TV to the war movies of the last couple of years: spectacular weaponry, deadly missiles, war as a video game. They presage our need. They rehearse our craving. Rage and resentment have accumulated and have no outlet. The pressure builds and finally bursts out in a war from which nobody can gain. The letting of bad blood.

When Lindsay Clarke, the author of *The Chymical Wedding*, was here working with me on the script, I took him to Glendalough, the site of a sixth-century monastery near my house. We stood together beside St Kevin's cell, perched over the lake. I have stood there many times pondering on the mystery of what brought Kevin to this remote place and why disciples flocked to join him. Glendalough was almost certainly sacred to the Druids before he and Christianity usurped it. I always have the sense that power, great power, is flowing from that lake. It is a power without purpose. Perhaps St Kevin felt this too. His patient prayer was intended to funnel that power to good. Before the monks, the Druids were probably in these same places, drawing the power to their own ends. I have the sense that in our godless times that power is running wild, untended, undirected, bent on destruction. Is it fanciful to believe that there are places where man and earth can connect and interact? Lindsay Clarke was a man to whom I could dare advance these tentative thoughts.

Chymical Wedding has a lake as its central metaphor, circular, reflective, deep. Under it is the past, the surface the present, the future reflected in it. This last autumn the holly was thick with berries, beech trees richer in nuts · than I have ever seen. Indeed, every tree was heavy with fruit. Owners of orchards use a cruel technique. They tighten wire around their trees, cutting through the bark. The tree believes that it is dying and produces a massive quantity of fruit in order to ensure its perpetuation. Nature seemed to suspect that the last summer had come, or, at least, that great forces of destruction were abroad. I hope that the 13,000 native broadleaf trees I planted this winter as an act of faith in the future of the planet will, in a minute way, help divert the force to a more positive direction.

There was a report in the paper that David Lean had been taken ill a month before he was due to start shooting *Nostromo*. I called yesterday and a very careful man answered, took my message, but would not say where I could reach David. This morning David called back. Through a croaking voice the old spirit burned. I said, 'David, what is all this? You have to shoot your movie, I want to see it.' He said he'd been suffering from a sore throat and that it had turned out to be cancer. He told me he was having radiation treatment. He took heart from the fact that the insurance company had agreed to postpone the picture for nine weeks rather than cancel it. He was very moved at the calls he had received. 'I didn't know so many people cared about me,' he said. I promised to visit him in London. A few weeks before he had invited me to his wedding. At eighty-three he was starting out on his sixth marriage and his seventeenth film. He had a lot more left to do. The lives of great men are too short. I saw a quote from him recently in which he said he had no interest in naturalism any more. He wanted to make transcendent cinema. In his combination of image and emotion he has often done just that. There are no great movies, as there are no great lives, only great moments. But he dreamt, as we all do, of a movie made up entirely of those moments. And by anchoring himself to simple, even trite, stories he has often been able to achieve those transcendent moments without losing his mass audience.

He wrote me a fan letter when he saw *Point Blank* and he doesn't know that he saved that picture at one point. Bob Chartoff, the producer, and I were called up before Bob O'Brien, who was head of MGM at the time. He didn't like my script. We knew O'Brien was either going to cancel the picture or demand substantial changes or replace me if I proved intransigent. We listened as O'Brien listed the charges against us. The script was confused. It made no sense. Before we could respond, his phone rang. He answered it brusquely. Then an unctuous smile appeared on his face. It was David Lean, the darling of the studio. He was making *Dr Zhivago* at the time. All we heard from O'Brien was: 'Yes, David. Sure, David. That's great, David. Sure, go ahead, David. Anything you want, David.' I assume he had approved another thousand extras or whatever it was that David needed. O'Brien looked up, rather surprised to find us still sitting there. He had clearly forgotten the purpose of our visit. 'OK, guys,' he said, 'make a good picture.'

1 February, London

Despite the discouragement of some unfavourable reviews I went to see *The Comfort of Strangers*, because Paul Schrader is an interesting director. It was playing at the Curzon in London, an immensely successful cinema cherished for its luxurious seating and long runs. The audience does not conform to the general movie-going profile, being middle-class, middle-aged and intent on a dose of easily digested culture. A Curzon film must be 'artistic', but not too difficult. It should be set in romantic or exotic locales. *Room with a View* is perfect, but Tarkovsky would be much too demanding.

The Comfort of Strangers qualifies on a couple of counts – the lush Venetian locations, a cryptic Harold Pinter script and a touch of sexual impotence with which, one suspects, this audience might easily sympathize. Schrader usually writes his own scripts. Pattie Hearst and Mishima are among his subjects. He manages to find finance for serious subjects which he treats with uncompromising gravitas. So it is surprising to find him here in bed with Harold Pinter. Although Pinter rarely writes plays these days, his film scripts proliferate. Tom Stoppard does quite a few too, and, as with Pinter, they are mostly adaptations. Tom told me that it is like doing crossword puzzles. All the characters and clues are there – you simply fill in the words, once you solve the problems of where they should go. It certainly simplifies life for these great men. They are relieved from the pressure of competing against their own reputations. They are well paid, and, if it goes badly, the director takes the blame, very properly, since he also takes the large share of the credit.

So screenwriting is a friendly haven for playwrights. When a project is being set up, a Pinter or a Stoppard adds a cachet to the credits. Most scripts are not made at all, of course, in which case no harm is done. Tom wrote *The Romantic Englishwoman* for Fassbinder, and *The Russia House* for Fred Schelpsi. He rewrote *Brazil* (mainly doing an editing job on 400 pages of brilliant delirium written by Terry Gilliam) and *Empire of the Sun* for Spielberg.

Pinter had a successful collaboration with Joseph Losey – *The Servant*, *Accident* and *The Go-Between*. Losey's hard-edged compositions, his awareness of the malignancy of objects, his tight hold on the actors, provided a suitable architecture for the Pinter dialogue. The trap of a Pinter script is that actors and director in searching for the subtext discover far more than is good for them. The recent revival of *The Homecoming* reminds us of the dense power Pinter can press between the lines, the almost solid mass of menace that fills the stage. Those cryptic arrangements of words are combinations that open the unsafe places where we lock away our atavistic terror.

The Comfort of Stangers is taken from the Ian McEwan novel and Schrader presents us with a fractured narrative that intercuts a young couple (Rupert Everett and Natasha Richardson) strolling around Venice trying to rekindle their flagging passion, and an older pair (Helen Mirren and Christopher Walken) living in a *palazzo*. The latter pair, having exhausted their considerable repertoire of S&M, are on the look-out for another couple they can include in their games. The older man obsessively watches the beautiful younger man. That comes awfully close to *Death in Venice*, except that here, for the most part, we are with the watched rather than the watcher. Also Schrader, perhaps uncomfortably aware of the similarity, shuffles time and place, mystery veering into mystification. Chris Walken, playing the older man, tells a long story about his father no less than three times. It is a story that resolutely refuses to resonate. It succeeds only in affirming what the young couple say: that the older man is a bore. The story with its obsessive, repetitious detail could be an out-take from Pinter's unmade Proust screenplay.

Venice is just too much for the movies. *Death in Venice* may be the best novella ever written, but Mann did not have the overwhelming physical presence of Venice to deal with. However admired the film was, I think it sank even the great Visconti. Beautiful shot succeeded beautiful shot until you wanted to scream.

In *The Comfort of Strangers*, Venice came rushing in to fill Pinter's pauses and measured empty spaces like cream in a meringue. Bursting with romantic decay and marinated in centuries of decadence, Venice simply smothered the story to death. *The Comfort of Strangers* ends abruptly with Walken suddenly cutting Rupert Everett's throat, exactly the fate Donald Sutherland suffered not a stone's throw away and about twenty years earlier in Nic Roeg's *Don't Look Now*, which could quite appropriately have been called 'Death in Venice' as could *The Comfort of Strangers*, and as, come to that, could most other movies shot in that city. Nic's perverse eye saw right through Venice. He was never for a moment seduced by the old whore. He probed out the depravity and cut through to the death-core that many artists seek in Venice, but which few have the skill or nerve to confront.

I have been tempted to try to adapt Jeanette Winterson's wonderful Venice novel, *The Passion*. She herself, her agent tells me, believes it to be unfilmable. Perhaps she is shrewdly aware of how treacherous Venice can be to a film-maker. Her story is set in one of Venice's most delightfully decadent periods: after the conquest by Napoleon. It concerns the daughter of a boatman. She has webbed feet, as all Venetian fishermen are mythically said to have, conveniently allowing them to walk on water. The heroine dresses as a boy and works in the casino as a croupier. The novel has a dangerous haunting beauty, a story of corruption of innocence in which the girl's brutal husband is finally murdered in a gondola by the boy who loves her. And how? Why, he gets his throat cut, as usual. It would be expensive to make, the studios would recoil in horror and, even if I could get it financed, Venice would be lying in wait for me, seductive, treacherous, irresistible.

My dilemma was solved by this letter I received from Jeanette Winterson.

Dear John Boorman,

Thank you for your interest in *The Passion*. I am sensible of the quality and power of your work, in fact, its very consistency and individuality have made it easier for me to be certain that you are not the right director for my book.

I do not say this lightly or with any arrogance. I have given the matter a great deal of thought and been honest with myself so that I can be honest with you.

While I was watching all your films again over the last weeks, I have not found in myself the response I need to begin the commitment. That response, crucial for me, would have to be an unequivocal feeling that, whatever the outcome, I wanted you to make *The Passion*. I have not felt that. It would be wrong then, using reasons more practical and more obvious, to go any further. I know you will understand.

4 February

Gilles Jacob, who runs the Cannes Film Festival, has written to ask me to contribute a piece for a book to celebrate its fortieth anniversary. To mark the thirty-fifth anniversary they gave a special prize to certain directors whose films had won honours over the years. This is what I wrote:

Billy Wilder and I turned up early for the rehearsal of the ceremony. The woman organizing the event asked us anxiously if we would mind waiting. 'Do I mind waiting?' said Billy. 'All my life I'm waiting, that's what making movies is, waiting. I'm waiting for the money, waiting for the actors, waiting for the cameraman, waiting for the sun. In fifty years of making movies do you know how long the camera was running? Maybe two weeks.' On the night itself we were all huddled together backstage waiting to go on, alphabetically, Antonioni first, Billy Wilder last. 'I'm always last at these things,' he said, 'unless Fred Zinnemann is present.' Volker Schlorndorff looked around at the familiar faces and quoted *Casablanca*: 'Round up the usual suspects.' But many of us 'suspects' owed our reputations to Cannes. Satyajit Ray on that occasion described how a Palme d'Or had made his career in India possible. Many directors from the Communist bloc were shielded from the wrath of their rulers by the recognition their films received in Cannes. By celebrating cinema, the festival helps protect our fragile art. More than that, Cannes is very much like movie-making itself. A mixture of art and money, greed and generosity, sex, glamour, vulgarity, envy and compassion, high aspirations and low life. Who can resist such a mixture?

5 February

Wrenching myself away from *Chymical Wedding* I am looking around for an alternative. I have been revising *Broken Dream*, a script I wrote with Neil Jordan some twelve years ago. It is about the ending of our world and the possibility, through magic, of finding another. Reading it again it remains poignant and bizarre, and deeply poetic. Yet I know in my heart that no one will want to make it. It would cost more than *Chymical Wedding*. It is riddled with magical effects. If I am sensible I will forget the *Final Analysis* débâcle and attach myself to a genre story, a thriller, an adventure/drama or a horror story and try to weave my patterns around it. Sneak up on them again.

I am attracted to a bad novel with a brilliant title, *Punish Me with Kisses*, an erotic thriller. I have been turning it over in my mind. It concerns two sisters and their relationship with their father. It touches on incest. It has possibilities, yet it remains stubbornly earth-bound. It needs a mythic or poetic dimension, yet the characters and story are doggedly trapped in their sub-porn naturalism. Naturalism is anathema to me, yet it is all the studios really want. They don't want my bag of tricks. I feel like Merlin, an old wizard who finds himself living in a materialistic world where there is no place for magic. I am caught in the middle. Either I should make a mainstream movie or I should lower my sights and do low-budget personal films with TV backing. My sin in the past has been to make films on movie budgets.

9 February, London

I came to London to speak at EXPO '91, an international festival of student films. I was in conversation with Simon Relph who was my First Assistant on

Zardoz and subsequently became a producer, as his father was before him. During the last five years he has headed up British Screen. Most British films, made or unmade, have passed through his hands during that time. He probably knows more about the state of cinema in the country at present than anyone else. He says that everybody knows that if you want to make a film all you are likely to get is a bit from British Screen and a bit from Channel Four, so scriptwriters censor their ambitions. This results in the present ghetto of modesty (my phrase, not his), small films with small ambitions. David Lean never made a film in America and his work was firmly British, yet his epic scope seems impossibly removed from anything Simon Relph might have sponsored.

Since I was in London, I took the opportunity to visit David Lean. He was staying in the home of his new wife in South Kensington. There was a blizzard raging and London was coated in several inches of powder snow. His secretary, a male assistant and his driver were busy clearing a path from the front door to the car. They were working with exaggerated fervour. Devoted to David, helpless in the face of his cancer, they seized on a small task, something they could do, something that at least would smooth his way. The house is very feminine, even exotic, quite different from David's sturdy warehouse in the Docks with its ocean-liner interior. I found him sunk into a sofa in the company of cushions. The great frame had collapsed. He looked frail. His impaired speech made it hard to make out what he was saying, but as he spoke the old fire flared up.

He told me in detail the history of his cancer and described his radiation treatment. He said the tumour is regressing, responding well, and he had hopeful signals from the doctors. He told me of a dream he had had. 'It was more than a dream,' he said. 'It was so real, so sharply focused, almost a vision.' He dreamt that he woke up with the feeling that there was someone in the house. He went downstairs and there he sensed that this dread thing was in the basement. He walked down the dark stairs and opened the door. There was a burglar. He stood there with an insolent grin on his face and David said, 'I know who you are.' 'Who am I?' the man asked. 'You are cancer,' said David, 'and I'm going to beat you.'

We had the most sweet and intimate conversation. The urgent sounds of the city were muffled by the snow. We sat there snug and warm with all barriers breached. 'I was always so stupidly shy,' he said. 'We should have had lots of talks like this.'

David turned to his wife, Sandra, and told her how he had seen *Point Blank* and told Bob O'Brien that he should hang on to me (which he did not) and I related to them how David's opportune phone call to O'Brien had saved the picture from extinction or mutilation. Sandra brought in camomile tea. Through the window, powdery snow drifted down in slow motion. It felt as though we were inside the ice house in *Dr Zhivago*. His head suddenly dropped and Sandra called his name sharply. He woke up. 'Damn radiation. The other day I was giving an interview – to prove I was still alive – and I nodded off in the middle of it. The poor journalist had to sit there watching me sleep.' He laughed, then his eyes drifted off a little, not to sleep but towards the past. He looked up and said: 'I started out editing silent pictures, John. When sound came in, it slowed everything down. Soundtrack became a tyrant. Having to lace up and run track and picture together. Bloody cumbersome. You need a rhythm to edit well. So I used to learn the dialogue by heart and lip-read the actors. Didn't need the soundtrack then. So I could throw the film about with the old abandon.'

He said that all his best ideas had been irrational and intuitive and that he wished he had followed them with more conviction, wished he had defended them against the opposition of others. I suspect that it was the other side of David, the rational, meticulous side that had opposed them.

I was elected to deliver the eulogy when he was given a tribute at the Cannes Festival a couple of years back. A thousand pillars of the international film community sat down to dine and celebrate the great man. I had read his wonderful script of *The Bounty* which, alas, he never made. In my speech I suggested that the conflict between Captain Bligh, the rigid disciplinarian, and Mr Christian, the man of feeling who embraces the sybaritic life, represented the two sides of David. It is when those two elements are in creative conflict in his films that they are at their best.

The generous sponsors of the event had thoughtfully provided a charming old motor yacht – all mahogany and brass and teak decking – for the use of David and myself. They moored it off the Carlton Hotel pier. I had it all to myself since David refused to set foot on it. He said that he had spent so many miserable hours on Sam Spiegel's yacht that he had never been on one since, nor did he intend to. In his own speech that night he told how Spiegel had never paid him his share of the profits of *Lawrence of Arabia* and had cut twenty minutes out without his consent. (It was restored in the revived version that year.)

Sitting up there between David and Omar Sharif on the high table, mellowing after the speeches, I was astonished by an exchange between them. Omar said that the tragedy of his life had been that he always went with the women who wanted him, that he never had the courage to go after the women *he* admired. David said, 'Exactly the same with me. We missed love. Afraid of rejection.' Omar nodded sadly. Here were two of the most glamorous, the most married men in the world, and even they were afraid of beautiful women. Meanwhile the beautiful Sandra, David's fiancée, sat listening to this with the most indulgent of smiles.

It reminded me of something Burt Reynolds said when we were making

Deliverance. He was the number-one sex symbol for a while, and women were throwing themselves at him. He said it was all very well, but these women were always disappointed. They expected multi-transcendent orgasms, violins, earth movements. 'The problem is, I'm just a fumbler, like everybody else,' he said morosely.

Sandra came back into the room. David and I had allowed our talk to wander where it would as we sat in our silent winter cocoon. It was time for him to go the hospital. His loyal familiars had cleared his path to the car. I rose to leave. He looked up at me and said, 'Haven't we been lucky? They let us make movies.' I said, 'They tried to stop us.' His face lit up with a boyish grin. 'Yes, but we fooled them.'

I walked out into the snow. The wind had got up, swirling it about. London's insistent drabness was banished. My heart had been heavy since the loss of *Chymical Wedding*. Now it sang with David's brave words. I have been lucky too. But can I fool them any longer or have they found me out? And can he, David, fool the Grim Reaper?

22 February

Still trying to decide what to do. Now *Chymical Wedding* is gone, Jeff Berg, my agent, has resumed the script barrage from LA by Federal Express. That efficient network which can deliver any package anywhere in the world in twenty-four hours breaks down when it has to reach me. A fellow in nearby Bray with a dented old van covers all the courier services for the Wicklow mountains. He waits till a few scripts pile up before he comes up here. Eventually, they accumulate in my office. I pick them over, wasting time on them, yet feeling I should somehow stay in the game, not wishing to be left out, hoping against hope that finally a script will come that I can connect with. Yet in twenty-five years I have never found one. Why should I now?

I sat down in anger to have another try at *Punish Me with Kisses*. Two sisters, incest and murder. I made a new plot, sketched out some of the scenes, even tried to see it in terms of Greek myth, but, when my anger subsided, imagination petered out. It lies here before me, scratchings in a notebook. Outside, the snow has gone and rain is falling. The deer have got into one of my tree groves and stripped seventy young rowan trees. Hares have slashed some of the young larches. My mind turns more and more to the trees and the care of them. It is my gift to the planet but also, selfishly, a curtain of privacy for my old age, a shroud for my end. To end among trees, there's a fine thing. My tree man, Maírtín MacSiúrtáin, claims a great oak in its lifetime consumes no more than a cupful of nutrients. Everything else it needs to form its great bulk comes from air and water.

My eye keeps drifting over to the script of *Broken Dream*, which lies on my desk maturing like a good wine. I had looked at it the other day, done some revisions and put it away again. Of all enthusiasms that come and go, it is the only script that lives on in my mind, rounded and real, alive and alight. When we wrote it in 1979, no one wanted to back it. Too poetic and mystical, they said. I did *Excalibur* instead – against which the same accusations could be made (and were, in some quarters), but it had enough action and adventure to carry it past the sceptics. After each film I always go back to *Broken Dream*, rewrite it, then put it away, hoping for better times to come. It will be thought of as an art movie and yet it is expensive to make, with complex effects. I tried to write it smaller, but that didn't work. I tried to make it bigger, but that failed too. It is a chamber work that needs a Wagner orchestra.

Having finished this latest rewrite, I can't think who to approach. The French distributor Paul Rassam who has backed several of my pictures? Canale Plus? It's no good going to the Americans with this one.

Like a call from the past, a script came along some months ago that had been first submitted to me twenty years earlier. Martin Ransohoff exhumed it and sent it to me: Waldo Salt's version of *Don Quixote*. Ransohoff's idea was Sean Connery. I was unenthusiastic. Much as I admire Sean, I could not see him as Quixote. As it happened, Sean, as he so often does, changed his mind. Ransohoff had taken an option on the script and when Sean dropped out of it he was stuck. As I was casting around for a project I gave it some thought. Who would be a great Quixote? Mastroianni came to mind. Sancho Panza? How about Gerard Depardieu? It suddenly felt very exciting – two of the greatest actors of today. I put it to Jeff Berg. He spoke to Ransohoff, whose option had lapsed two weeks earlier. He scrambled to extend it and we are trying to put it together. It seems to excite everyone.

23 February

Sean Ryerson was my production manager on *Where the Heart Is*. He is a large Rabelaisian Canadian in love with Ireland. He came back with me after the picture and has been here ever since. He runs Merlin Films for me, a company we have formed to help people make Irish films. He is wildly enthusiastic about *Broken Dream*. It has encouraged me to send it out, tentatively.

We are lashed by gales, but this morning it was a balmy sunny morning. The land is littered with twigs and branches torn from the trees by the storm, and the river is fat and furious. I discovered that rabbits have destroyed even more of my trees. My mind has been as dull as the weather but with the sun warming the dead earth, the imagination also stirs. The BBC has asked me to make a documentary in a series they are doing called *The Director's Place*. I am making notes for a script. It should be about trees, the mature ones I inherited here and the young ones I am planting; it should include some of Maírtín's forest wisdom and sketches of my friends and neighbours, Garech Browne and Jeremy Williams; a tour of my sacred places, St Kevin's bed at Glendalough, the Hamilton Oakwood, my river. As I think about it, other ideas insinuate themselves: my inner landscape, the ghosts haunting this house; J. M. Synge, who wrote in this room where I now write; the Druids, the dark ages, the monks in the monastery up the way, the cruelty of man and nature, and the quest for harmony, for an end to that endless conflict. As these thoughts tumble out, I begin to sense a style of film that hardly yet exists, an intimate journey of images, music, words that would connect this landscape with my inner one. I suppose I am positing something close to the novel, internal and external interlaced. A flow of thought and image. But films should be poems, not novels. Film is about compression, leaving things out, subtext. Find the metaphor.

The power of *Broken Dream* is its central metaphor. The world is coming to an end. It is simply crumbling away. People are forgetting and whatever is forgotten is lost forever. Old Ben, the illusionist, discovers how to make objects disappear. He teaches it to his son, who perfects it. The old man then declares his intention to follow the objects to the place where they go. He obliges his son to send him across. Young Ben's lover, Nell, and indeed anyone who witnesses the crossing over, yearns to go too. It is a metaphor for all our endings, for death and the possibility of redemption and transcendence.

The BBC movie, springing as it does from my personal parthenon, lacks drama or metaphor. I think the drive must come from humour, that is the safest bet.

I am writing this as a refugee from the Gulf War. Sky News pumps it out twenty-four hours a day. The TV sits in the corner of the kitchen dominating our lives. I am in the drawing room. My three Ivon Hitchens paintings have finally arrived from London. There are two landscapes and a still life of poppies in a vase. His slashes of colour – dynamic, daring – seem to represent the inner life of the landscapes he paints. The compositions of colour, mass and form have a peculiar effect on me, calming the turmoil of that Gulf War. They are violent paintings, yet profoundly harmonious. They correspond to this inner landscape of mine that I want somehow to express in the BBC film. When I read a poem by Seamus Heaney or look at Hitchens, film seems so clumsy by comparison. Even a Tarkovsky film has moments of banality which a poet and a painter would expunge from his work. I am profoundly dissatisfied with movies. All movies are bad. Mine are often acutely embarrassing. They are mounting a retrospective of my work in Dublin in April to coincide with Dublin's tenure as European cultural city of the year. All I should do is apologize when I go up to accept my Waterford glass trophy from the President of Ireland, Mary Robinson.

25 February

I have sent *Broken Dream* to Jeremy Thomas. I spoke to him tonight. He is on his way to Toronto where he is producing *Naked Lunch* for David Cronenberg. He is a brave producer. I love his courage, and courage is what *Broken Dream* requires in buckets. After his triumph with *The Last Emperor*, his next collaboration with Bertolucci, *The Sheltering Sky*, was not so successful and his outing with Karel Reisz, *Everyone Wins*, was a financial disaster.

Meanwhile I wait. As Billy Wilder said, movie-making is mostly waiting.

So I am sketching out *The Director's Place*, the BBC film. Things to include: Mrs Curley, Bridget's laugh, river things, the heron, swimming, the new bridge, the plan to build a pagoda where the two rivers meet, extracts from *Excalibur* and *Zardoz* where they express the moods of the Wicklow mountains. Those mountains and this river must be the core of the film. Maybe that should be the title – 'Those Mountains, This River'.

2 March

The Dublin Film Festival is under way. It runs for a week and, like most festivals around the world, is also a sell-out. It was founded six years ago by Michael Dwyer, the film critic of the *Irish Times*. It has a permanent staff of one part-time woman. Dwyer is unpaid. He shows about fifty movies, almost all seen by him during the year's other festivals and screenings. He gets grants and sponsorship of about £70,000 which enables him to bring over directors and actors. He showed *Where the Heart Is* yesterday and I spoke afterwards. It was painful, opening those wounds, but the audience seemed warm and receptive. I had dinner later with Dwyer and Wilt Stillman, the young writer/ director of *Metropolitan*, the tale of a group of yuppie New Yorkers who at first seem execrable, but gradually attract our sympathy. It is elegant and poised and funny and made on a shoe-string. It expresses its story in a style that breaks the rigid plastic mould of American movies and is, therefore, refreshing. Given that, I was surprised to find him such a Hollywood-watcher, up-to-the-minute on gossip and anxious for advice on how to deal with the studios. He is shrewd and cautious and may well survive. Wisely, he is not falling into the arms of Hollywood after this success, but is doing another low-budget production called *Barcelona*, concerning two love affairs in that fine city and using two of his actors from *Metropolitan*.

I saw two films yesterday in the Festival, *White Palace* and *Bullet in the Head*. James Spader is a young Jewish wimp who falls for a tough old waitress played with brio by the glorious Susan Sarandon. The performances are excellent. It satirizes middle-class Jewish family life; the script works hard on quarrying the gritty gravel of truth from a modern relationship, but it is fatally rooted in naturalism. It carries all the baggage of a TV movie. It never flies, yet in TV and mainstream movies this is staple fare, it is the dominant style, and it is deeply depressing. What is still more depressing is that Sarandon's *tour de force* could be overlooked for an Oscar nomination in favour of Julia Roberts in *Pretty Woman*.

Bullet in the Head is a Hong Kong gangster opera by Johnny Woo. Over two hours of remorseless mayhem: balletic deaths, ingenious killings, delightful detonations, rivers of blood, acrobatic fights, all larded with treacly layers of sentimentality. The film is like Hong Kong itself, an explosion of vast energy, expertly made but childlike and innocent. Three young men in trouble with the police in Hong Kong and frustrated by its claustrophobic deprivations go to Vietnam during the war to get rich on drug dealing. There are marvellous moments, as when they are captured by the Vietcong and forced to shoot American prisoners. Occasionally it confronts real terror and throws up authentic responses to human degradation and cruelty, but it is mostly comicbook stuff. The Hong Kong section was a great success in the London Film Festival, and the audience last night revelled in the film. They were able to laugh at it and enjoy all its violence because it was at a convenient cultural remove. I was conscious of something else. These three sweet young Chinese guys exploding in an orgy of violence is surely suggestive of what may happen in Hong Kong itself, which is in turn a pressurized version of the Greater China.

Sean Ryerson was delighted by the film, exploding with mirth, gloating and gleeful. He is a gentle, kind man, yet he revels in the obscenities of *The Cook, the Thief, His Wife and Her Lover* and roars with delight at the brutal violence of *Wild at Heart*. It seems to me that there are two ways to express violence on the screen: to show it as fact and to explore its consequences as I tried to do in *Deliverance*, which is a sombre and harrowing experience for audiences, akin to suffering violence against oneself or loved ones; or to celebrate violence as spectacle. If this has a poetic dimension, whatever that is, it can have a kind of terrible beauty, it crosses into dream, it corresponds to images of the unconscious, making the atavistic connections that link us to our racial past. But the audience that roars its approval of a spectacular decapitation is probably responding as people did who attended executions. It is an outlet for frustration, it is about hate. It is to do with the repression of savage responses. It is a release of our deep-seated secret contempt for other people. There are too many people in the world and they jostle and crowd us and we would like to kill them. Greenaway's films are full of disgust for other people, and they touch a chord. Baudelaire said, 'When I hear laughter, I hear the roar of the wild beast.' That is what I hear in movie theatres, particularly in the United States.

5 March

I saw two films in the Festival which are nominated for the Academy Award
for best foreign film – the Chinese film, *Ju Dou*, by Zhang Yimou and the
Italian entry, *Open Door*, by Gianni Amelio. Together with *Cyrano de Bergerac*,
also short-listed, they offer a depth and scope which far surpasses the Oscar
nominees in the English language. There is so much emotional manipulation
at work in American cinema, that the absolute honesty of *Open Door* was
wonderfully refreshing. It is set in pre-war Fascist Italy. A civil servant
murders his boss, and then his own wife. He denounces the corruption of
Fascism and freely admits his guilt. Gian Maria Volonte plays a judge who
gently probes for the truth while the mob bays for the blood of what they are
convinced is a bestial killer. It is mostly a courtroom drama, but it is played
with such restraint and shot with such grace. One of the jurors is a farmer,
a peasant who inherited a great library from which he has gained the wisdom
to support the judge against the mob. The film makes no easy assumptions;
it is always aware of the complexities of human motives. It avoids triumphant
climaxes. Yet it is elegiac, even poetic. You feel absolutely connected to the
period and place (Palermo) and, most of all, utterly safe in the hands of the
director and engaged by his wisdom. Wisdom is a rare thing in a film. But,
more than that, the movie has a kind of poise. It speaks of a flattering
confidence that the director puts in his audience. The tone of the film reminds
me of the way men who have deep, compelling voices are able to take their
time, confident that the timbre of their speech will wash over us, hold us,
possess us. I am sure Amelio, the director, has one of those enviably deep,
soft voices that commands attention. I don't, so I tend to blurt out provocative
remarks, trying to grab attention, to shock, surprise, amaze, to conquer the
audience. I am always nervous that I will not be amusing enough to hold
them, and that results in a tendency to be over-assertive in my films.

9 March

The festival concluded with Neil Jordan's *The Miracle* and Woody Allen's
Alice.

The *Miracle* was shot in Neil's home town of Bray, a once-fashionable and
now seedy seaside town near Dublin. An adolescent boy with a drunken
father, brilliantly played by Donal McCann, falls for an older women who
visits the town. It turns out to be his mother. There is a circus in town. The
boy has a girlfriend who wants to be a writer and puts down her observations
in a notebook. Neil made it last summer. Philippe Rousselot, who shot *The
Emerald Forest* and *Hope and Glory* for me, was the cameraman and he stayed
with me during that time. There was enormous enthusiasm among a packed

Dublin audience, delighted with characters and places they could recognize. The movie is beautifully observed, full of sly wit and glancing humour. I was delighted to see the Neil that I knew and nurtured had made a film so true to his vision. Philippe's work is subtle and replete with atmosphere. I asked Philippe how he felt about the morality of making Bray look so much better than it really is. He said it would have been quite immoral to inflict its true ugliness on audiences. After the showing I was able to express my delight to Neil and he was equally delighted to receive it.

The Miracle was eclipsed, however, by the final film in the Festival, which I saw on the same evening, *Alice*. It is simply exhilarating. Neil told me that in the sneak previews in the States audiences did not respond to *The Miracle*, and *Alice* has failed miserably at the US box office. Coming in the wake of my own failure, it is sad that people are not interested in these movies – all of them very gentle films, if that means anything. It throws back in my face the question: Can I stay in the mainstream while being true to myself or has that always-strained relationship come to an end?

Depardieu, who has a reputation for doing every picture offered, has turned down the part of Sancho Panza. He said he felt he was Don Quixote, not Sancho Panza, and that he had already played Don Quixote in *Cyrano*. Paul Rassam has still not responded to the *Don Quixote* script. When I told him about the idea he was roused from his morose pessimism to express joyful enthusiasm, but I cannot get him to read the script. There is also a deafening silence from Jeremy Thomas on *Broken Dream*. The rains persist. Ireland can be very depressing in this weather. March is the harshest month, but this morning as I walked out with the dogs the trees were shrill with legions of birds. Frog-spawn is thick in the new ditches we have dug for the tree groves. The river is all but bursting its banks.

I write awaiting the arrival of John Hurt and his wife Jo for lunch. I wanted John to play one of the leads in *Chymical Wedding* and he has loyally called friends in the States urging them to put up money for the picture, but to no avail. I sometimes get the feeling that my life is over. My family is grown and gone, and I can't do the work I want to do. But I keep David Lean's remark in mind: 'Haven't we been lucky?'

11 March

Jeremy Thomas just called from Toronto from the *Naked Lunch* set. He liked *Broken Dream*, but put his finger on some of the problems. It is intimate, poetic, yet expensive to make. He felt it petered out at the end and was less than satisfied with the conclusion. He thought it should be more accessible and more like *Mad Max*. The problem is the script remains stubbornly itself, however hard one tries to change it. I was happy to get a positive response, but I am afraid I will not be able to satisfy him. He made no commitment. I spoke to Paul Rassam in New York. After three weeks he has still not read *Don Quixote*, so I drift on in this limbo of a wet Irish Monday. However, the daffodils and tulips are venturing out to take the place of the drooping snowdrops and the trees are a cacophony of bird song as the mating season begins.

Last night Desmond (The Shit) Mackey summoned his admirers to dinner at the Tree of Idleness in Bray. This legendary Dublin character was knocked down four years ago by a car on New Year's Eve. He has been unable to walk since. He is nearly eighty and to our amazement he can now walk with sticks. Gerry Hanley, the novelist, was there, John Hurt, Garech Browne and Noel Person. The fate of *The Field* has brought Noel down to earth a bit after the euphoria of *My Left Foot*. His Oscar successes have made him a hero in Ireland. *My Left Foot* was his first film as a producer. Until then he was a Dublin theatre impresario and chairman of the Abbey Theatre.

We all swapped stories about how we and others had been charmed out of various sums of money by Desmond Mackey. In *Where the Heart Is* I have a character called The Shit, played by Christopher Plummer, which is based loosely on the original. The Shit Mackey is threatening to sue me, claiming that he is the one and only genuine Shit. I used an exchange in the film that originated in a famous moment when The Shit said to Garech Browne, who had inadvertently called him by his nickname in public, 'At least I'm *the* Shit. You're just *a* shit.'

Noel told a story about how The Shit was holding court in a Dublin pub just after the war when a drunken American soldier interrupted the flow of his oratory by claiming to be Gloria Swanson's fourth husband. 'Jaysus,' said The Shit, 'if you couldn't get into the first three, I wouldn't brag about it.'

I must find a way of getting The Shit into my BBC film.

Talking with Noel about Jim Sheridan reminds me that during the Dublin Film Festival Jim and I conducted a seminar on screenwriting together with the playwright Frank McGuinness. The theatre was packed. Everyone in Ireland wants to make movies. When Stephen Roach won the Tour de France they all took to bicycles. After the success of U2 everyone formed a rock band. When Ireland got into the finals of the soccer World Cup, the country went football crazy. Since *My Left Foot* they are all mad to make movies. The familiar cry went up. The same whining plea I've heard here and in England for twenty years: 'When will Ireland have a proper film industry?' Jim answered: 'Ireland doesn't have any other industry, why should it have a film industry?' They all wanted to know what kind of stuff they should write which would interest Hollywood, and how to prevent their brilliant ideas from being stolen. Jim said Irish plays were always about people waiting for something that never happens, whereas American stories are about characters making things happen. Frank said that modern Irish theatre had been heavily influenced by movies, that they were plays trying to be movies. I agreed.

I first came across Sheridan's work when he was running the Project Theatre. I thought his style very cinematic and encouraged him to write for the movies. I tried to guide and advise him for the next ten years and I was delighted by his success with *My Left Foot*. Oddly, although his theatre work was cinematic, his film work has, so far, been a little theatrical. But he has such a vivid, tensile mind and such an enviable ability to connect with people at all levels that he has a good chance of staying the course. Jim said the only stories worth doing were ones that try to make sense of your own life. He is currently writing a script based on the period he spent in abject poverty in New York running an Irish theatre company.

He and Noel have a rich development deal with Universal, but I doubt if that studio will go for Jim's kind of story. I was tempted to tell that to Jim, to save him the trouble, but I bit my tongue. Maybe I'm wrong. I hope so.

There were more than a dozen of us, The Shit's friends and admirers, and he had entertained us royally at the Tree of Idleness, a restaurant aptly named for an occasion celebrating The Shit's life. We began to worry about how he would pay the bill. His income during the past four years had mainly derived from bank loans shakily secured by his upcoming litigation against various insurance companies. Noel, Garech and I got together and quietly paid the bill between us. It was only afterwards that we discovered that John Hurt and others had made cash contributions direct to The Shit. Having invited us all to dinner, he came out with a handsome profit. He didn't earn his proud sobriquet for nothing.

23 April

Although Dublin is the European City of Culture this year there has been scant sign of any burgeoning of imagination or flowering of art. The most notorious event has been a savage attack in the *Irish Times* on Seamus Heaney's reputation by one Desmond Fennel, who has published a pamphlet called *Whatever You Say, Say Nothing*. Seamus has always been immensely generous to fellow writers and poets but as someone once said, 'In Ireland no good deed goes unpunished.' An acquaintance of mine suggested they should raise a statue in Ireland to the Unknown Begrudger, and they should raise one in England too. David Lean died. I was disgusted at how mean-spirited many of the obituaries were.

Philip Molloy, a film buff, and news editor of the *Irish Independent*, was determined to organize a tribute to me and my films as part of the cultural celebrations. Despite my reluctance, and in the absence of any official support, he rounded up sponsors and bullied the film distributors who own my films and succeeded in mounting a week of screenings. I had deposited the personal copies of my films in the National Film Archive in London on the understanding that I could take them out whenever I wished. This was the first time I had asked to borrow them. The nature of archivists is to collect and hoard and hang on to what they have. One of my campaigns as a governor of the BFI has been to press for an accessible archive. They always complain that they have no money or resources to make prints to be seen, that they must devote all their cash to preserving films for posterity. But when does posterity start? I soon discovered that it is a lot easier to put films into the Archive than to get them out. I wanted to examine one film for fading. They informed me that no viewing facilities would be available for at least three weeks and, in any case, they would not be able to find and ship my films in time for the tribute. What is more, they required written confirmation that the distributors were agreeable to the screenings. I said we had spoken to them all and they had readily agreed. My word was not enough. 'They are my films,' I screamed. I do not intend sending them back after the tribute. I shall buy a dehumidifier and store them myself.

There was a week of screenings climaxing with a dinner in the Great Hall of Trinity presided over by the President of Ireland, Mary Robinson. A number of people associated with my films turned up. Bob Chartoff spoke, acknowledging that in *Point Blank* he had given me a lousy script from which I had somehow made a great movie and that this had launched his own career as a producer. Michel Ciment, author of a book on my work, made a witty and perceptive speech and Bertrand Tavernier was wonderfully generous.

Mary Robinson got up to speak. Her brilliant campaign for the presidency advocated liberal policies that have been anathema to Catholic Ireland in the past. With only a 10 per cent political base she swept to victory, breaking forever the rigid mould of tribal Irish politics. In her speech she described how she had seen *Leo the Last* in Paris in 1970 and had met me shortly thereafter. Since then she has loyally supported all my films. She presented me with a large Waterford glass bowl. As I stood up to speak holding this object, a memory flashed into my mind of a scene from Hugh Leonard's play *Da*. A friend brings a similar bowl as a wedding present to the son, who is as puzzled as I as to its use. The friend says it can be used for floating roses in. 'Ask your Da,' he says, 'he's a gardener.' The Da growls back: 'I grow them, I don't teach the buggers to swim.' My story was not entirely inappropriate since Hugh Leonard had written a generous appreciation of my films in the programme of the tribute. I was also required to contribute a piece which I reproduce here.

A Foreign Language

Water looks wonderful on film and there is a lot of it in my movies; rain, oceans, lakes, rivers, especially rivers. *Hope and Glory* was about my early life, London in the Blitz and then a childhood touched by magic at Shepperton on the Thames. That turgid old Thames, tamed by locks and weirs and hemmed in by embankments, is still, in my memory, a wild and primal place and throughout my life at bad moments I could always close my eyes and watch the sun of my childhood days play on its waters and be consoled.

I sought out and found a river in the American South that was as wild as my memory-Thames and made a movie on it, *Deliverance*. The Chatooga runs through angry shoals and down stomach-churning rapids. That river too flows in my mind, a nightmare version of the dream Thames.

Finding a landscape to fit the film has always been vital to me. I scoured the South Pacific until I discovered the Palauan archipelago with its eroded mushroom-shaped islands, an alien-scape for a war story removed from war and reduced to a conflict between two warriors – American and Japanese – in a setting that suggested the world before men were upon it.

The Emerald Forest brought me to the ultimate river, the Amazon. It drains 40 per cent of the world's rainfall, it is 70 miles wide at its mouth, and thrusts fresh water 80 miles out to sea. I went out to the middle of that river mouth and swam in it and felt its power. If there is a centre of the planet, that was it for me.

Seeing the films of Michael Powell in my youth, particularly his use of fantasy, gave me an insight into what cinema could be. I have always felt close to him and was privileged to know him. I felt closer still when he began his autobiography with this: 'All my life I have loved running water. One of my passions is to follow a river downstream through pools and rapids, lakes, twists and turnings, until it reaches the sea. Today that sea lies before me, in plain view, and it is time to make a start on the story of my life, to remount it to its source, before I swim out, leaving behind the land I love so much, into the grey, limitless ocean.'

This tribute has set me thinking. Around the next bend in the river there has always been another movie waiting to be made, but the open sea gets ever closer.

I came to Ireland and found the Wicklow mountains awaiting me, a landscape that perfectly coincided with an inner spiritual landscape. For the last twenty-two years it has been my home.

The Arthurian legend has been the abiding myth that has shaped many of my films – most, in fact. Having found the landscape I was finally able to address the story directly and I made *Excalibur* on locations mostly within 10 miles of my house. Lough Tay at Luggala is a special place of mystery and beauty and in the film it became the setting of Camelot. It also featured in my film *Zardoz*, another Arthurian surrogate. The bogs of Sally Gap served as the Wasteland. Folded into the river valleys of the Wicklow mountains are fragments of primal oak forests that I have filmed and walked among all these years.

The mountain waters of Sally Gap flow into Lough Tay and pause at Lough Dan before passing in front of my house at Annamoe. I have recently thrown a sword-bridge across that river to give access to land on which I have planted 13,000 native broadleaf trees. I can watch them growing from the window where I work on the scripts of the several films I still hope to make.

Film is a foreign language. It is easy to understand, but hard to speak. However clear your vision, when you make a film, you grope and fumble. I used to imagine that the great masters knew exactly what they were doing all the time. *8½* blew the whistle on that. Fellini showed that it is only by groping blindly towards an undefined goal that a good movie can come into being.

I went to visit Sir David Lean recently. He had fallen sick just four weeks before he was due to start shooting *Nostromo* and he was feeling frustrated. He is eighty-three. He said he wanted to go on making movies because he felt he was just beginning to get the hang of it. When I look back over the films I have made, I feel the same way. I think I am beginning to know how to do it.

Meanwhile, time goes by. So much is wasted in abortive attempts to get projects financed. So many ideas fail to get support and are set aside. Most directors these days spend more time on movies they don't make than on ones they do. And the river flows on. Travelling up through the Amazon and its tributaries, with the jungle pressing in on all sides, I always felt the presence of a great mystery, and that each new turn in the river might reveal it. I have the same sense of anticipation each time I look through the camera lens, each time the lights go down in the cinema, that same flutter of excitement, that this time, at last, all will be revealed.

I once had a dream that I had made the ultimate movie. I was showing it to a preview audience. As it ended the crowd leapt to its feet cheering, weeping, laughing. Then I saw that one man was still in his seat, shaking his head sceptically. I went over to him and saw that he had my face. He said, 'Aren't you ashamed of yourself?'

The house was full of friends during the week and entertaining them was exhausting, more so than the lectures, seminars and speeches that Philip Molloy had talked me into doing. We got new prints of *Point Blank*, *Deliverance* and *Hell in the Pacific*. I had not seen them for many years. I was surprised by their force. There is an intensity about my work which often makes it painful to watch, but which also gives the films an integrity. There is also a silliness which crops up with irritating frequency. I recognize this in my character. It is an English silliness. There are moments of it in every movie, and they make me cringe. It comes from a fear of being serious, of embarrassment, of a lack of belief in self, of not being rooted in a strong cultural tradition. Englishness is almost entirely negative as an identity. You are not Scots, Welsh or Irish. You are the mish-mash in the middle. The film that had its fair share of silliness, but which had the greatest impact on me and others at the screenings, was *Excalibur*. I had forgotten the powerful effect of compressing and telescoping the entire legend into two hours and twenty minutes. The movie verges on critical mass. It gives the impression that it might combust at any point from sheer density. Its underlying system of symbols somehow holds it together so that it exists as a kind of spiritual ritual as well as a mythic movie. It is dangerously portentous, but Nicol Williamson's Merlin thankfully undercuts that.

When I look at this work I have done I feel a stranger to myself. The man who made these movies is someone I hardly recognize. I felt a fraud claiming authorship. I have been addressing this strangeness of my work and the strangeness of myself in writing the BBC film. Perhaps Jim Sheridan is right and it will help to make some sense of my life. My films have become more personal in recent years, but perhaps not sufficiently so. Perhaps *Where the Heart Is* was a failure because my daughter Telsche and I, in writing about our experience of family, discovered so many no-go areas that the film finally took refuge in farce and evaded the real emotional issues. *Hope and Glory* evaded the dark side of my childhood. I omitted the acute fear of my father which dominated my early life and translated into a lifelong fear of authority. My secretiveness and mendacity all come from that fear. Yet in the film I portray my father as the figure of fun that he only became when I had outgrown my fear of him. Although it seems obvious, I never understood that my obsession with the Arthurian story with its central triangle of Arthur, Guinevere and Lancelot reflected my mother's love for my father's best friend. I saw this only when I had completed *Hope and Glory* and saw it with an audience, saw it with their eyes, finally able to detach myself from it. So it is that little by little we unravel our own mystery. Why did I evade the dark side? I suppose I felt I had to be entertaining and funny and that those murky areas are best left unexplored. A family trait. Look on the bright side. My mother's way.

So now I am going to make a film directly about myself. I will be in it, acting myself. In recognition of my limitations as an actor (not as an evasion this time) I have written in an alter ego for myself, to be played by John Hurt. He will act out the mystical and imaginative scenes. For although it is commissioned as a documentary, Merlin, the Green Man and the Lady of Lake have intruded themselves and the thing is gradually becoming dramatized. I am seeking to show the various ways in which I relate to my chosen landscape. John Archer of BBC Scotland proposed this project more than a year ago. It set me thinking. Inevitably, since I am so passionately involved in planting trees my thoughts turn to them, to my immediate landscape, the land I husband. Then I move outwards to the Wicklow mountains that I have grown to love deeply over the last twenty years. Why does one connect so passionately to a particular configuration of landscape? The film explores this question. In this first draft, at least, I am more perplexed at the end than when I set out, but, curiously, more emerges about my relationship with film than with landscape. I suggest that being uncomfortable in my own skin, feeling the world to be an alien place, I have sought out actors, surrogates, to send out into worlds of my invention.

Making movies is hard enough, yet I seem to be intent on making the process as hard as possible, insisting on controlling everything – writing, producing, directing – and always taking the hardest road. Why am I so set on punishing myself? Why do I feel guilty if I find I am enjoying my work? When I make a picture I seem to be several people, all at war with each other. The writer's unfettered imagination irresponsibly puts down scenes that are impossible to shoot. By dint of prodigious hard work and invention, the director not only solves these problems but sets new impossible targets, threatening to plunge the film over budget and lurch out of control. In steps the producer, who ruthlessly cuts back the ambitions of director and writer. And when I am editing I am someone else again, cleaning up the mess made by the other three.

Acting myself, putting my own face on the screen, a face which I find ridiculous and self-conscious, is something that I fear and dread. I don't know why I'm doing this, except that I have the feeling that the only way I can confront myself with honesty is on film. When I look at myself with a director's eye, an editor's eye, only then will I know something of myself.

16 May

En route to Los Angeles.

Went last night with Matthew Evans and Caroline Michel to see *Ai No Corrida* (*In the Realm of the Senses*). I saw it in America when it first came out. It was banned in the UK and has only now been given a certificate. The second time round it had the same deeply disturbing effect as before. Why should it be so compelling? In most movies the sex scenes stop the action and one simply waits for them to be over so that the story can continue. Here is a film that consists entirely of sex scenes yet, astonishingly, they not only progress the action, but tell the story and illuminate the characters. The film is beautifully constructed and acted. The colours and compositions, the positioning of the camera are all perfectly balanced and controlled. As the film ventures into this forbidden and dangerous territory you know yourself to be in safe hands. The continuous scenes of sexual congress make the fucking in most movies seem as fake and absurd as they mostly are. A kind of ritual grammar has emerged for sex in movies in which the man displays his virtuoso athleticism while the women are all multi-orgasmic. In *Ai No Corrida* the fucking is actually taking place. We see the penis entering the vagina. And although most movie sex is acutely embarrassing, this is not so at all. On the face of it, it is a story of obsessive passion. It explores the relationship between sex and death. But what is passion? It is surely the *becoming* of a person. Are we not, for most of our lives, marking time? Most of our being is at rest, unlived. In passion, the body and the spirit seek expression outside of self. Passion is all that is *other* from self. Sex is only interesting when it releases passion. The more extreme and the more expressed that passion is, the more unbearable does life seem without it. It reminds us that if passion dies or is denied, we are partly dead and that soon, come what may, we will be wholly so.

The kimonos are important; the sensual way Oshima arranges the bodies

in the kimonos is magisterial. They make superb compositions that connect
with Japanese erotic paintings. The Woman is, from the beginning, over-
wrought. She is hypersensitive and her orgasms are intense but painful. The
Man forces ecstasy through her pain. All sensation has extremes of pleasure
and pain. Pain sharpens the sensibilities, just as extreme pain dulls it. Pain
is the absolute way of affirming life. Pleasure is its companion. When they
come together through passion they confirm the fullness of that person's
aliveness. The film poses the question: if those moments of sublime pleasure
can be extended, prolonged, even made a permanent condition, why not? A
path of ecstasy leading to death is surely to be preferred to a long gradual
deadening and dying. It is a mark of the success of the film that a packed
audience sat silent and still throughout. Of course, cries of horror and disgust
went up when the Woman cuts off her lover's genitals, and Oshima shows
that unflinchingly too. As you emerge, you feel you have witnessed something
true, an event at the very centre of the human experience, a reminder that at
the limits of pain, of passion and pleasure, lies death. As we went off to
dinner with Caroline and Matthew, we all felt rather ashamed of our mild
passions and it took some good wine to regain our seats among the gods . . .

    . . . and now here I am jammed into a centre seat of a packed 747. The
man next to me is trying to read what I am writing, so I am hunched over
my notebook. I feel far removed from the lofty passions of last night. All you
can do on these long-haul flights is to put your life on hold, forgo your
humanity and accept your sardineness. At least I can write up my notes of
recent events.

    Even though when I visited David Lean a few weeks ago he was already
dying, the actuality of death never loses its power to shock. He was a few
weeks away from shooting *Nostromo* and part of me, the wishful dreamer,
believed he could make it. I thought again of how we had sat alone that winter
afternoon in London, as big, fluffy, phoney-looking snowflakes fell in slow
motion outside the window, and we had talked with such a sweet intensity
and gentleness. I often think of that dream he related to me of the burglar
in the basement. He dreamt he woke up. Those are the most frightening of
dreams, because you are convinced you are not dreaming. I have made that
the opening line of my documentary, and perhaps its title, 'I Dreamt I Woke
Up'.

    Another friend died recently, Bill Stair. He was a painter, a writer, but
most of all a frantic, comic chronicler of his own desperate life. I took him
with me to Los Angeles when I made *Point Blank*. He worked on the designs
and I kept him at my side in that alien place. His familiar personal insanity
somehow protected me from the wider, blander insanity of that crazed mega-
lopolis. Later, we wrote *Leo the Last* together. Bill was a paid-up lifelong
paranoiac. Extensive analysis made him aware of that, but in no way amelior-

ated his conviction that we were all out to get him, and he lived his life in a state of acute anxiety. When I first knew him in my BBC days in Bristol, he was teaching at a comprehensive school. He became persuaded that the headmaster, his fellow teachers, his wife and parents were all conspiring to have him committed to an asylum. He conceived a plan to thwart them. He took the bus to the mental hospital and presented himself at the door. He told them he was giving himself up, that he knew they were all trying to get him inside so here he was: 'Take me.' When they refused him entry, he was shattered. The imagined conspiracy had become the sustaining centre of his life and, without it to struggle against, he collapsed into a mental condition that did seem to warrant his family and colleagues committing him. When they attempted to do so it reaffirmed his conspiracy theory and he quickly recovered his equilibrium.

Bill was also endlessly on the look-out for signs of a fatal disease. He wove all his horrors into maniacally funny monologues. He was that rarest of creatures, an entertaining neurotic. His mind spun wildly. It was out of control. He always reminded me of a balloon that you inflate and then let go, and it farts off around the room in all directions. His ideas and images were like that. Many of them were spurious, some were wonderful. If he was given responsibilities his mind froze. As a freewheeling free spirit, as a child in a playschool with life as his toys, he was brilliantly inventive. More than anything else he wanted to design a movie. I gave him the job on *Zardoz*. No sooner did he assume that responsibility than he seized up. He sat rigidly with a notebook on his lap and wrote down whatever I said, but became incapable of contributing. His eyes were wild with panic. He was staying with me in Ireland. In the night a scream of pain rang through the silent house. In his sleep Bill had scratched his eyeballs. They were bleeding. Thankfully the cuts were superficial, but his eyes had to be bandaged. He could not continue as designer. Tony Pratt took over. The moment Bill was relieved of responsibility, the ideas flowed again.

When he was given three months to live, Bill was almost relieved. The death sentence he had expected for so long had finally arrived. He told all his friends, revelled in the attention, made terrific jokes about dying. I went to see him and presented myself with a suitably funereal face and within minutes he had me splitting my sides. I said, 'I was so depressed when I heard you were dying, but you have really cheered me up.' All his friends pilgrimaged to Bristol to make their farewells. To his acute embarrassment, the three months elapsed and he was still very much alive. He lasted another year. I made several farewell visits during that time. 'This is positively my last appearance,' he would say.

As well as writing for film and television, he taught over the years. Dozens of his ex-students turned up at the funeral. I had no idea he had affected so many lives. His anarchic mind, spinning and turning, had sent off sparks among the students and set their lives on fire. On a movie you need a title, a specific job. Bill never fitted in, not in films nor in life. He was a maverick. I miss him.

It is well known that Stanley Kubrick will not fly, does not travel, is a famous recluse. But he uses the telephone a lot and he calls me from time to time, usually looking for information. Information is the pretext. He likes to chat. I asked him what he was doing. 'Writing,' he said cryptically. He asked me what I was doing. 'Writing,' I replied. Why should I reveal more to him than he would to me, for in neither of our recent talks would he vouchsafe the subject of his next film? I think he is right. I wish I could say nothing as effectively as he does. He asked me if I still wrote my scripts in the traditional format. Well, yes, I said, I did. I always feel stupid in conversation with Stanley. He challenges every convention, questions all received wisdom, and here am I doing things the way others do them without a critical thought in my head. He argued that scripts were impossible to read, because your eye always went to the dialogue and skipped the directions. This was because of the layout. It put undue emphasis on what was said. To stop the reader doing this he reverses the order, spreading out the dialogue and narrowing the descriptions. The conventional way is like this (a script fragment from *Broken Dream*):

They are sitting round the fire, sharing the food that MOTHER unwraps from little parcels she has in her basket.

> OLD BEN
> Don't worry, son. This has
> to be done. We have sent
> objects flying like birds
> into another world. The
> question is, can a man follow?
> If I can get there, others
> can too.

He reaches out his hand. BEN takes it in his. OLD BEN lowers his voice, a whisper that only his son can hear.

> OLD BEN
> You've seen, as I have, in
> that moment before things vanish,
> the wonders of that other place,
> and the terrors of the journey
> there. So, remember, when the
> time comes, if you falter for
> one instant, I will be forgotten
> and lost forever.

BEN turns away, overcome. NELL gazes at father and son anxiously, understanding what has passed between them.

Stanley's way would have it like this:

> They are sitting round the
> fire, sharing the food that
> MOTHER unwraps from little
> parcels she has in her basket.

> OLD BEN

Don't worry, son. This has to be done. We have sent objects flying like birds into another world. The question is, can a man follow? If I can get there, others can too.

> He reaches out his hand.
> BEN takes it in his. OLD BEN
> lowers his voice, a whisper that
> only his son can hear.

> OLD BEN

You've seen, as I have, in that moment before things vanish, the wonders of that other place, and the terrors of the journey there. So, remember, when the time comes, if you falter for one instant, I will be forgotten and lost forever.

> BEN turns away, overcome.
> NELL gazes at father and son
> anxiously, understanding what
> has passed between them.

Reading it over, I think Stanley may be right.

Before getting on the plane, I dropped off my rewrite of *Broken Dream* at Jeremy Thomas's funky Soho office. Jeremy was in Cannes at the Festival. I fear that he will find the script insufficiently changed. As I've said, however hard I try to change it, it remains obstinately itself. I have at least attempted to make it clearer, to let the audience in earlier, and have emphasized the race against time to rescue our characters from extinction. And that is about all.

Jeremy has come up with the idea that we might shoot *Broken Dream* in Australia, where some money might be available. He suggested that shooting it there could impart to it some of the energy of *Mad Max*. The implication was that it might also purge the script of some of its Irish whimsicality. A fair comment. I like his enthusiasm and directness and his way of finding ways to make things work.

The reason for my trip to Los Angeles is to attend my friend Bob Chartoff's third wedding, and as I write *Green Card* plays on the plane, a film about a modern marriage of convenience that has its admirers. I had seen the trailer and was put off by the arch tone. No film should be judged by its inflight performance, but this one reminded me of a friend's verdict on a film playing on plane: it was so bad people were walking out at 30,000 feet. Peter Weir has done good things, he has touched his films with poetry, but this is bland, social unrealism and it is lit like a TV sit-com. The Disney effect can be seen at work once more.

This is the same Peter Weir who made terrific pictures like *Gallipoli* and *The Year of Living Dangerously*, and knew just how to handle Mel Gibson's boyish shyness. I saw Mel's *Hamlet* the other day, or 'Omelet' as it has been cruelly renamed. It has been greeted by the critics with surprised cries of 'It's not that bad, quite good in fact.' Zeffirelli set *Romeo and Juliet* in its true Italianness. He understood doomed young love. Although he shot *Hamlet* in a Scottish castle, its light looks Italian. It is bright rather than gloomy. As if still pumped up from his action pictures, Mel leaps and lurches about Elsinore with manic energy. Hamlet as a man of action, bursting with adrenalin, is a novel view of the indecisive prince. Zeffirelli has rearranged the play, so as to make everything subordinate to the plot, always the least interesting part of a Shakespeare play, and in *Hamlet* he clearly did not spend much effort on it or assign it too much importance. Zeffirelli puts all that right. Oddly, the film version of Tom Stoppard's play *Rosencrantz and Guildenstern Are Dead* is also playing in the cinemas. I had contemplated directing it twenty years ago. Tom was a good friend. We had worked together in television. I had employed him as an actor. He was an unemployed newspaper man whose temporary poverty in no way diminished his air of aesthetic aristocracy. When we sat down to make a screenplay of the play, Tom responded to the possibilities of film and we made both minor and radical changes. I've yet to see the film, but from what he has told me he has changed the play even more. This leads me to wonder how Shakespeare would have shaped up as a screenwriter of his own work. Certainly Zeffirelli rearranged *Hamlet* in startling ways. Clearly he wanted to shake free of Shakespeare's authority. The credits announce: Screenplay by Zeffirelli and another fellow (no mention of Will), then, ah yes, based on the play by ...

I believe Shakespeare would have relished cinema. His plays are bursting with exteriors, forests, glades, castles, blasted heaths, storms, ghosts, battles, horses. He would have understood that dialogue has to be rooted in action and would have written accordingly. Film has its own agenda. What comes to mind when we think of Olivier's *Henry V* is that great flight of arrows. Perhaps the best renderings on film of Shakespeare's work were the Russian *Hamlet* and Kurosawa's *Throne of Blood*. Since these were both done in foreign tongues, the directors were liberated from the text. Shakespeare's poetry is a tyranny that no film director in English can throw off. Despite Zeffirelli's restless camera movements and mobile actors, the speeches define the pace.

They root it to the stage where they belong and make Zeffirelli's direction seem like the fidgeting of a fretful child.

Paul Rassam has still not read the script of *Don Quixote*. A while back I sent him a fax saying: 'Dear Paul, I know how hard it is for you to find the time to read the script, but if you had decided to read it a page per day when you received it, you would now be up to page 30.' Right now he would be at page 70.

I asked Jake Eberts to read it and he did, overnight. He liked it, but with reservations. He thought it was too episodic. Well, he'll have to blame Cervantes for that, rather than Waldo Salt. The script is owned by Ronnie Lubin, a gracious man with whom I have played tennis from time to time. He has made a habit, over the years, of selling options on the script to other producers who are never able to get it made, and in due course the rights revert to Ronnie. Jake said he was not thrilled at the prospect of working with Marty Ransohoff.

I decided to ask Edgar Gross, my business manager, to talk to Ronnie Lubin, who had been away in Europe. When Lubin got back it transpired that Ransohoff's option had run out and Ronnie had gone to Europe and sold an option to a Norwegian financier, Stein Iversson, who was supposedly putting up $15 million to make the movie and wanted John Cleese to direct it. Edgar was furious with Ronnie. He said to Ronnie, 'How could you go off and sell it to someone else when you knew John wanted to do it?' It transpired that Ransohoff had threatened to sue Ronnie if he took the project to me or Sean Connery, because Ransohoff had introduced us to it. The good news was that with Marty Ransohoff out of the picture Jake would be more willing to get involved, that is, if there is still room for him, and for me, come to that. What a mess.

What is there to be said about *Dances with Wolves?* Jake put the finance together. No studio would touch it, the conventional wisdom being that Westerns are box-office poison. I believe Jeremy Thomas wanted to make it at one stage, but because of other commitments had to relinquish it. He told Guy East, who runs Majestic Films, it was a great project and urged him into it. Everything about it was wrong. It was three hours long. There were subtitles. It had narration. Yet critics, public, the Academy embraced it, were utterly seduced by it. Jodie Foster said to me, 'It's long, it's low-brow, but it works.' Almost the only voice raised against it was Pauline Kael. She said it was a film made by a bland megalomaniac, that his Indian name should not have been 'Dances with Wolves' but 'Plays with Camera'. Its enormous and universal success (for it has done as well in Europe as in America) hastened her retirement from the *New Yorker*. She felt profoundly out of joint with the times.

What the film has is a gentleness, a very ordinary charm. The film speaks of more innocent times, of an America of endless lush landscapes. The Indians are good and wise and humorous. The white man comes along and destroys all that. It is simple and, yes Pauline, bland.

LA is looming up out of a yellow haze and we are starting our descent. The Indians knew about LA fog long before the white man came, so the motor car cannot take the whole blame.

17 May, Los Angeles

It is 3.30 a.m. I am in Los Angeles wide awake with a headache, breathing smog. Countless times over twenty-five years I have made that eleven-hour flight across the Pole. It used to be in the old Boeing 707s. I remember the elation of drinking wine, with Beethoven in the headphones, looking down for the first time at the ice-scapes of Greenland. Sometimes the air is so clear that you feel you are only a few feet above the ice-floes. Yesterday, cloud covered it all – from Hudson Bay right across Canada. Las Vegas was the first town that was visible. I was flying Virgin Airlines, £200 each way. Since I was jammed into a middle seat, the view was irrelevant.

The plane was packed, but there was a vacant seat next to me, the only one on the plane. I was praying that it would remain so. Just as they closed the doors, a man sat down. His face lit up. 'John Boorman!' My face dropped. Ten years ago he was in Ireland and engineered a meeting with me through Garech Browne, and I could never shake him off. At that time he was trying to direct a script he had written. He had spent four years struggling to get it off the ground.

Now he droned on in a dull monotone acquainting me with every minute detail of his struggles of the last decade. He is one of those bores who never finish a sentence. There is never a moment when you can break in, interrupt or excuse yourself. Ten years ago I found myself helping him out just to be rid of him, but that only made it worse. He bound himself to me ever closer. My children, everyone, hid when they saw him coming. Finally, he disappeared. I felt badly about it because he was a decent fellow with a good heart.

And here he is ten years later, sitting down next to me. I can feel his breath on my neck. He is still trying to make a movie, the same one. By now he has written other scripts and one of them is finally about to be made. He has spent the years, mostly in Hollywood, trying and trying. The money comes from some financial manoeuvring and manipulation involving exchanges of stock between companies. My mind wandered as he went on about it and I failed to grasp the scheme even though it may have been useful to me. Of all the people in the world, it had to be him who sat down beside me on this eleven-hour flight. It was an appalling prospect. This man would spend a long day with his face inches from mine, with one of those voices that somehow saps your will. He creates a boredom that is so pervasive that you drown in it.

By a supreme act of will I finally cut into his flow, brutally interrupting. 'I promised myself I would do some writing on this trip,' I said. With that I opened this notebook and started writing up notes that I had made over the past month but had not developed because of *Broken Dream* and the BBC film; they had taken up all my writing time. I wrote for several hours. Every time I paused or looked up from my notebook he was poised, ready to speak. It was the most sustained piece of writing I have ever done. He did get up and go down to the back of the plane at one point. This gave us a chance to have our picnic of fine cheeses and pâté with the fresh French bread which I had brought that morning in my son-in-law Tom's shop. Not only is airline food bad, but on long trips they stretch out the meals to help pass the time and it interferes with whatever else you want to do.

All through the plane people were poring over scripts. Cheap flights to LA are bursting with Brits going over to pitch their stories. Fourteen long years this man has been plugging away. It is not as if he had some great vision. His stories are all exploitation thrillers, so it is impossible to consider his struggle heroic. I know many like him. They get caught up in the miasma of dealing with agents, lawyers, tax shelters, territorial advances. It is a narcotic litany that they become addicted to. They are always one deal away from glory. The plane was full of them. A ghastly thought occurs. Perhaps I am becoming one of them myself.

Last night, determined to stay awake, we forced ourselves to go out for dinner across the street here in Santa Monica. We wandered into Giorgio's, which turned out to be a media place. The talk at the tables was the same: the tangled problems of a TV series; development deals at a studio; whose picture was being cancelled; which executives were being fired; how many zillion dollars stars were getting; that Spielberg's version of *Peter Pan* was costing $100 million. Nothing changes in this town except that the numbers go up.

Spoke to Edgar Gross on the phone, better news on *Don Quixote*. He had talked to Ronnie Lubin and directly to the mysterious Norwegian. It turns out he had made no commitments to John Cleese or anyone else and was interested in talking to Jake and me. Meanwhile I sit here in Los Angeles; it is 5.00 a.m. I have that special jet-lag headache. I think the brain must take longer to decompress or something. It is the black night of the Los Angeles dog-watch. But outside the swish of rubber on concrete never ceases. Cars traverse the city without rest. When I drive out of the airport on to the San Diego freeway, I am always awestruck that in all the months since I was last here those twelve lanes have been full of cars, night and day, just as in rooms across the city, also without cease, scripts are being written by dreamers who, if they can only connect, score once, they will be rich and famous and live for ever.

18 May

Last night I attended a stag night for Bob Chartoff's wedding. The traditional American ritual usually involves a lot of booze and a naked girl jumping out of a cake and the guys making lewd jokes – a final crude, drunken brawl with the boys before the groom is carried off into domesticity. It probably harks back to the pioneer days. Men came to this country, hacked out a living from the wilderness, then sent for the women. This was rather different. A book called *Iron John* has swept the land with new notions of manhood. Bob belongs to a men's group which comes together once a week, sits in a circle, beats drums and honours their fathers and grandfathers, and speak their hearts on manly matters. The stag party took that form. Forty of us sat in a circle. Drums were beaten and an Indian talking stick was passed around and each of us said a few words about Bob. They all found it quite comfortable to express their feelings, to express love. I felt my toes curling. Many of these men had been in various forms of therapy. Inevitably, many or most of them were connected to the entertainment industry: lawyers, business affairs executives, producers and so on, all thoroughly therapied but still valiantly searching for themselves.

It is easy to scoff. Every year I come to LA there is a new fad. EST held sway for a while. Channelling was big. Every so often a guru rises from the East and sweeps them all away. Many of them have recently been to meet the Dalai Lama. I sometimes feel that LA people need to make this huge effort to be human beings. Everything that we take for granted, that we learn from our mother's milk, they have to relearn, find a book about it or go to a weekend seminar on it. When they talk so exhaustively about their feelings and constantly articulate their love for one another, I have the suspicion that they say these things so compulsively not because they have those feelings, but because they don't.

Is this the sour response of an inhibited Englishman? After all, people left Europe for America to find new ways of living, rejecting the oppressive societies they had endured. Is America not a place for experiment, for this great quest into the self? But in Los Angeles it gets tangled in hype, fraud and silliness. There are legions of religious and psychological flim-flam men out there ready to exploit the desires of the rich to self-indulge. Bob is one who is always ready to try the new thing and goes on meditation courses, psychotherapy weekends and so forth. But because he is also an indefatigable traveller and knows the East, he is more discriminating than most.

It was moving to hear speaker after speaker extol Bob's virtues, his generosity, his kindness, his consideration. So many there have been helped emotionally, financially or spiritually by Bob. He has used his wealth and power as a successful producer to help other people, as well as to seek himself. When it came to my turn to speak I told them that I had come to honour Bob, but that I felt obliged to express my profound unease with the situation. I said that I had always hated gatherings of men where women were excluded. Although the crassness and vulgarity of the locker room was happily absent, I nevertheless found it distasteful. But, when I reflected on it, I realized it was not the maleness of the thing that was troubling but the femaleness of it. It was men behaving as women. They talked about their feelings all the time. That might be good. They find these meetings give them back an identity that has been lost and stolen away by society, by women. But it feels contrived, too serious, lacking in irony, even pompous. A great deal was said about the importance of giving up the quest for power, giving attention instead to spiritual growth and to nurturing relationships. After fighting and scheming for money and fame, a lot of movie people just ease up when they achieve it, and do just enough to stay in the game. Bob has an office, employs five people, a script reader or two to assess material. But, I suspect, his heart is no longer in it. You can find others like him at the tennis clubs, golf clubs, talking about last week's grosses, justifying their inactivity by damning the ineptness of the studios, the crassness of audiences, much as I do myself. Ronnie Lubin is such a man, charming, hangs out at the tennis club every day and nurtures *Don Quixote*, gently waiting. He maintains a status because he owns a few important properties, yet leads an easy life as an elder, a wise old man who can reach back further than we to the brief history of film.

21 May

Barton Fink won not only the Palme d'Or but the director's prize and best actor at Cannes. This must be unprecedented. As a Coen fan I was delighted, even though the awards seemed excessive. I can imagine that Roman Polanski as president of the jury would be attracted to their scabrous black humour. Alan Parker was also a member of the jury. Like Polanski he is cynical, irascible and impatient with 'arty' films.

The papers are full of Madonna, whose presence dominated the Festival. She is making an art form out of celebrity. She has become Andy Warhol's ultimate superstar, for he invented this way of celebrating celebrity. She has discovered how to devour her audience instead of them devouring her. This weekend her documentary concert film *Truth or Dare*, called in Europe *In*

Bed with Madonna, did nearly $5 million at the box office. It is an accomplished piece of autobiography – raunchy, outrageous and fun. She brings the private language and morality of modern American into public view. Like Warhol, David Lynch and the Coen brothers it is a celebration of trash. She trashes religious icons, sexuality, fashion, by subsuming them into her trashy act. She revels in vulgarity, just as Hockney and other modern artists have painted freeways and street signs and beer cans. She also makes art out of the detritus of the world around her. You may transcend the shoddiness of life, she is saying, only by being a star. You then give yourself back to the public. And the public may transcend the trashiness of their lives for those brief hours when she is theirs. Warren Beatty berated her in the film for living her life on camera, for having no interest in doing anything off camera. But we are on her side. This is her life, the camera is her only true love.

Edgar and I got Lubin into a room and called Jake up in Canada and arranged for him to meet the Norwegian, Stein Iversson, in London. Lubin and I would also go in for the meeting next Wednesday. Lubin told of all his near-misses with this project over the years. He was in Spain and on the verge of shooting when the musical, *The Man from La Mancha*, hove into view and scuppered him. We talked about casting, where it could be shot, and so on.

Dinner with Jon Voigt. Jon cannot accept a role without suffering agonies of doubt and vacillation. It took me weeks of patient coaxing to lure him into *Deliverance*. When I was at my wits' end, desperate for a decision, I said at the end of an hour's telephone conversation, 'Jon, I'm going to count to twenty and if you haven't said yes by then I'm going to hang up and find another actor.' He said, 'John, why twenty? At least count to fifty.' I counted to twenty. No response. I put the phone down. He called me back immediately. 'OK, I'll do it, but this is a brutal way of working.' It is several years since he found a part he could commit himself to. To my astonishment, when I mentioned *Don Quixote* he offered himself up for the role without reservation or hesitation. I am his greatest fan. I believe he can do anything, but he has let his career slip into the doldrums. I fear the distributors would not greet his candidature with enthusiasm. He has always followed the spiritual path. The Jesuits got him early. He studied for the priesthood for a time. Now he has become a convert to Judaism. He studies the Talmud. He reads the great Jewish teachers. He has become a Sephardic Jew. But, unlike some of the other seekers for the truth I have encountered on this trip, Jon is profoundly serious, deeply spiritual and pursues his ends with fanatical obsession. He is even learning Hebrew.

Jon was at the wedding. We sat together with Burgess Meredith, who Jon remarked had become an old shaman. 'A few years ago nothing he said made sense,' Jon said. 'Now everything he says is wisdom.'

Burgess is writing his autobiography, which I look forward to with great enthusiasm. Mike Medavoy was another member of the wedding. Late of the failing Orion, he now reigns at TriStar. He has many millions of Japanese money to dispense. I went to his office and told him about *Don Quixote* and *Broken Dream* and he told me of some of the projects that he was developing. He was responsible for making *Excalibur*, for which I am eternally grateful. He asked me if I was still interested in the mythic past. The conversation turned to the Vikings and then we spoke of the power of the Tristan and Isolde story. Rashly, I suggested combining the two and setting the great love story in the crazed hallucinatory context of the beserker Vikings. It sounded like a brilliant stroke in his office. We both got excited. Driving back along Santa Monica Boulevard, it seemed absurdly remote and unlikely. He also gave me coverage on a Nabokov novel *Laughter in the Dark*. A couple of TriStar readers had voted it unsuitable as movie material. Interesting that Mike was able to look past those judgements. But was it not already filmed by Tony Richardson? I never saw the film but I remember the story of how Richard Burton was playing the lead, behaved very badly, was constantly late, and Tony went to see him and fired him. Burton was at the height of his power and fame. They had a furious row. Tony left, slamming the door behind him. Only then did he remember that he was on Burton's yacht which at that time was moored in the Thames. He was obliged to go back and ask for a boat to be taken ashore. Nicol Williamson replaced Burton.

Silence of the Lambs is a preposterous thriller that is absolutely compelling. Anthony Hopkins essays a cannibalistic psychiatrist who, despite being incarcerated, exercises a mesmeric power over Jodie Foster's FBI trainee agent. They are hunting a serial killer, who murders and skins young women. Hopkins eats people. The pursuit of the killer conventionalizes the film – although those scenes are well done – but the savage heat of the movie lies in the interviews between Hopkins and Foster conducted through the glass of his cell. They are profoundly sexual. He probes her background, intuits her private terror and gains control over her. It is a remote sexual conquest and it offers a unique metaphor for the sexual act. I've discussed before the difficulties of doing sex on film. Finding this is pure gold. Both actors are superb.

On the way back from Los Angeles I stopped in Paris to see my daughter Telsche and her daughter, Daphne. We had a rendezvous at La Doyenne where Régine, Telsche's mother-in-law, reigns. Daphne is allowed the run of the place. Carole Bouquet was there with her son. Carole's personality differs completely from her appearance. As she looks out from the Chanel ads or appears in *Too Beautiful for You* (the marvellous Blier movie) she is the cool perfect beauty, unattainable, remote, the kind of women men dream of, but fear to approach. Yet in truth she is a tomboy with an earthy humour and raucous emotions that are always ready to spill over. She was sixteen when she became Buñuel's *Obscure Object of Desire*. Telsche is in great demand as a screenwriter and Carole is coaxing her to write a script for her.

I met Michel Ciment at the Café Flore in St Germain and he gave me his impressions of Cannes. I thought he would bridle at the excessive honours heaped on *Barton Fink*, but he agrees it was by far the best film. He also liked Pialat's film on Van Gogh. Pialat is a contentious figure. When he won the Palme d'Or four years ago for *Under the Sign of Satan*, he was greeted with boos when he went up for his prize – which was probably very much to his taste. Michel said that when he praised Pialat's first film Pialat said, 'Are you insulting me? Do you think that's the best I can do? It's a piece of shit.' As Pialat was about to descend the steps of the Palais du Festival with the band playing and the crowd clapping, Michel slipped up behind him and shook his hand and said, 'Bravo.' Pialat whipped round and snarled, 'You shit on my last picture – well, I agree with you about that. But how could you praise *Jean de Florette*, which is far worse than my movie?' Michel said that he did not like *Jean de Florette* and had never praised it in print or in private. 'Well,' said Pialat, 'you must have terrible enemies, because that's what people are saying.'

25 May, Paris

Dinner at L'Ami Louis with Marcello Mastroianni.

We re-enter that little world we made twenty years ago in Notting Hill Gate – *Leo the Last* – and celebrate our mutual survival. We comforted each other that the passing years have left us comparatively unscathed. We both have hair and teeth. Marcello says that his brother, the film editor, has lost those accessories. 'He doesn't need them,' says Marcello. 'I need them to act.' The conversation turned to acting. Marcello was puzzled that so many American actors found the craft so painful and difficult and that they agonize over it so much. He said that for him acting is like making love. 'It is wonderful while you are doing it, but when it is over you forget about it, and hope that you can do it again tomorrow.'

I told him that I have never understood why people are prepared to expose themselves in front of a camera. I am very grateful that they will. This reminds me that I will shortly have to face that ordeal myself. I felt a sick flutter in my stomach. I told Marcello of my apprehension. He said yes, he feared it at first, but soon he entered into complicity with the black eye of the camera. 'It is like a mistress. I know her ways and I know how to be in her good graces.' The lens is not the only victim of his charm. Marcello's devastating effect on women has to do with his air of helplessness. He offers himself to their mercy, and they rush in to help. He sees human behaviour with absolute clarity. He is a brilliant observer; that much is evident from his work, but he views the pettiness and frailty about him with a kind and forgiving eye.

Two young girls came over for his autograph. Marcello said ruefully, 'They used to say it is for my sister, then twenty years on, they said it's for my mother.' He turned to the girls. 'I suppose this is for your grandmother!'

He spoke of Fellini. Even he is finding it impossible to get finance. He wants to make a film about acting with Marcello, rather on the lines of *The Orchestra Rehearsal*. Marcello's eyes narrow with desire. 'I want to make a film about this strange beast, the actor.' Of course, we speak of *Don Quixote*. He gives me some indications of how he would play it. It is dazzling, of course. His disarming modesty goes even further. He says maybe because of his English he did not understand what I wanted. His friends said, 'Surely Boorman wants you to play Sancho Panza,' and he replied, 'No, I think I am Don Quixote, maybe not. If he wants me to be Sancho Panza, that's good also.' I reassure him that he's Don Quixote. I've sent him the script and he called me to say that he couldn't read it in English, it was too difficult; could I have it translated into Italian for him? He said, 'Of course, you know I can act in English, but I cannot read it too well.' And then he told me the story of the film he made with Julie Andrews. He'd also assured her that once he'd learnt the lines there was no problem with his English, even though he didn't speak it so well. The first line he had to say to Julie Andrews was 'Close your eyes,' and it came out 'Close your arse.' He said that Julie Andrews is a very proper lady and was a little bit startled.

Whether I can persuade my masters that Marcello and Depardieu would make a wonderful pair for *Don Quixote* is another matter. To get a US distribution deal, which is necessary to trigger the project, pressure will be brought on me to employ American actors. A meeting has been set up in Jake's office on Wednesday next, 29 May, with Lubin and the Norwegian Stein Iversson to take the project further. If this man really does have $15 million, there should be nothing to stop us.

29 May, London

The meeting was arranged for 12.30 in Jake's office. Jake called to say he had spoken to Stein Iversson, who had confessed that far from having $15 million dollars he had secured a $10,000 option from Ronnie and then intended to shop it around the studios. I called Ronnie and told him; he was shattered, as was I. Was it worth going over to London for the meeting? I have not heard from Jeremy Thomas about my rewrite of *Broken Dream*. I suddenly felt desperately abandoned. Yesterday's man. Could it be that I would try and fail with three projects in a row?

We all assembled edgily in Jake's office. Jake was terrific, he laid it out:

'I'll back *Don Quixote*, produced and directed by John Boorman.' He was ready to put up development money to get a rewrite, assess costs, locations and budget as long as control passed to me and Stein did not figure as producer. Stein turned out to be a rather young, very blond Scandinavian. Ronnie Lubin, as much a dreamer as Don Quixote, had imagined Stein had $15 million in his pocket; Stein claimed he had merely said he felt $15 million was what would be needed to make the picture. I said to Ronnie, 'Why would you sell this to Stein when you are just as capable of sending the script to the studios as he is?' No answer, but they both squirmed in their seats. A mess.

30 May

When I got home, I found that Jeremy Thomas had phoned to say he loved the new script of *Broken Dream*. My spirits lifted. Then came a call from Jake to say that Stein does not want to do *Don Quixote* with me. I suppose Jake's forcefulness made it evident to him that there would be no role for him. When Jake discovered that Stein's deal included paying Ronnie $600,000 for the script and his services, he lost interest in it anyway. Stein wanted John Cleese to direct it. He wants a comedy director. In the meantime I spoke with Depardieu, since I learnt from Jeff Berg that Ridley Scott's film in which he is to play Christopher Colombus may not go ahead. Depardieu was full of enthusiasm. Yes, he would love to play Sancho Panza and he greatly admired Marcello. Marcello called. He had received the Italian translation of the script, read it and loved it. It was shattering: I had two of this era's greatest actors, Jake would put up the money, and now the script had been snatched away from me.

5 June

Jeremy is serious about *Broken Dream*. He promised that his own production fund will put up 40 per cent of the budget. We can maybe get 20 per cent from tax shelter money here. He is looking for the rest. It is the piece I most care about, yet also the most dangerous, in commercial terms.

A script drops out of the sky called *The Boxer and the Blonde*. John Heyman, who also has one of these Japanese funds, offered me $2.5 million to make it. Pay or play. It is well-written, diverting, if unoriginal. I could do with the money. It is two years since I earned a fee. I am doing the BBC film for what amounts to expenses. Yet I am fifty-eight. It would take a year to make. It could be my last movie. To hell with it. My last movie should be *Broken Dream* – shit or bust. So I go on turning down lucrative offers in the hope of distant prosperity. Meanwhile, I am looking to see if I can write an alternative *Don Quixote*. I am wading through the book. It is daunting.

21 June

En route Dublin–London.

Midsummer's Day. It will certainly be a long one for me. We start shooting the documentary on Monday and I am on my way to interview actresses to play the role of the Lady of the Lake, my dream woman, who also transmogrifies into a bitchy journalist who challenges all my cherished beliefs. I should get back in time to celebrate the solstice at home and probably at Luggala, where last year on this day I planted a tree with due ceremony to take the place of the one that Merlin stood under when he called Excalibur from the lake. That tree fell and died a couple of years back.

Marianne Faithfull was to have played the part of the woman in *I Dreamt I Woke Up*, but she is rehearsing the *Threepenny Opera* and her director would not release her. I tried Charlotte Rampling, but could not reach her. I wanted to make this film with friends, entirely with those I knew and liked. I put off the problem until the last moment (which is now), and I am obliged to seek a stranger. So, here I am flying to London in a DC9 on Midsummer's Day on my way to find my dream woman.

Sean Ryerson and I have been in a state of gathering panic this last week. The film is very ambitious and we are doing it on a shoestring. I was hoping to go back to my beginnings in documentary. How often I have yearned for a small crew without the pressure of the meter running on 200 people; to be able to wait for the light; take a day off; have time to reconsider – in other words, function as one does in normal life instead of at the frantic, fevered pitch of movie-making where, in order to survive, you must find access to a kind of mental overdrive that compresses information and decision-making into ultra high speed. I suspect it also uses up your life at a rapid rate. However, I seem to have made this little film so complex and ambitious, packing so much into each day, that I find I have put myself under the same pressure, but without the resources, equipment, crew or facilities with which to solve them. I am increasingly alarmed at the prospect of acting, of appearing. What have I got myself into?

The other attraction of this was to make a film that my career would not stand or fall on. It does not have to be a box-office smash or win prizes. Nothing depends on it. Except that now I see that I could make a complete fool of myself. Yet in the film I present myself as a fool, a ridiculous man, trying hard to make sense of his life and to connect with the world, to nurture nature. In my better moments I feel a sense of grace settling upon me and this enterprise. In those moments it all seems to lie under my hand, complete and true. Then a nagging voice says, 'Don't relax, be vigilant, worry about everything, otherwise it will all fall apart.'

22 June, London

I saw several actresses and finally chose one I was not able to see – Janet McTeer. She was on a distant location making a TV film. I saw some tapes of her work and, after some agonizing, made a leap in the dark.

I had a long talk with her on the telephone. I told her she had three days' work. I would put her up in one of my cottages, feed and wine her, pay her £3,000 and she would have to wear her own clothes. She said yes without hesitation. She seems bold and brave.

I now definitely call the film *I Dreamt I Woke Up*. Here is the script:

INT. GLEBE BEDROOM. NIGHT
JOHN HURT (*John Boorman's alter ego*) *is sleeping alone in his big brass bed. He awakes, hearing voices murmuring below.*
JH: (*Voice over*) I dreamt I woke up.

INT. GLEBE STAIRS / DRAWING ROOM. DAY
JH *descends. He stops, looks down at the hall and drawing room, which are decorated with leaves and branches. People are gathered round a coffin. It is made of stone and carved with elaborate Celtic runes.*
JH: I bought that as a coffee table. It's not meant to be used.
   (*They appear not to hear him.* JH *is not pleased to see that he himself is lying in the coffin.*
   Now he is inside the coffin, looking out as the lid slowly closes. The faces of his family and friends look down. They are smiling. There is a stranger among them, a veiled woman. She looks at him with ineffable love and sadness. Her lips are moving but he cannot hear her.)
JH: (*Voice over*) Being dead seemed such a pity when the woman I had been waiting for all my life had finally appeared. I felt no pain, just regret for other lives unlived.
   (*The lid closes. Darkness.*)
   So this is it. You let go and you fall. How good it is to let go at least, to give up the struggle. But wait. Hold on. That woman. I must . . . before I . . . Noooo . . .
   (JH*'s face impacts on a sheet of glass. The camera is under the glass and records his flattened features and startled eyes.*)
   and then I was back, watching . . .
   (*The branches decorating the room are now bare and autumn leaves fall from the ceiling. The mysterious woman is running her finger along the runes*

John Boorman and John Hurt in County Wicklow during the filming of
I Dreamt I Woke Up

carved into the coffin lid. Her lips move soundlessly as she translates their
meaning. The mourners watch tensely. The woman makes a gesture: voila!
The lid opens and JH *sits up, blinking and shaking his head. He is warmly*
embraced. He searches the room for the woman. He catches a glimpse of her
back as she slips out of the room without looking back. The swish of her hair.
In the way of dreams JH *is watching all this from the stairs. He turns and*
goes back up to the bedroom.)

INT. GLEBE BEDROOM. NIGHT
JB *the dreamer is sleeping in the bed.*
JH *climbs into the bed and into his own skin. The dreamer and the dreamed are*
reunited.
JB: (*Voice over*) Soon I would have to re-enter the waking world and resume
   the pretence of being one person, and that a ridiculous man, a stranger
   to himself.
   (*Close on* JB *lying asleep on his back, his profile revealing an absurdly pointed*
   nose.)
   When I look at my face it does not look like the person I feel I am. So
   I don't look at it if I can possibly help it.

INT. GLEBE BATHROOM. DAY
JB *is shaving in a fine eighteenth-century Waterford glass mirror. Big close-ups of*
chin and cheek following the path of the razor.
JB: (*Voice over*) I just look at the bits I'm shaving. I'm embarrassed by me.
   (JB *pulls on his pants clumsily. He overbalances.*) I trip. I stumble. I stutter.
   I'm self-conscious. I am not comfortable in my skin. I have never got
   used to myself. I'm not my kind of person. (*He recovers, gets to his feet,*
   looks in the mirror unhappy about what he sees. Fleeting images of
   Mastroianni, Voigt, Marvin, Connery appear in the mirror to replace JB.)
   Fortunately, making movies has allowed me to engage the charming,
   handsome, rugged men I ought to have been and to send them off on
   my adventures. (JB *towels his face and goes to the bedroom window.*)

INT. GLEBE BEDROOM. DAY
JB *looks out to the east at the new morning.*
JB: (*Voice over*) And the world itself has never looked quite right to me. But
   when I came here to Wicklow in Ireland twenty-two years ago, I felt
   I'd come to a place . . .
   (*The view out of the window. Towering limes lead the eye down to the river*
   and across a meadow planted with thousands of young trees, and on to the
   folds of foothills.)
   . . . that had always existed in my imagination, that here I could

somehow come to myself at last. Is that what home is? Finding in the
outer world a place that coincides with an inner landscape?

EXT. THE GLEBE AND MOUNTAINS. DAY
From outside looking in at JB *at the bedroom window.*
*The Glebe itself from the river meadow, its reflection wavy and insubstantial in the
water.*
*The house, small and square like a child's drawing, couched in trees, the Wicklow
mountains stacked up behind it.*
*The soft folds of the mountains. Cloud shadows scud across them, light and shade,
playing havoc with the cartography of colour – gorse-yellow, bracken-brown, granite-
grey, moss-green, lichen-white, heather-heather.*

JB: (*Voice over*) What makes a landscape? Is it the contours, the colours, the
light, the rock, the things that grow upon it? What is the mysterious
thing that touches us, that says, 'This is your place?'
(JB *is looking at Djouce mountain. Its shape resembles a reclining woman.
He stares at it with intense concentration. A woman's body appears faintly
superimposed, closely following the contours of the mountain.* JB *blinks in
surprise and the apparition disappears.*
JB *walks the bog at Sally Gap. He is an awkward figure. His feet sink into
the soggy soil.*
JB's *foot sinks into the squelching bog. The next step sets his foot alongside a
rotting sheep's jaw.*)
The roof of the Wicklow mountains is a sponge, a bog that soaks up
the relentless rain. It is bleak and desolate up here. I like that. It's a
salutary corrective to my tendency to romanticize nature. The soft folds
of the mountains give them a feminine aspect, but that softness came
about by the glaciers grinding at the hard granite. Djouce Mountain
was sacred to the Celts. They saw the Mother Goddess lying there,
wrapped in moss and heather with the fickle light playing on her slopes.
Ha! There I go! Remember, there's a stony heart under all that. In
winter it's the bleakest place on earth. A wasteland – which is exactly
what I needed for my film *Excalibur*.
(Excalibur *Excerpt: A knight rides across the bleak land where peasants grub
among their rotting crops.*)

JH: (*Voice over*) A great hurt has been done by man to the earth. Crops will
not grow. The knights set out on a quest to find the lost Grail. Only
the Grail can heal the sick King and make the land fertile once more.
(JB *comes across two men cutting turf in a peat-bog. They are pulling a heavy
object out of a pool of black water. It is a man perfectly preserved by the
sterile bog. The* TURF-CUTTER *looks up shiftily as* JB *approaches.*)

TURF-CUTTER: Finding a few of these, lately. Could be a thousand years old, this lad. The old bog'll preserve them for ever.
(The figure is tanned the colour of the bog. As the water runs off it, JB studies the leathery ancient face.)
JB: If only it could speak, eh? What tales he could tell.
(A hiss of air escapes the bog-man's mouth. JB is replaced by JH, who looks urgently at the BOG-MAN. He stoops close as the creature whispers.)
BOG-MAN: They buried me alive.
JH: Who did that to you?
BOG-MAN: The Druids. They made me half-dead.
JH: Why?
BOG-MAN: My sin was great. I did rape on the holy mountain.
JH: The Druids. Where did their power come from?
BOG-MAN: Down there. The lough.
(JH turns to look at Lough Tay, a silver dish of water far below. He looks back at the BOG-MAN, who is trembling, his body caught in convulsions.)
Be warned, you who dig and delve,
You who knows no peace himself,
Never waken those who die,
Let sleeping bogs lie.
(JB is back. He looks at the BOG-MAN, now lifeless and inert.)
JB: You'd better get in touch with the National Museum.
(The two TURF-CUTTERSS wink at each other and grin with the special joy that men who do hard work derive from easy money.)
TURF-CUTTER: Ah, no, Mr Boorman. There's a fellow in Roundwood makes them up for us. We sell them to the tourists. It's softer work than cutting turf.
(A stream runs down from the bog into the magical valley of Luggala. Lough Tay lies below couched in mountains, a mirror for the heavens, a chalice.)
JB: *(Voice over)* The rain, bog-filtered, beer-coloured begins its fall to the sea. It drops into Lough Tay at Luggala, and a few miles on it will pass my house.
(JB moves down towards the lough, pushing his way through tangled branches.)
There's an easier way down, all right, but I favour the steep slope to the lake with its tortured oaks entangled in the mossy rocks – a memory of how life looked after the ice receded.
(Views of Luggala in all its aspects from above and below.)
This valley of Luggala is an enchanted place, a chalice cupped by mountains. I felt sure it was here, in the heart of her mystery, that the Lady of the Lake might offer up the sword of power – Excalibur.
(Excalibur excerpt: The sword Excalibur, held in the hand of the Lady of the Lake, rises from the water.

JB *stands where Merlin stood. The lake is a mirror reflecting an upside-down
mountain. As* JB *watches the lake, two strange creatures appear before him,*
GARECH BROWNE *in norfolk jacket, bearded and pony-tailed, and* MAÍRTÍN
MACSIÚRTÁIN, *the tree man.* MAÍRTÍN *is peering myopically at a leaf
while* GARECH'S *head is temporarily concealed by the young tree he is carrying.
In fact he looks like a mobile tree. It is an extremely rare Korean tree and they
are disputing its history and provenance.* MAÍRTÍN *suddenly disappears into
a hole and* GARECH *hands him the tree for planting.*
JB *watches* GARECH *and* MAÍRTÍN *as they walk towards the house, a Gothic
hunting lodge at the foot of the mountain commanding views of the lake.
Many trees have been planted in little cages to protect them from the deer that
abound in the valley.*)

JB: (*Voice over*) Here is the habitat of the Hon. Garech Browne, my friend
and neighbour. He is the custodian of this valley of Luggala. He
nurtures it, as he nurtures Irish music and poetry. Maírtín MacSiúrtáin
is the tree man who plants for Garech and me. I put down mostly native
broadleaves, whereas Garech favours rare and exotic species. That goes
for his life. He is a collector of the rare and exotic – whether it be
objects or people. He is a rare bird himself.

EXT./INT. LUGGALA. DAY
JB *looks through a window of the house. A number of people are draped about the
room. There is an air of shabby decadence and exquisite good taste, a potent mix.*
GARECH *and* MAÍRTÍN *enter.*

JB: (*Voice over*) Here he collects poets and pipers, druids and drunks, landed
and stranded gentry.
(*Faces are picked out for* JB *to identify: the poet* JOHN MONTAGUE, *the
piper* PADDY MOLONEY, *the novelist* GERALD HANLEY, DESMOND
MACKEY, STAN GEBLER-DAVIS.)
He likes to have his friends about him and when they die he keeps
their death masks close at hand, and indeed their hands.
(*Moving across the death masks on the wall and a pair of bronze hands on
the sideboard among the vodka bottles. Across the open pages of the visitors
book, over the Irish Georgian furniture and on to the portrait of a young
Garech hanging on the wall.*)
His own likeness by Lucien Freud is a death mask of his youth, for
the face has gathered the wisdom and sorrow of years to itself since
then.
(*Dissolve to* GARECH'S *present face, his eyes sad. He is now standing by the
window looking out at the lake and the little temple on its shore.*)
About Gareth and this place the poet John Montague wrote . . .

(MONTAGUE, *seated in the room, has his* New Selected Poems *open in his lap. A close shot of the poem 'Luggala' on the page. He reads.*

JM: Again and again in a dream I return
to that shore . . .

EXT. LUGGALA. DAY

JOHN MONTAGUE *walks to the tomb by the side of the lake.*

JM: (*Voice over*) There is
a wind rising, a gull is trying to skim over the pines, and
the waves whisper and strike along the bright sickle of the
little strand. Shoving through reeds and rushes, leaping
over a bogbrown stream, I approach the temple by the
water's edge, death's shrine, cornerstone of your sadness.
(JM *stands against one of the pillars. He looks down at the circular stone basin filled with water like an echo in artifice of the lake beyond.*)
I stand inside, by one of the pillars of the mausoleum, and
watch the water in the stone basin. As the wind ruffles
cease, a calm surface appears, like a mirror or crystal.
(*Dissolve to* GARECH's *face at the window. Superimpose the image on the stone basin of black water.*)
And into it your face rises, sad beyond speech, sad with an
acceptance of blind, implacable process. For by this grey
temple are three tombs, a baby brother, a half-sister and
a grown brother, killed at twenty-one.
(*The lake, circled by gulls, falls into deep shadow, forbidding.* MONTAGUE, *a small figure, leaves the tomb and walks back towards the house.*)
Their monuments
of Wicklow granite are as natural here as the scattered
rocks, but there is no promise of resurrection, only the
ultimate silence of the place, the shale littered face of the
scree, the dark, dark waters of the glacial lake.

INT. LUGGALA. DAY

The guests are engaged in conversation.

JB: (*Voice over*) Magic leaks out of that lake and people and things are
intensified in this house, made better or worse, and whatever they are,
they are made more so here.
(*In the drawing room one of the guests is looking through an album of photographs of Garech's wedding in which he wears an enormous turban and ornate robes.*)
Garech's marriage to an Indian princess gave full rein to his pleasure
in ritual and regalia.

(*Garech is there in the drawing room, back to the fire surveying his guests, who are in animated conversation.*
PADDY MALONEY *has picked up his pipes and plays a haunting air that seems to touch the very spirit of Luggala. It silences the clever tongues.*
GARECH *is moved by the music as he looks out over his guests. Still standing by the fire, he levitates slightly. His guests applaud. 'That's powerful piping, Paddy,' they say.*)
GARECH: Paddy, put me down.

EXT. WICKLOW MOUNTAINS. DAY
From high above Luggala a view sweeping down from Lough Tay across the mountains to Lough Dan.
JB: (*Voice over*) From Lough Tay at Luggala the bog water begins to form a river in the glacial valley and it cuts a path into a second lake, Lake Dan. (JB *on the grassy edge of Lough Dan, which is tamer, more benign than Tay. He turns and walks through the dark, tangled thicket and emerges in the oakwood that rises from the shore. The floor of the wood is dusted with a haze of bluebells amid the holly and bracken.*) On the lower shore a tangled thicket discourages intruders, but if you can pass through it you come upon a secret corner of the valley where lies one of the last fragments of primal oak forest. Much of northern Europe looked like this a thousand years ago. The oak was sacred to the ancient Celts. They cut it down on pain of death. They feared the wrath of the Green Man, the malevolent spirit of the woods. If the Green Man lived still, he would live in such a place.
(*A figure gradually emerges from its surroundings of bark and leaf. It appears to be a soldier in camouflage.* JB *has become* JH. *He studies the face.*)
JH: Is this a military exercise? In here of all places?
MAN: Come closer.
(JH *studies the face. The face is camouflaged in brown and black. Lichen and moss grow out of his beard and eyebrows.*)
JH: Camouflage?
MAN: You could say that. (*He raises a hand. The fingernails are long, spiky points. The eyes are malevolent.*)
JH: It's you again. The Green Man. Can't you leave me alone? I just want to take a walk – ALONE!
(JH *walks away; the* GREEN MAN *calls after him.*)
GREEN MAN: Alone? Only a fool would come to a wood like this to be alone. You're in the midst of life, death-dealer. You're in the heart of the world.
(*The* GREEN MAN *is suddenly in the branches of a tree in the path of* JH, *who stops and looks up.*)

Trespasser! Desecrator! Tree-feller!

(*The* GREEN MAN *makes a slashing pass with machete-like blade. A branch crashes down on* JH. *He falls to the ground, pinned by it.* JH's *face pops out from the leaves that cover him.*)

JH: (*Angrily*) You've always been at war with us, long before we began to destroy you.

GREEN MAN: Because you're the enemy. Always have been.

JH: (*Furious*) Peace! Peace and harmony is what we want, you malignant bastard!

(JH *hauls himself out from under the branch, then gets tangled in briars, trips and falls headlong. The* GREEN MAN's *laughter rings in his ears. Although it is* JH *who falls, it is* JB *who painfully stands up in his place, freeing his feet from the briars.* JB *looks up at the tree above him. Frayed ropes hang from several branches.*)

JB: (*Voice over*) The ropes are still there after more than ten years. It was in this same wood and on this very tree that we strung up . . .

(Excalibur *Excerpt: Knights in armour hang from many of the tree's limbs, swaying and creaking. A rook picks out the eye of one of them.*)

. . . the knights of King Arthur, who had failed to find the Grail and heal the land. They hung like rotting fruit. This oakwood, so vibrant with life, is also a place of death and decay.

EXT. ANNAMOE. DAY

The camera follows the river as it sweeps past an oak-banked escarpment, through silver birch and gorse and meadow-sweet to the bridge at Annamoe.

The camera passes under the bridge and down into JB's domain.

The Glebe house, reflected in the river. Young trees planted in cages line the banks. The great lime trees standing about the house are in the first flush of leaf, their colour at its limest. Pan to the slender bridge which spans the river.

Dissolve to the pen-and-ink drawing of the design of the bridge.

JB: (*Voice over*) Just below Lough Dan the river passes my house and divides my land. We built a bridge across it, which the architect Jeremy Williams designed. I wanted a sword-bridge, so narrow that one man with a sword could defend it against an army. It gives access to thirty-five acres on which we have planted thirteen thousand native broadleaf trees. Jeremy helped Maírtín and I plan the series of groves and the network of walks and rides between them.

INT. GLEBE DRAWING ROOM. DAY

JEREMY *is drawing a perspective view of the house set among the groves of trees giving an impression of how they will look in maturity.* JB *and* MAÍRTÍN *lean over him as he works. Spread out on the table are Maírtín's plans of the groves, indicating the species planted. They remark that they will all be dead when the woods look like this.* MAÍRTÍN *comments on the suitability of the soil and the ecological effects.* JB *tells of his wish to restore the valley to its original natural condition.* JEREMY *speaks of landscaping, Capability Brown, and the forgotten people who planted the mature trees here. They also were dead before their trees came to their full glory.*

EXT. GLEBE. DAY

MAÍRTÍN *and* JB *walk the land, inspecting the young trees, the damage done by rabbits, the trees cut by hares angry that trees have been planted on their runs.* MAÍRTÍN *points out that although our aim is to restore we are also imposing an ecology. All growth is resisted, all nature is in competition. 'What about reaching a state of harmony?' asks* JB. *'We drain, plough, fence, plant, banish the gorse. Are we doing the right thing? Some experts claim that we shouldn't plant at all. We should allow these forests to regenerate naturally.'*

The GREEN MAN *appears at their side.*

GREEN MAN: Exactly. Nature? It's become a third world country. We live on hand-outs of fertilizers. Look at those groves with their barbed-wire fences – refugee camps for trees.

JB: You are so melodramatic.

(The GREEN MAN *has disappeared.* MAÍRTÍN *wonders if the remark is aimed at him. But then* JB *often talks to himself, so* MAÍRTÍN *just ignores it.*

MAÍRTÍN *talks about trees, how that great oak, in its lifetime, will consume only a cupful of nutrients. These, the largest living things, take their sustenance from the air. They live on carbon dioxide and replenish our oxygen. They temper our climate and provide the environment for all forms of life. They are noble, they have no malice nor aggression. They provide us with everything from newsprint to furniture.*

JB *becomes passionate on the subject. This is a tree planet, he claims. It belongs to them. We should revere them as our ancestors did. I've come to know these trees, he says. When I stand among them they calm me, they steady me down. Is that fanciful? When I was in the Amazon there was a species being killed by a virus that was slowly moving across the forest. A strange thing occurred. Trees in the path of the virus but which it had not yet reached, developed antibodies. When the virus arrived, they were able to withstand it. Did the dying trees send out some kind of signal? Do trees have minds, Maírtín? He thinks they do.*

They walk among the groves, examining the tender young leaves flushing on the fledgling trees. Close shots of a leaf of each species, veined and vibrant. On the soundtrack MAÍRTÍN *recites their names, oak, ash, beech, willow, black walnut, hornbeam, etc. It is a litany of profusion.*

They examine oaks planted five years ago and now becoming sturdy.

MAÍRTÍN, JB *and* JEREMY *are joined by* PADDY KENNY *as they approach the point where two rivers converge. They discuss JB's wish to build a pagoda at the point of convergence.* JB *says that the meeting of rivers have always been considered sacred places. They discuss holy places, wells, lakes, springs – holy meaning whole, complete, harmonious. Is it proper to mark this place with a pagoda or should it be left wild, untouched? Why does man have this compulsion to impose meaning, order, form?* JB *says it is a way of connecting the real, turbulent, chaotic world to our dream world.*

A large stone boulder sits in the grass a few yards from the Glebe house. BROTHER ANTHONY, *a Benedictine monk, hammer and chisel in hand, chips at the hard granite. He is carving a series of Celtic spirals into the reluctant stone.* JB *questions him.*

Why did he want to do it? Because it is so hard, almost impossible? Like being a monk in modern Ireland?

BROTHER ANTHONY *points out that the glacier took much longer and more care to produce this beautiful shape. He explains that this was a glacial valley and that* 14,000 *years ago we would have had hundreds of feet of ice above us.* JB *asks why we have this urge to take an artefact of nature and improve it.*

Not improve it, BROTHER ANTHONY *replies, but try to know it, reveal it, release it. The spirals follow the style of those found at New Grange.*

Some illustrations of the New Grange spirals.

JB *comments that the spirals suggest tension within the rock, powerful opposing forces held in balance. Is that ridiculous? Do we impose our imaginations on the inert and lifeless, needing to find meaning everywhere?*

BROTHER ANTHONY *might respond that he seeks God in all nature. The hard rock reminds him how hard He is to find.*

What about the river? Like me, says JB, *you have the urge to submerge, only you do it winter and summer. Is it a sensual pleasure or a way of scourging the flesh?*

Both at once, BROTHER ANTHONY *laughs.*

BROTHER ANTHONY *and* JB *swim in the river. They speculate that the river is the opposite of the rock. It is all movement and change and reflects whatever is in its path. What is a river? Its path, its course, its flow? It changes at every moment of time. Yet when we say 'river', we see it in our minds, we know it. Change is the only constant of a river. A river is an idea, not a thing. It is like a movie, which we know is a big reel with a start and a finish but we experience it one frame at a time. So it is with the river. We know it has a source and runs down to the sea. But we experience it a bit at a time.* JB *says that rivers, for all their elusiveness, are a great comfort to him. 'I can't be far from one for long.'*

JB *swimming in the river.*)

JB: (*Voice over*) As a child on the Thames I fell into the river by a lock and was sucked down by an open sluice-gate. When I could hold my breath no longer, I breathed water – the lungs close off automatically – but the stomach sucks it in and out. The water roared in my ears. I opened my eyes and stopped struggling. I was breathing the river. I felt completely at home in this alien element. I had become the river. (JB *ducks under the surface of the river.*) *Deliverance* was a film about rivers. When Jon Voigt falls, he plunges into a nightmare, for the man he has shot is brought back to apparent life and seems to embrace his killer. (Deliverance *excerpt: Ed (Voigt) is lowering the dead mountain man by rope down a cliff-side to the river. The rope breaks and they both fall into the water. Beneath the surface, the mountain man's limbs appear to move and grasp at his killer. The rope entangles the two men. Ed's eyes are full of horror.*) In *Excalibur*, Percival is set upon by the people he had betrayed. Failing to find the Grail, he has lost all hope. He is sucked under by the weight of his armour, by the weight of his guilt. (Excalibur *excerpt: Percival is hurled into the river by angry peasants. His armour drags him under. Beneath the water he struggles to rid himself of the armour, the weight of which is holding him under. Finally naked, he bursts to the surface gasping for air.* JB *surfaces from the black waters of the river.* (Excalibur *excerpt continues: Percival hauls himself out of the water to find himself at the Grail Castle.*) Stripped of his pride, and all he possesses, and having breathed the water of despair, only then – when all hope is lost – does he find himself at the gate of Grail Castle. So, finally, he is able to fulfil his quest and heal the King, and to bring the Wasteland back into fruit and flower.

EXT. THE POWERSCOURT WATERFALL. DAY
The slender waterfall feathers down the rock face into a pool of spray. Dissolve to . . .

EXT. GLENDALOUGH HOUSE. DAY
. . . the cascade at Glendalough House. It spills into a culvert which guides the water down a series of pools and lilyponds through exuberant and wildly various rhododendrons and azalias. DANNY ROCHEFORD *weeds and nurses it.*

JB: (*Voice over*) All is flow and all water has a longing for the sea. One of the many streams that join our river is captured by my neighbour, and her gardener, Danny Rocheford. He guides it through a series of pools and canals to make this water garden, a dream of what nature could be, or was once, perhaps, or is still – in another world.

(DANNY *clips and weeds, and digs and tells of the endless struggle to keep it beautiful.* JB *asks him what would happen if it was left wild.*)

EXT. THE GLEBE RIVER. DAY

DANNY *is fishing in the river. He speaks of the fish he caught as a boy, how much larger they were then, and how the old men in his day remembered tales of salmon. A tall man in long waders appears in the middle of the river. He is* NICK GREY.

JB: (*Voice over*) Nick Grey is engaged in a study of this whole river system from the Wicklow mountains to Arklow, where it meets the sea.

(*He fills a bottle with a sample of water and holds it up to the light. Leaves of mica sparkle in the soupy water. He comments on its contents. A map is spread out.* NICK GREY's *fingers trace the tributaries and he describes the water shed. He shows our river coming from Sally Gap and Lough Tay and the other branches of the system spilling down from Glendalough, Glenmalure and Glenmacanass. He points to Avoca.*)

EXT. RIVER AT AVOCA. DAY

NICK GREY *and* JB *are wading in the river.* NICK *describes how the old copper mines are still leaching metal into the river. Several old mines release other metals and the Arklow river is one of the most polluted in Europe. He describes how a fungus reacts with the copper ore to produce sulphuric acid, which runs into the river. It eats his rubber boots away.*

EXT. NITRATE FACTORY. DAY

A grey pall of dust is permanently settled over the factory and the surrounding vegetation. Not a weed will grow within a quarter of a mile of it.

JB: (*Voice over*) This factory produces nitrate fertilizers which are supposed to promote growth and bounteous crops. The Holy Grail of Science. Ironically, it kills every living thing about it and produces this wasteland. No salmon could ever pass this place. And, if it did, the sulphuric acid would be waiting for it upriver.

(PADDY MOLONEY *plays a dirge on the soundtrack as the wounded river finally dissolves into the Irish Sea. It is a bleak, featureless place. The camera moves in on the murky swirling water...*)

A river that begins in hopeful springs and magical lakes, ends here in a kind of lurid, green death.

INT. GLEBE/DRAWING ROOM/HALLWAY. NIGHT

A reprise of the first scene. JH *in the coffin rises out of the casket, guided by a woman's hand.*

JB: (*Voice over*) The opening scene. A man has a dream of death. A mysterious woman draws him back to life.

INT. GLEBE/STUDY. DAY

JB *is trying to write a script. He moves from his desk to a drawing board where he has made a chart on a large sheet of paper. On it are lines and arrows and words like 'plot', 'themes', 'the woman'. There is also a storyboard of the dream seen at the beginning of the film.*

JB: (*Voice over*) He meets her later, by chance. He recognizes her from his dream. Does she recognize him? No. He follows her obsessively. She is elusive, mysterious. She's wounded by life in some way.
   (*His name is called. A visitor. He rises from his reverie and leaves the room.*)

INT. GLEBE DRAWING ROOM. DAY

JB *enters the room where a woman is awaiting him. Her hair, clothes and make-up are very different but it is unmistakably* her, *the woman from the dream. Her manner is brittle, aggressive.* SHE *holds a miniature tape-recorder in her hand which* SHE *shakes at him.*

SHE: You don't mind this? People deny they said things. Journalists make things up. It keeps us honest.
   (JB *sits down. Her stares at her, astonished.* SHE *does not sit but moves about the room, inspecting it brazenly.* SHE *looks at some paintings.*)
   Ivon Hitchens?

JB: Yes.

SHE: He just kept on painting the same landscape over and over. Never got it right, I guess. (SHE *laughs rather unpleasantly.*)

JB: Well, I happen to believe he was trying to penetrate that landscape. In the end he wasn't painting trees and rivers, but their meaning.
   (SHE *raises an eyebrow*)

SHE: I'll do you a favour. I won't print that. It would read so pretentious.
   (JH *appears at* JB's *side on the sofa.*)

JH: It's her!

JB: I know.

SHE: You know it's pretentious? Then why say it?

JH: Say something. Do something.

JB: Shut up.

SHE: Take it easy.
   (BRIGID *the housekeeper comes in with a tray of coffee and puts it down on the stone coffin. The woman runs her fingers over the carved runes just as her dream sister did.*)
   Creepy coffee-table.

JB: As a matter of fact, it's a Celtic sarcophagus.

SHE: Some critics have said there is an unhealthy obsession with death in your movies. How do you feel about your own death?

JB: Right now I feel I'd rather die than do this interview.

SHE: Why did you agree? You surely know my reputation.

JB: I wanted to use your magazine to promote my film.

(SHE *smiles sweetly, sits.*)

SHE: Great. We want to exploit each other. Perfect grounds for a modern relationship. Speaking of which, I read somewhere that you are very taken with that quote from *Citizen Kane* where the guy says that he glimpsed this girl getting off the Staten Island ferry. Never saw her again, but there wasn't a day went by for twenty years when he didn't think about her. Is that how you see women? Mysterious, elusive?

JB: The women in *Hope and Glory* were earthy and raunchy, weren't they?

SHE: But they were your mother and aunts and sisters. They probably disgusted you. So you reach out for this 'idea' of woman. Sort of distant and unattainable and therefore safe. And also she has to carry all this symbolic baggage, like she's Mother Nature and Isis and the Lady of the Lake, etc. I mean do you really believe all this mystical stuff?

(JH *appears at* JB's *side again.*)

JH: This is disastrous. Can't you stop her? Can't you rewind this? Make her how we want her to be? Start again?

SHE: Have you ever actually had a mystical experience?

(JB *looks anxiously at* JH *then turns to* SHE.)

JB: You can't see him, can you?

SHE: Who? Are you putting me on? You call yourself a Jungian. Wasn't Carl Jung just a convenient scientific justification for your pet ideas about man's alienation from nature, Merlin as a magician–mediator and the quest for the Holy Grail, all those woolly notions about harmony and oneness?

JB: Do I get a chance to answer some of these questions?

SHE: Go ahead.

JB: Well, let's take Merlin. Yes, he is very real to me. He lives in my imagination. We converse all the time.

SHE: But has he ever appeared, physically, like in this room?

JB: No, of course not.

SHE: So it's all just so much fantasy and whimsy?

(MERLIN *appears, in the conservatory window, behind* SHE. JB *jumps to his feet, astonished. He points.*)

JB: Can you see him? It's him, Merlin.

(*She smiles, cynically.*)

SHE: You pulled that one already.

(SHE *looks over her shoulder.* SHE *screams.* MERLIN *puts his hand on her arm, confirming his corporality.*)

Look, I absolutely do not believe you can possibly exist.

MERLIN: You are not yourself.

(SHE *starts to sob.* SHE *looks younger and vulnerable. The brittle shell has fallen away.*)

SHE: I know. I'm not like this. I'm someone else.

MERLIN: All men are liars and you have devoted your life to finding them out.

SHE: Yes. And it's made me into someone I don't like.

MERLIN: It's a terrible thing, not to feel at home in your own skin, to be a stranger in a strange land. You are not alone. So it was with me. So it is with him. (*Indicating* JB) But you have come to the right place, for close by is Glendalough. Long ago a man called Kevin came there. He also was lost to himself . . .

EXT. GLENDALOUGH. DAY

The mountains rise sharply from the lake. It is more forbidding, powerful and ominous than Lough Tay and Lough Dan. Paddy's music echoes across it.

JB: (*Voice over*) In the sixth century, the man Kevin came to this remote place and lived as a hermit up here in a tiny cell and stared at the lake and mediated.

(JB *stands at St Kevin's Bed, looking down at the lake.*)

Such was his reputation that he attracted hundreds of fervent followers and a great monastery grew up.

(*The churches, the round tower and the graveyard clustered in the valley at the foot of the lake.*)

Probably Kevin came here because the Druids had found it a holy place before him. So what was the power it possessed? What was Kevin doing? Praying, I suppose. But, why here? And why did this supremely passive act arouse such wild excitement? His disciples knew he was on to something.

(*Tourists wander about in a desultory way. They stare out at the lake as though waiting for something to happen.*)

Glendalough is one of the essential tourist stops in Ireland. They are told it is a holy place, the holiest of all. They flock here as Kevin's followers did. But when they arrive, they are disappointed. They look at the lake hoping to feel something, but there is no ritual, no ceremony to help them. At shrines all over the world you see the same blank expressions as the secular present peers at the magical past. Is it quite dead, that past?

(*The tourists have gone.* JH *is alone at the lake. He is climbing up to St Kevin's Bed. It is very steep. He clutches at roots to haul himself up.*)

JH: (*Voice over*) I dreamt I was trying to reach Kevin's Bed. I knew if I could only get there, some important mystery would be revealed.

(*He reaches the top, panting.* JB *is standing there. They look. A deep hum seems to come from the lake.*)

JH: Can you hear that?

JB: No. What?

JH: There's a great force coming from the lake.

JB: I often come here hoping to feel something, but . . .

JH: Surely you can feel it. It's terrifying.

(JH *is trembling, his eyes fearful.* JB *has disappeared.*)

JH: (*Voice over*) A great force was coming from the lake. It was . . . How can I describe it . . . like naked power. It was terrifying because it had no purpose, no objective, not good, not evil. It was just itself. (JH *is trembling, his eyes fearful. A wind has got up, lashing the trees around him, buffeting the water off the lake.* JH *starts to scramble down the hill.*) And I understood that what the Druids and the monks were doing was to harness that power to the cause of good and now nobody is watching, nobody cares, and it is running wild, blind, destructive.

(JH *is running along the shore of the lake, terrified.*

A WOMAN'*s face is rising from the lake, forcing itself up through the turbulent water. As she bursts through the surface, the humming stops.*

JH *looks back over his shoulder at the lake and sees the* WOMAN *emerging from the water. She wears a silver wetsuit. She looks at* JH *and he sees that she is the* WOMAN *in his dream. She reaches the shore some fifty yards away where twisted trees overhang the water. The surface of the water is calm again.*

The WOMAN *smiles at him. Even though they are far apart and speak softly they are able to hear each other's words.*)

JH: I have been looking for you all my life.

WOMAN: And in other lives. And you will. The word is not . . .

(*Before she can finish her sentence, the* GREEN MAN *emerges from a tree beside her. He draws her into the wood.*)

JH: (*Voice over*) I tried to help her, but my feet would not move.

(JH'*s tormented face. Flashes of limbs seen through branches. Fallen leaves churn into the air in the turmoil of the rape. The spiked fingernails of the* GREEN MAN *rip open the rubber belly of the* WOMAN. *Blossoms and berries spill out of the wound. The* GREEN MAN *claws them with his cupped hands and buries his mouth in them.*

JH *screams soundlessly. A hand touches his shoulder and he swings about.*)

JH: Merlin!

MERLIN: You cannot stop it. It happened long ago. Before Kevin, before the Druids. It is the wound.

JH: I can I must.

(MERLIN *gestures towards* JH's *feet. He looks down. His feet are tree roots going deep into the ground. He screams.*)

INT. GLEBE DRAWING ROOM. NIGHT

JB *is sleeping on the sofa. A book lies in his lap. He wakes up with a start. He rubs his feet. Pins and needles. He stands up but his feet will not support him properly. He circles the rug as though walking on glass. He suddenly sees Merlin sitting in an armchair by the window. He goes towards him.*

JB: How can we heal the wound, Merlin?

MERLIN: Ah, there's a question.

JB: Is there nothing I can do?

MERLIN: Well, you have made this film.

(JB *looks out the window, at the clear, summer's afternoon light. He turns towards* MERLIN *and smiles.*)

JB: OK. Cut. It's a wrap. Thank you very much, everybody.

8 July

Yesterday we completed the ten-day shoot. The crew consisted of Seamus Deasy as cameraman, his brother Brendan on sound and Shane O'Neil as focus puller. Seamus's son, also called Shane, is clapper-loader. The Deasys had come to my attention when they made *The Making of Excalibur* for Neil Jordan. They are quiet and resourceful. Seamus is a superb camera operator and he lights with subtlety. We got by with one electrician, who worked only two days out of ten. Sean Ryerson acted as production manager and first assistant director. David Keating, a young writer/director who is a protégé of mine, worked as a kind of second AD on an occasional basis. Propping, set-decorating and gripping we did between us. John Hurt played my alter ego in the dramatized sequences. My son Charley was the Green Man, the malevolent spirit of the forest, and Janet McTeer played the woman who appears in three manifestations: a mysterious stranger in the opening scene, a bitchy journalist and finally the Lady of the Lake. Other parts were done by non-actors, all friends: Stan Gebler-Davies, a Swiftian columnist, played Merlin; odd-job man Philip Giles, Andy Byrne who helps plant my trees, Brigid and Mrs Curly, who help in the house, did other small roles.

My fears about acting were well founded. As a director you must stand outside the action and watch objectively. You must put out of mind what you know of the actor's thoughts and feelings and believe only what you see and hear, but as an actor you are blind. I was shocked that I could not see myself. Unlike the director, the actor must exclude everything – the camera, crew, everything – from his consciousness and depend on his feelings, or his simulated feelings. I found myself watching the camera out of the corner of my eye, checking on its movements, worrying about the light on my fellow actors. I would block and rehearse with a stand-in, sometimes Charley, sometimes David Keating, then sit in myself. I got into it, eventually, after a shaky start. I had carefully alibied my self-consciousness and awkwardness by owning up to these characterisitcs in the opening scenes, by admitting that I have always felt uncomfortable in my skin. So, in a sense, it was difficult for me to be worse than I said I was. Curiously, I found the documentary elements – chatting to people – much more difficult than the acting scenes. It is hard to say how well the drama scenes will fit in with the documentary sections. They could be oil and water.

With these cautious reservations disposed of, I have to say that we all, actors and crew, had the most delightful and exhilarating time. Not to be encumbered with a huge crew and convoys of trucks was liberating. We moved fast – shooting it on 16mm of course helped – and where the resources of the feature film were not available, we improvised. The film is quite complex with special-effects sequences, underwater shots, dream sequences, complex make-up, including prosthetics. We used lightweight plastic tracks and levelled them with the rocks that are in such abundance here. Where conditions would not allow us to move the camera, we devised complex choreography for the actors to take its place. Fast film and fast lenses allowed us to shoot inside with only minimal lighting.

For example, in the opening dream sequence John Hurt is required to descend the staircase and to see himself lying in a Romano-Celtic stone coffin in the drawing room. He has awoken from sleep in the night – or rather he dreams that he wakes up. It is night, of course, in the bedroom. To achieve a night effect in my drawing room, which is decorated in pale colours and has five large Georgian windows, would mean either shooting at night (out of the question) or blacking out the windows, which is much too time-consuming and expensive. My solution was to make a night effect on the stairs and hallway and track through into the drawing room which was in full daylight, thus deliberately overexposing the shot by four stops. We added a fog filter which helps to make the light from the windows 'halo'. The final effect is that he witnesses his death in a blinding white light. The dream-like effect is achieved by passing from the night-time hallway into the daytime drawing room in a single shot.

We made an average of thirty-three set-ups per day as against the eight to twelve that I would achieve on a feature. Working without lights on exteriors I had to use other techniques. We had small reflectors that could provide some fill light where the subject was backlit, but I always had to be ready to shift location to suit the light, using the foliage of trees to break up harsh sunlight or moving to a less dense part of the woods if sunlight was absent. I also had to plan my shots to coincide with the direction of the sun. I learnt in the Amazon that overhead light is the most effective in forest. When the sun is at a low angle it increases the amount of foliage it has to penetrate. In most other exteriors a low sun gives much more interesting light and more shadow, which gives more shape and modelling. Backlight or three-quarters backlight helps to separate the various planes, giving the illusion of depth. Backlight also gives a luminous quality to objects which helps them escape the two-dimensional nature of film, its natural conditon of flatness.

In every set-up we seek what Sam Fuller calls 'the one thing' – that ingredient that will transform photography into cinema, make magic out of emulsion, the alchemical catalyst. Shooting an emblematic scene like the Green Man raping the Lady of the Lake ('the wound in the heart of God' is how Lindsay Clarke put it), I had a number of elements: the brooding lake of Glendalough as a background, and a copse of twisted oak and birch as a setting. There is John Hurt's anguish as he watches it, and Paddy Moloney's pipes will eventually give it a shrill and melancholic voice, and yet and yet . . . It still required 'the one thing'. I asked the few spare hands of my sparse crew to whip back and forth the branches of bushy birch under which the rape was being committed. The thrashing tree suggested that it was nature herself that was raped. In *Deliverance*, I shot the mountain men as though they were emerging from trees: like malevolent spirits of the forest coming to rape these city men who had in turn ravaged the forest. So, too, here I have bounteous Mother Nature ravished by that other potent force of nature, its cruel and predatory side, for the nature of nature is that it feeds savagely upon itself.

10 July

It is nearly two years now since I agreed to give a paper at a seminar in Salado, Texas, for a Jungian Group that Lee Marvin espoused. He and Pam used to go there every year, and the founder, Harry Wilmer, finally persuaded me to go. While it was two years away, it was easy to agree and now suddenly it is upon me. He has written to say he wants my paper. I thought I would be able to go along and just improvise, but I sat down finally and wrote this piece. The subject of the seminar is to be Dreams and I call my piece 'Day-Dreams':

What do we mean by day-dreams? The 'day-dreamist' stares into space, trance-like, unaware of what goes on around him or her. In other words she is not present, she is elsewhere, 'far away' we say, or 'miles away'. Dreaming, night or day, is only possible when we are able to free ourselves from the solid tyranny of space and time. Being here and now. Most of us are incapable of either condition – being totally here, or being totally absent. To be totally present, to be here and nowhere else, to exist in this very moment without referring to past or future, without a rogue corner of the mind flitting hither and thither, stepping out of that moment and the self, looking back at us, making us self-aware, self-conscious and therefore unable to be entirely present – that is a wondrous thing. It means to be completely alive. We say about an actor that he has great presence, and it means just that. They are here and nowhere else. All the great movie actors have this in common. They are able to be wholly present. This lends them great power because we believe in them, because about them there is no hint of self-consciousness.

But to dream it is necessary to be free of here and now; in the unconsciousness of sleep we are liberated. In day-dreams, only partially so. There are a few people who can achieve a total 'waking absence', but, for most of us, we only experience something like it at the movies, which approximate the condition of dreaming. Films move freely in space and time. They present an impression of reality, yet they consist merely of light playing on a flat surface. They suggest a contiguous world, as dreams do. We can watch a film over and over as we experience a recurring dream.

When I was preparing to make *The Emerald Forest*, I spent time with an Amerindian tribe in the Xingu region of the Amazon. They had had almost no contact with the outside world. I forged a close relationship with Takuma, the shaman of the tribe. At one point he enquired about my work. I struggled to explain the work of a film-maker to people who had never been to the cinema or watched television. He was puzzled until I told him how the images could move from place to place and shift about in time. 'That is what I do in trance,' he said. 'You do the same work that I do.'

D. H. Lawrence in his novel *The Lost Girl* described coalminers in Nottingham watching early silent films. Gone were the embarrassed leering expressions they wore when seeing live performers. Their mouths now gaped, their eyes stared, unblinking. When we are frightened in the movies and we clutch our companion's hand, how does this action relate to how we might react to the same incident in real life? When we cry in the cinema at loss or separation are they the same tears we shed for our own losses in life? (I have to admit that I have cried at the movies at situations where in life I could find no tears – there is a contradiction to conjur with). How can we be utterly lost in a movie, yet still be aware that we are sitting in a theatre? That is day-dreaming: to be both absent and present at the same time.

So the movies can transport us into a trance of dreams. What then, what do we encounter there? We meet mostly film-makers who are unaware of the power they wield. Many are simply greedy and manipulative; some, more than a few, are driven by misogyny. Then there are the natural movie-makers like Griffith, John Ford, David Lean or Michael Powell, who have a direct line to the unconscious, but are unconscious of it; their simple story-telling is framed in mythic compositions and played out by archetypal characters. Almost the best that cinema has thrown up is the work of these intuitive movie-makers. D. W. Griffith and his cameraman Billy Bitzer contrived an entire technical grammar of film in a couple of years during the time when millions of men were dying in the trenches of the First World War. In Russia, Eisenstein systematized these techniques and devised his theory of film, particularly the notion of montage. For example, if you juxtapose a shot of a man's face with a child crying, the viewer will ascribe compassion to the man. If the same shot of the man's face is cut next to a clown doing a trick, you would imagine the man is amused.

Eisenstein was perhaps the first structuralist. With Prokofiev he developed a theory of wedding music to image. Eisenstein saw how audiences' emotions could be manipulated by film technique and thus used for propaganda purposes.

The power of the movies, and its potential power, is enormous and hardly tapped. Hollywood today works mostly by manipulating audiences' emotions in the quest for money. Cinema has produced only a handful of artists who give us an inkling of what this art could be; artists who connect, both intimately and consciously, to this parallel world of dreams; artists who can take us there and give us perfect day-dreams. These dream-movies are rare, but they reward us for the endless disappointments we endure. We know deep down that film can be revelation, and the excitement we feel each time the lights go down is the expectation of that. All but a few fail. Some have great moments, flashes of revelation; we get caught up in their stories, follow the action, but finally they mostly disappoint. Now and then a Tarkovsky or Buñuel will take us all the way and we are transported. We are shown – I was going to say – the after-life, but I think I mean the life of the spirit, a life that is hidden from us by the hard surfaces of the waking world, this Other Country that we, otherwise, only enter in the confused tumult of dreams.

I have just finished making a film for the BBC called *I Dreamt I Woke Up*, so-called because it begins with just that, me dreaming that I wake up. Except it's not me, but my alter ego, who pops up throughout the film whenever the world of the spirit intrudes on the everyday. All my life I have had waking-up dreams. They are terrifying because you believe you are awake. Often in a dream, when nasty things happen – well, you know it is a dream and that eventually you will wake up, just as, however caught up we are in a movie, we know we are in the theatre; but when you dream that you wake up you are convinced that these horrors are befalling you, that you are actually awake. I have had those dreams all my life.

The film opens with my alter ego dreaming that he wakes up. Hearing voices below, he descends the stairs, looks into the drawing room and sees himself lying in a coffin. The lid closes over him and he falls into blankness. I show him falling happily through space. 'How good it is,' he says, 'to let go, to give up the struggle, to fall.' Finally, he remembers there is something he must still do. He starts to struggle, he exerts his will and he hauls himself back to the land of the living. So I re-enact in the film a dream that has frequently visited me, a dream of dying. I am falling, it is very pleasant, then I become aware that if I don't fight to live, I will, as the old joke has it, wake up dead. At which point I do wake up – so far, anyway! With heart pounding I leap out of bed, the treacherous bed through which I can so easily drop into the void. The film continues moving in and out of dreams, so that, insidiously, I suggest that whether waking or sleeping, in film, all is dream.

The subject of the film is man's, this man's, relationship to the natural world. In particular, to the landscape in which I live in the Wicklow mountains of Ireland. I plant trees. We put in 13,000 last winter. I am surrounding myself in forest, restoring what was once here and was lost. 'Trees', Carl Jung said, 'are the thoughts of God.' Landscape is metaphor. I suggest that we all have an inner landscape of the spirit and we yearn to find an outer landscape to coincide with the inner one.

Dreamscape you could say. I present myself in the film for what I am: an awkward man, uncomfortable in my own skin, a man trying to connect, trying to find a condition of harmony with the world. The night before I started shooting I had a dream in which someone said to me, 'You are an absolute shit and that should be in the film.' Perhaps I am, perhaps it is.

So I had a dream about a film which is about me dreaming that I wake up. Am I the butterfly or the man? Jung argued that since the unconscious was part of the universe it must obey the laws of the universe, and his hope was to find a unifying theory that would account for the contents of the unconscious. I'll leave that to the scientists. My modest task is to make a few forays down there and to bring back the evidence on film.

15 July

Jean Luc-Godard once said, 'All you need for a movie is a gun and a girl.' In *Thelma and Louise*, Ridley Scott has a gun and two girls, women rather, and what glorious women they are: Geena Davis and Susan Sarandon! The same cannot be said for the characters they play, two dumb broads. Much has been made of the movie. Here are two ordinary women, we are told, breaking out of their drab lives, shooting the man who sexually harasses them and having a great, liberating time. Ridley Scott's restless, caressing camera wraps the women in American landscapes like a lavish dress designer. He probes for phallic symbols, finding them in the most unlikely places. The supporting cast is brilliantly put together, mostly nasty males; the extras are chosen and placed with cunning skill – they always illuminate the action and are expressive of the place. Ridley's camera work is as stunning as ever, and he makes extraordinary use of the strengths and limitations of anomorphic lenses. One of the problems of the system is the lack of depth of field. Even in this movie there are one or two close-ups, which I imagine are exposed at F2 or 2.8, where the eyes are in focus but the nose is not. However, he builds up the light in most of the close and medium shots to what looks to me between F5.6 and F8, so that the wide portion of the frame not occupied by the face can be filled with appropriate action, extras and so on that are sufficiently out of focus not to draw the eye, and yet who they are, and what they do, can easily be perceived. There are many scenes between the two women in the moving car and, hard as I tried, I could not detect the use of rear projection. The road tracking shots were superb. The steadycam has become a standard piece of equipment that has liberated the camera from its mooring. The most acute pleasures of the movie are those wonderful camera movements which mirror the new-found freedom of the women.

However, the actresses are over-qualified for the roles. You feel the women they are playing would never do and get away with the things they do, but that Geena and Susan would. You do not quite believe the characters' reactions to killing the rapist nor to their subsequent actions. I got the impression that the actresses were fighting Ridley all the way for the space they needed to play out their drama. They are in constant competition with his army of images, but it is a creative conflict, a male–female thing. Ridley conveys the exhilaration and grandeur of American landscapes, but I missed any sense of the boredom and endless repetition of driving across America. Ridley even defies common sense by keeping the top of their convertible firmly down.

When you drive along those flat desert roads, you put it up thankfully and turn on the air-conditioning. But you get better shots with the top down. Those women must have eaten a lot of dust.

20 July

I'm on my way to Taormina in Sicily as a guest of the Arts Festival. They are to show *Where the Heart Is*.

I have completed the first cut of *I Dreamt I Woke Up*. The ten-day shoot has left us with very little fat, but the fast pace of the making has given it an invigorating dynamic. The experience has been invigorating for me too. When you make a movie today the stakes are so high, there is so much money riding on it, reputations and careers are at stake and we are all conscious that so many films fail and so few are hits. Kubrick once said to me, 'It's not that I want to make a hit, I just don't want to make a failure. But to avoid that you have to make a hit.' This experience liberated me from all that and put the sheer pleasure of film-making back in. Although the resources were so limited, it was nevertheless thrilling to have the instruments back in my hand and to find I could still play them with some skill. Now, each day, I take my breakfast and walk down to the guest cottage where Ron Davis awaits me on the Steenbeck.

So, what about myself on film? Surprisingly, in the scenes in which I am required to be an actor and speak written lines, I sneak by, passably. It is in the documentary bits that I seem inept, muttering and stuttering. Worse still, in the pieces about the life of the spirit, about connecting my deepest self to nature, to history, to God, the figure on the screen seems a dull man lacking in passion for this passionate subject. He seems out of place. True, I make the point that I have never felt at home in my own skin, but even so there is little to indicate what lies under it.

21 July, Taormina, Sicily

The high-vaulted room in the San Domenico Palace looks out on to a balcony and, below, the Ionian Sea is spread out before me. The town is cut into a mountainside and hangs over the azure sea. The hotel was a Dominican monastery, then served for a while as Nazi headquarters during the war, and now is at the disposal of film directors and other guests of the 37th Festival Arte. It has served the privileged down the years. The opening ceremony and screening took place at the Greek amphitheatre under a half-moon. Antonioni arrived on the arm of his beautiful and attentive wife. He was limping from the after-effects of a stroke he suffered a few years back.

At dinner afterwards I spoke with him. I reminded him of his visit to my house in Ireland when he had told me the story of how Dino de Laurentis had heard that Antonioni had a story he wanted to make. It was *L'Avventura*. Dino sent him a plane ticket to come to Rome (Antonioni was in Milan). 'You tell me the story. If I like it, I make it,' said Dino. Antonioni was always laconic. (He once proposed a film for me to direct for which he was to be the producer. 'What is the story?' I asked. 'It is about a woman,' he said. I waited but he added nothing further.) So he told the story of *L'Avventura* to Dino, of the girl Anna who mysteriously disappears and how the rest of the film is spent searching for her. At the end of it, Dino said, 'So what happened to Anna?' Antonioni shrugged. 'I don't know.' 'You wrote the story and you don't know what happened to her?' 'No.' Dino held out his hand. 'Then give me back my money for the plane ticket.'

Antonioni had been visiting Ireland, where he hoped to make a film called 'The Crew'. 'It is about a man on a boat,' he told me cryptically at the time. He wanted Robert Shaw to play the role, and I introduced them. He still hopes to make it, perhaps co-directing it with Mark Peploe, who wrote the screenplay.

22 July, Taormina

Last night in the Teatro Antico, under the moon and the stars, we watched Chen Kaige's (*Yellow Earth*, *Big Parade*, *King of the Children*) new film *Life on a String*. Its polyglot, polyphonal producer Donald Ranvaud told us of the enterprise. Chen has suffered persecution and the banning of his films in China. Although this new one is non-political it is a complex allegory and the Chinese authorities have yet to give their permission for it to be shown. Even so, it is deeply subversive and I will be surprised if it slips through the net. The finance came entirely from the West: Channel Four, German, French and Italian money. Donald avoided any investment from the Chinese government, which would have given it the right to stop its distribution abroad. The rushes were sent out and processed in Berlin, where the post-production was done.

I could make very little of the Italian subtitles, which, interestingly enough, were not on the film but on a kind of electronic scoreboard under the screen. What I picked up was this: an old blind minstrel and his young blind apprentice are discovered walking across the desert. They seem lost, doomed. High crane shots show hundreds of miles of desert all around them. Even so, they eventually come to a place at the edge of a cascade where they are fed by a beautiful, provocative woman. There are some crazed people in attendance around her. The old man's banjo-like instrument and his astonishing voice have the power to heal conflict and bring joy. Yet this power seems to be connected to his state of blindness. The young man falls in love with and makes love to a girl in a village they visit. This appears to be a betrayal. The boy wants sight. There is a remedy, but the quest for it somehow breaks the old man's banjo strings and his powers are lost.

The imagery is of such beauty that it wrings your heart; the music, the singing, are sublime. You know yourself to be in the presence of a great work of art that will reveal layers of meaning on re-viewing. It recalls Tarkovsky in that you feel that film was invented for such a movie. This is what it is for. It is a journey into the landscape of the spirit. It reveals the overwhelming ache in the Chinese soul. If I were a Chinese Communist ruler, this film would frighten me to death. The need of the Chinese is enormous, unstoppable and yet it also seems to be connected to spiritual eruptions that are bubbling up out of the unconscious across the globe. It can be set alongside Tarkovsky's *The Sacrifice* as a masterpiece of cinema. Both films are curiously similar in theme and style. And they both reveal that the purpose of the beautiful image is to puncture the hard surface of reality, and reveal the meaning beneath. *Barton Fink*, which swept the prizes at Cannes, leaving *Life on a String* empty-handed, must be truly amazing. More likely, in the spirit of Cannes, Polanski and fellow jurors were irritated by the inordinate length and stately progress of Chen's film, daring, as it does, to wear its soul on its sleeve.

23 July, Taormina

Last night on the stage of the Teatro Antico, Bertolucci presented Antonioni with a special prize. They showed the last reel of *L'Avventura*. Bernardo said it was the seminal film of his generation, that it represented the birth of modern cinema. And there was Monica Vitti on the screen once more, her face a mask of bruised *angst* as she searched the rooms and corridors of (I'd quite forgotten) the very hotel in which we are staying. After the ceremony, I introduced *Where the Heart Is* from the stage. I added my homage to Antonioni and I said what a wonderful place this was to see movies. 'Sitting in the warm fragrant air under the stars I felt sorry for the Greeks,' I said. 'They built these beautiful theatres, but they had no movies to show.'

We did not stay to watch *Where the Heart Is*. The memories are still to me too painful to re-see it at present. We went to dinner at La Botte with Michel Ciment and Evelyn. Michel has seen the film five times already and is a great supporter of its virtues, so he could miss it too. People came into the restaurant at the end of the screening. Antonioni embraced me and held me in a surprisingly strong grip. 'Bravo, bravo,' he said and kissed me on both cheeks. Others arrived, critics, journalists, film-makers, and their warmth seemed genuine. Bertolucci came in with his wife Clair. He was very generous too; he said it was original and wonderfully entertaining. 'That must be your family on the screen,' he said.

This morning Bernardo and I gave an informal seminar to critics and journalists on the subject of exile. Bertolucci said he could no longer find inspiration in Italy. He cited the fragmentation of popular culture brought about by television. He felt that, more than elsewhere, Italy has been colonized by American culture. He preceded his remarks by again, and in public, praising *Where the Heart Is*. He said it was a completely original work; although it is playful and witty, it is a serious film with serious themes.

I told the assembled audience that I have the same reluctance as Bernardo has to engage with contemporary life in England or Ireland as film material. I am not sure why. Partly, I suppose, because our small islands seem so peripheral in world terms. *Where the Heart Is* was orginally an attempt to make a film in modern London. Although I was bitterly disappointed when I failed to finance it and was forced to transpose it New York, nevertheless it immediately took on a different kind of power and resonance there. When it was set in London, I felt it necessary to explain why these events and characters were there and apologize even for being there, whereas New York is simply *there*. It is where you expect movies to occur. The enterprise immediately took on a swagger of confidence. Would it have been a better film had it been more closely connected to its roots, my roots? Yet it is a long time since I've lived in London. I explained to them how liberating it was for me to go to America. It was only when I was there, making *Point Blank*, that I realized how oppressive the English class system had been for me. But then I found it impossible to live in LA. It was fine as long as it seemed bizarre, a fragment of science fiction, but once it began to seem normal, I took flight. I could not return to England and I could not stay in the States. Ireland was the refuge. I lived in the hills, sheltered in the Celtic twilight, and tried to heal my bruised soul. *Point Blank, Hell in the Pacific, Deliverance* – those pictures took a lot out of me, nearly broke me. They stretched me to my limits; but, more than that, I was always profoundly disturbed by making them within the Hollywood ethos. For there, those values always insidiously prevail. So there we were, myself and Bernardo, marooned, lost to our pasts. I told the journalists that, as national cultures crumbled or were swept away by the American cultural bulldozer, film was evolving into a global form which chartered a land as yet undiscovered, a spiritual country which could help to connect people across the world. That is perhaps only a fond hope. Can film live up to that? After all, the movies that unite the world are *Pretty Woman* and *Dances with Wolves*. But there is a lesson in that too for the Boormans and Bertoluccis.

I go to the beach each morning. The water is perfect. I swim far out to sea. I lose myself in water; my limbs move but I have no consciousness of myself, I am part of the ocean. I have no weight, no thoughts, no feelings, no self.

In the afternoon in the heavy heat I shelter in the shuttered room, read, write, check the messages on the answering machine in Annamoe. I talk to Sean Ryerson. He tells me that the helicopter shots which we delayed making because of the bad weather are finally done. Seamus says conditions were good. The one I most need is to connect Lough Tay in Luggala with Lough Dan – an essential link in my progress down the river valley. We are still having problems with Warners; they want to charge huge fees for using brief extracts of my films. It is galling that directors have no rights over their work once completed. I spoke to Paddy Moloney of the Chieftains and arranged to plan the musical score with him on 17 August in Annamoe. It is only then that the peripatetic Chieftains finally touch down and pause from their endless world tours.

26 July, en route Taormina–Ireland

Dinner with Michel Ciment last night. As a passionate advocate of *Where the Heart Is*, he was thrilled at the success it enjoyed here, even more than I. Enrico Ghezzi, the director of the Festival, who is shyly inarticulate in several languages, arrived on his moped to say goodbye as we left the hotel. I gave him a bottle of Irish whisky and thanked him for giving such a welcome home to my orphan film. He and his colleagues have such a love of the movies. That might seem a precondition for running a festival but, in practice, most festivals are mounted for other reasons, often for the glory of the organizers. I had several encounters with young film-makers, writers, critics, who passionately believe in the potential of film to transform the human condition, to change the human heart. Such meetings strengthen my resolve to aim at the highest level of achievement, rather than allow myself to settle for less. Film directors are mostly iconoclastic. We have to stand apart, but these contacts are reviving and nourishing.

9 August, London

Dinner party at Groucho's for my daughter Katrine's birthday. She has taken on a new role for her brother-in-law, Jasper Conran, as his 'girl'. His designs will be built on her body. She wore a white dress of his that set heads spinning when we came in. Timna Woollard, who did the *trompe-l'oeil* body painting for *Where the Heart Is*, was there and her sister Emma as well as Jasper, my son Charley and his fiancée Olivia. We talked about *Edward Scissorhands*. Timna pronounced herself enchanted by its magic and so was Emma. Katrine thought that magic was what it lacked. The movie has echoes of *The Wizard of Oz* and *Beauty and the Beast* and is a brave and welcome excursion into fantasy – a tradition stifled by the brutish sci-fi or numbing naturalism of

American cinema. One of the film's problems is the central conceit that the eponymous hero has scissors for hands. His gentleness is undercut (if I may be allowed the pun) by the inherent hostility of the device. Although we see him cutting women's hair and shaping hedges into animal figures, the act of cutting is essentially reductive. This is not the right equipment to bring magic into these suburban lives. The brilliantly stylized 1950s suburb, elaborately constructed and painted in the pale candy colours of the period, is peopled by a grotesquerie of housewives and beer-bellied husband slobs. Tim Burton's background as an animator intrudes as he sketches them with savagely extravagant parody against these cartoon backgrounds. The flat lighting, so effective and appropriate in achieving this cartoon effect, casts much too harsh a light on Edward's snipping and cutting. This shadow creature is not allowed the shadows he needs. It is a matter of two clever ideas that conflict with each other. Cinema works best when separate elements combine in an alchemy that produces something new and magical. Here we have two constructed artifices which bump against each other with a resounding clunk.

Backdraft is about Chicago firemen fighting fires. It seems that fires in that city have an hysterical fervour they lack elsewhere. They leap across rooms, crash through walls and explode through ceilings. I saw it in Bray. Halfway through, the lights went up in the middle of a scene. I asked the manager why. 'Two hours twenty minutes,' he said, 'is too long to get on one reel, so I have to break in and sell some ice-cream.' The projectionist had been having problems with the focus, the soundtrack was a continuous bombardment, and all that fire was scorching my brain. So I decided to catch the second half another time and go home and hose myself down.

The trade papers are full of news about Interactive, a combination of video game and film where the viewer controls the characters and plot. Lucasfilm and Disney are pressing forward with this and claim that 'passive' films will soon be a thing of the past. Already audiences are dictating the outcome of movies in sneak previews. More and more studios insist that the film-maker reshoot to follow the dictates of the audience. Yet I wonder if watching conventional movies is altogether passive. Timna projected her hunger for fantasy into *Edward Scissorhands* and made it a much better movie than the one Katrine saw. The other night I found myself seated opposite Salman Rushdie at dinner. He had seen *Thelma and Louise*. 'Don't ask me how I saw it,' he warned, and, as a man incarcerated, he was exhilarated by the flight of these two women across America. Ridley Scott's floating camera carried Salman in his arms in flights of joy. Needless to say, he has forged close and emotional ties with his Special Branch bodyguards (four of them hovered in the kitchen, washing dishes), and he was fascinated by the scenes in the film where the FBI agents camp out with the husband of one of the fleeing women, particularly the way the man asserts his role as householder by controlling the TV zapper, switching channels on the FBI agents.

I screened *I Dreamt I Woke Up* for John Archer at Ealing Studios, where the BBC film unit is based. Although he had admired the script he looked slightly askance at the end, wondering perhaps if he had not gone too far in giving me *carte blanche* on behalf of his employers. I can see the virtues of the film, but being confronted by myself on the screen prevents me from relishing it or indeed judging it. I was hoping to find out more about myself, and although I am in accord with what he stands for, I do not find the man on the screen sympathetic.

I recorded the voice-over at Pinewood with Ron Davis. There was very little activity in the studio, and business is generally bad. The rumour is that Shepperton Studios is to close. Elstree has gone already. Bray Studios is threatened. It looks as though Pinewood could be the only one left. Twickenham will go on, but its stage space is very limited. It is really a post-production facility.

I met up with Phil Stokes, the able special-effects man who built the miniature of the dam for *The Emerald Forest* and convincingly destroyed it. He also managed the rogue barrage balloon in *Hope and Glory* and the re-enactment of the scenes from the Blitz. He is all fired up by the script of *Broken Dream*. He has been consulting with a team of whizz-kids in London who are working on a new digital system of special effects similar to the one which was so admired in *Terminator 2*. The problem to date has been that in order to use the panoply of electronic special effects available to television you have to transfer your film to videotape and eventually back to film again. Even HDTV only boasts 1,250 lines, whereas 35mm film is equivalent to around 3,500 lines. The degradation of quality involved is clearly quite unacceptable. The new digital system avoids this transfer. It digitally scans each frame of the film. With this information in the computer the scene can be manipulated using Paint Box and all the technical wizardry available in electronic imagery. The final digital information directly instructs a new film negative telling it how much light and which colour should appear in each of its thousands of dots. There is no loss of quality at all. Since the story calls for objects and people to disappear in startling and poetic manners, this facility will enrich the film. Phil had come up from Dorset where he had wangled a ride on a Chieftain tank. It has a gyroscopic gun mount which keeps the aim steady, even when the tank is hurtling over the roughest country. He wants to adopt the idea to the needs of film. His plan is to mount a steel boom on a truck which would carry a camera and operator. The boom would remain steady and the operator would have foot pedals, as well as the usual controls to get elevation and swing. He has also acquired two jet engines which he will mount on each side of the same truck to provide the enormous wind that we need. I love his enthusiasm.

19 August, Kinsale

John Hurt, extravagantly, keeps a yacht with a crew of two down in Kinsale. He offered it to me and I am taking a cruise along the coast to Union Hall, where I will entertain Stan Gebler-Davis and his wife Paddy to dinner on the boat. Here we are, cut off, as the news reaches us of Gorbachev's arrest. Suddenly, I didn't want to be on a boat, but at home, hunkered down watching cable news.

Last Friday we caught the 5.30 performance of *Terminator 2* in Dublin on its opening day. The line stretched round the block, 85 per cent were young boys between fifteen and twenty. The film arrived wrapped in legend. It supposedly cost $100 million. The rumour was that Carolco had given Schwarzenegger their corporate jet as a fee. It had taken $100 million at the box office in the US in two weeks. American critics were saying it was the best science-fiction film ever made. The digital special effects were said to be revolutionary. And so they are. Perhaps for the first time, film is able to approach the wilder flights of imagination that literary science-fiction has enjoyed. In this case, a 'cyborg' is able to alter shape at will, notably into a mercury-like metal. When it is destroyed, it quickly re-forms itself. Arnie's cyborg is an old model and therefore not as resourceful. Arnie is able to slow down his antagonist by blasting holes in him which take a few moments to heal. Some of the cyborg's re-formations have a surreal beauty about them, as when he takes human shape from the unpromising beginning as a piece of chequered hospital corridor floor. In another case he is submerged in liquid nitrogen. He freezes and his body cracks into hundreds of splintering fragments. This movie is a landmark, like *2001*.

The digital effects apart, the movie is mostly an orgy of destruction and mayhem, with chases and a huge array of weaponry. It sets out to outdo whatever has been done before. The car chase is the most spectacular ever. The guns are bigger than we have ever seen. They are enormous.

It started with Clint Eastwood's .44 Magnum in *Dirty Harry*. (Lee Marvin used the same gun in *Point Blank*, but there it represented an impotent phallic symbol.) Since then, with its implied statement, 'My dick is bigger than yours,' every macho movie star has been finding bigger and better guns. But there has never been a bigger one than Arnie's.

It was Lee's idea in *Point Blank* to shoot into the empty bed of the wife who had betrayed him. Since the Magnum was so powerful, we assumed it would have huge recoil. But we were using blanks, which give no recoil, so Lee faked it, his arm whipping back a foot or more after each shot. It suggested the enormous power of the thing more than anything else could. Later, when we were filming on Alcatraz, we got some live ammunition and fired the big Magnum for real. There was no recoil at all. Lee grinned at me. 'Our way sure beats the real thing,' he said.

When was it that movie actors all started shooting guns with both hands? It happened overnight. All those years, all those Westerns and gangster films, where you only used two hands if you were using two guns. Now, if an innocent girl when confronting her assailant manages to grab a gun, why, she clutches it in both hands and holds it in outstretched arms, just like she's seen it in the movies.

28 August, London

Heading for London to mix the tracks of *I Dreamt I Woke Up* at Pinewood. I will also work with the grader at Technicolor. On Thursday last we recorded the musical score at Windmill Lane Studios. In the spirit of the film, Paddy Moloney made do with five musicians, including himself. Derek Bell, harpist of the Chieftains, also played the keyboards and operated the synthesizer, which we used to thicken things up. Paddy played the pipes and the tin whistle. In addition, we had flutes and fiddle. I had discussed the score with Paddy, and he had studied the script, but it was not until last Sunday that we sat down and spent the day together spotting the cues. Ron Davis and I had prepared a music cue sheet with the starts and ends of each piece. Although his musical background is in the Irish folk tradition, Paddy is eclectic and sensitive to the needs of the film. He also appears in it, his piping at Luggala so powerful and moving that it caused Garech Browne ('doom and gloom de Brun', as Paddy calls him) to levitate. Getting a vodka-marinated Garech into a harness and hoisting him up convincingly proved difficult and tiresome. Garech was obstructive and contrary in that mood and my deep affection for him was severely tested. Consequently, in that atmosphere, Paddy never achieved the soaring poetry of which he is capable and which would justify Garech levitating. But in the studio, he put that right. We recorded all day. Nothing was written down. Paddy would sing a phrase and the musicians would pick it up, but he had prepared each piece and knew exactly the instrumentation he wanted. He fished tunes out of his vast folk reservoir and invented a couple of new ones.

It was 10.30 p.m. before he did his solo on the Aeolian pipes. He was exhausted. We had recorded twenty mintes of music during the day and he had performed in nearly every cue as well as conducting and composing.

Every time I meet Paddy I am shocked at how small he is, yet as soon as he talks and laughs and plays, he swells up, he grows before your eyes. His presence quickly fills the room, he sets the table at a roar, he pulls out the tin whistle and enchants us like Pan. He is suddenly a giant. So Paddy dredged up the last of himself and piped like an angel, at Windmill Lane, late at night. I almost levitated myself.

We mixed the tracks of *I Dreamt I Woke Up* in three days, as opposed to a normal schedule of four weeks for a feature. Since *I Dreamt I Woke Up* is half the length of a feature, you would expect it to take two weeks, so it had to be a quick job: although the dub is good, there were things I let go that I would have liked to correct. Nevertheless, Paddy's music and Ron's effects, together with my re-recorded commentary, have enhanced the piece considerably. It's all a bit of a rush because the Venice Film Festival has asked for Oshima's film and mine to be shown in the Festival. The BBC are very excited about this and they have urged me to get it ready in time. We managed the mix, but the lab work had been fraught with problems. We had to get permission from Warners to include five excerpts from *Excalibur* and *Deliverance* which are part of the film – images that connect my life and landscape. These amount to less than two minutes of screen time. Warners' policy is to charge $8,000 per clip. They wanted us to pay $40,000 for less than two minutes in a fifty-minute film whose total budget is $150,000. I pointed out that it was I who had made the films for them, that those films had earned them millions of dollars and that these clips were to be included in a personal film I was making for the BBC. This failed to move them: 'This is our policy.' A film-maker is obliged to give up all rights in the films he makes. I could not even show them in the Dublin retrospective without their permission.

I was dismayed at this. I had felt sure they would give me the clips *gratis*. Columbia agreed to do so for a clip from *Hope and Glory* which I finally decided not to use, and so did ABC Films for a line from *Hell in the Pacific*. We confronted Warners with this. They were shamed into falling in line. They offered to make no charge for one showing on the BBC and one Venice screening. I pointed out that my contract with the BBC required me to deliver the film free and clear. After several expensive, wrangling transatlantic phone calls I finally hassled them down to $15,000. Still exorbitant. Even more damaging was the fact that, until the deal was struck, Warners would not issue the Laboratory Access letter without which no lab will allow any of the negatives in its keeping to be duplicated. We could not strike a print of *I Dreamt I Woke Up* until the excerpts were inserted. When we finally got them, the extreme haste involved in getting the print out for Venice led to series of errors which resulted in severe misgrading of colour and density. We were making a 35mm blow-up direct from the 16mm negative, a process fraught with problems. I was planning to take the print down to Venice with me – I am serving on the jury this year – but it was not ready in time. I left it in Ron Davis's care. The lab technicians were gloomily predicting that it would not be ready in time for the scheduled screening in Venice. It is on a double-bill with Oshima's contribution to the series, a portrait of his mother's life in Kyoto.

3 September, Venice

The sleek motor launch from the Hotel Excelsior met us at the airport and we skimmed across to the Lido with Venice just a fleeting Renaissance skyline on our right. The hotel is vast and vastly expensive. Anything that does not move is marbled. The dining room with its high ceilings and hard, bright surfaces reminded me of the Hotel Rossia in Moscow. Happily, the back of the Excelsior lets on to the beach and I hastened to plunge into the Adriatic. Despite its reputation, the water looked and tasted more like sea than sewage.

The Festival building is just along from the hotel. Built by Mussolini, it is a brutal white concrete block, an architectural jackboot. At the behest of Guglielmo Biraghi, the mild-mannered and persuasive director of the Film Festival, we, the jury, climbed its curved staircase and assembled in the jury room for our briefing. We eyed each other uneasily. It was comforting to find Michel Ciment among them, not only as a friend but also as an old hand at jury work. He knows how things are done. I introduced myself to James Belushi, who was dressed up in suit and tie and on his best behaviour. He was chewing gum with great urgency. He told me it was nicotine gum and that he was more addicted to it than to the cigarettes it was replacing.

We waited around to be presented to the president of the Senate. He was half an hour late and arrived with a phalanx of acolytes. They pushed into the small room, outnumbering we jurors. They all wore very dark, silky suits and we found ourselves pressed much more intimately together than was comfortable for this kind of formal encounter. The president, a large and larded man, loomed over us, moved amongst us, shook our hands over-firmly, and looked deeply but briefly into each pair of eyes. He asked us to award an extra prize, called the Senate Prize, for a film that promoted social and humanitarian progress.

Back at the hotel, the determined Italian glitz and glitter was rather enervating. We fled to Venice, where we shuffled through the twenty-seven rooms of the Celtic exhibition at the Palazzo Grassi in a state of weary wonderment. A lost chapter in the history of civilization has somehow been recovered and pieced together. The images and objects leapt at me. I recognized them. My dreams of Druids, the imaginative intuitions in *I Dreamt I Woke Up*, all found confirmation here. Perhaps nothing is ever really lost. If the need is great enough, strong enough, the past reappears in the imagination.

The exhibition demonstrated that what we think of as the heart and bastion of Celtic culture – Ireland, Scotland, Wales, Brittany – are, in truth, the faded fringes, the dim twilight of a once vigorous and vital civilization.

Walking back to catch the elegant Excelsior boat at the Gritti Palace, we weave through the suffocating beauty of the city. Shop after shop offers exquisitely expensive objects. Because the streets are so narrow, the produce seems to caress you as you pass. You slip into the door before you know it. Buying is so sensual here: you make love and you walk away carrying your purchase in a stylish plastic bag, glowing with well-being, leaving no trace behind you except the impression of a plastic card.

Garech and Purna have arrived. They decided that the screening of *I Dreamt I Woke Up* was sufficient reason to spend a few days in Venice. The secretary to the jury is a black American woman called Gloria. It transpires that she attended Garech's wedding in India. She tells me that Garech called her Gloria Noir to distinguish her from his very blonde friend, Gloria McGowran, who was also at the nuptials. Although she is American, Gloria Noir takes a very Italian view of her work. She smiles charmingly at our frustrations over the general condition of chaos, then, just as we are about to explode, everything falls perfectly into place at the very last minute, in the Latin fashion.

We saw the first film in the competition at 10.30 p.m.: *A Simple Story* (*Una Storia Semplice*), by Enidio Greco. It suffers in comparison with *Open Door*, which I saw earlier in the year at the Dublin festival. *Open Door* is drawn from a tale by the same Sicilian author, Leonardo Sciascia, whose stories have also inspired Rosi, Petri and others to film his intriguing criminal investigations.

A Simple Story and *Open Door* both begin with a violent crime in which the criminal and his motive appear to be obvious and clearcut – open-and-shut cases. In each story an investigator insists on probing deeper, angering his superiors and setting himself apart. The truth about the crime, in each case, implicates the community and uncovers much that officialdom would prefer to conceal. In this process, *Open Door* illuminated a community and gave a vivid portrait of a place, whilst holding us in a state of tension, every simple image composed to create suspense, uncertainty, anxiety. The film had a calm, stately surface, yet such was the skill of the director, Gianni Amelio, that we searched and probed every frame for its meanings. *A Simple Story* also had interesting characters well-portrayed by some fine actors, Ricky Tognazzi in particular. The two films share the great Gianmaria Volonte, and in those short periods when he is on the screen, *A Simple Story* assumes the complexities and resonance that it otherwise lacks. The direction is static, simplistic rather than simple, and although photographed by the great Tonino Dell Colli, it is visually flat. There is a limit to what a director of photography can do if the director provides him with dull set-ups. In this instance many of them occur in offices where men stand statically against walls and speculate on past events. It recalls Hitchcock's admonition that what makes a thriller is not who-done-it but who's-going-to-do-it. *A Simple Story* lacked the thrill of impending events that Hitch demanded; so did *Open Door*, yet that had me on the edge of my seat. The first law of film theory: whatever works works.

4 September, Venice

Last night's film finished after midnight and at 9 a.m. this morning my fellow jurors and I fell into our seats and were required to watch *La Plage des enfants perdus* by Gillau Ferhati. The film is in Arabic with Italian subtitles, so there was a scramble for headsets with simultaneous translation. Michel, the linguist, asked me why, in English, we require three separate words for the same adjective: Arab, Arabic and Arabian. I could not help.

A flat, home-counties voice was superimposed on murky Arab (Arabian?) passions. Biraghi had explained that because of the strikes that one expects in Italy at this time of the year, all the prints had arrived late and there had been no time for the projectionists and translators to rehearse. In this film, the director employed a rather perverse technique, which was to start scenes out of focus and allow his characters to step into focus. The projectionist would tweak his focus, but of course could not get it sharp, and by the time it was sharp on film, the projector was out. Visually mangled and aurally bland, the film had an uphill struggle to engage this early morning audience. How important it is to ensure that your film is shown in the best conditions, at the right time of day. Next time I have a film in a festival I shall audition the translators, rehearse them like actors, and encourage them to reflect the emotions of the story. Come to think of it, I do have a film in this Festival, albeit a minor one.

Even making every possible allowance for these problems, it was not an engaging film. After a poor night's sleep, I found it almost unendurable. With the wisdom of age, one no longer feels compelled to finish bad books or watch lousy movies through to the end, but as a jury member you cannot walk out, fall asleep or even fidget. Eyes are upon us. The rigours of this task are beginning to dawn on me.

The 35mm print of *I Dreamt I Woke Up* will not, as we feared, be ready in time, so we will attempt to show it in 16mm. Sean Ryerson hand-carried the print and arrived today. Recalling the giddy delirium of this morning's floating focus, I insisted on a rehearsal. It was just as well. The 16mm projector in the main theatre proved too weak to make an acceptable picture. We measured the light at 3 foot-candles instead of the 14 required. The projector scratched the film badly, ruining the print. Much to the dismay of the Festival organizers, I cancelled the screenings. I phoned Ron Davis and told him to press ahead with the 35mm blow-up and get it down here as soon as possible. Oshima's

film, made for the same series, will now be shown alone. They will try to find
a slot at the end of the Festival for me if the blow-up makes it in time. It is
disappointing. Garech and Purna came specially. Seamus Deasy and wife are
on their way.

Our jury meeting was Hamlet without the prince. The president, Luigi
Rondi, failed to turn up. We were told he had an important political meeting.
Biraghi explained the rules to us: strictly one award per film, no sweeps like
Barton Fink at Cannes. Michel Ciment whispered to me that every festival
director in the world is horrified at what happened at Cannes. Spreading the
prizes around keeps the national delegations happy and ensures their co-
operation next year. There are too many festivals chasing too few films. The
flags of the participating nations fly along the Fascist façade of the Festival
building. I pointed out that the Irish flag was missing, and that my film was
Irish if it was anything. Biraghi said he would try to find one.

Naum Kleiman, the Russian juror, curator of the Eisenstein museum, has
just arrived, straight from the barricades in Yeltsin's Moscow. While on the
subject of flags, I asked him what he thought about the hammer and sickle.
Did it any longer properly represent the Russian film in the competition,
which, incidentally, was shot entirely in Chinese Mongolia? I have always
been opposed to pinning flags on movies. Good films leap over the barriers
of nationality. And what defines a film's citizenship anyway? Is it the subject
matter? The country it was shot in? Or where the money came from? Naum
smiles wanly. He was exhausted but exhilarated by the tumultuous events in
the Soviet Union and obviously felt that my fussy problem with flags was
trivial stuff.

Oja Kodar, the Yugoslav actress, is a very beautiful and charming jury
member. She is also the widow of Orson Welles. She has a wonderful opening
line – she said to me (as I am sure she has to others), 'Orson loved your
films.' She is terribly worried about her family. They are Croatians. She does
not know if she can go back. She phones every day.

After the meeting we reassembled to see *L'Amore necessario* by Fabio Carpi.
Ben Kingsley and Marie-Christian Barrault (both dubbed expertly into Italian)
play a couple on vacation whose relationship allows them to take lovers as
long as they do not intrude on their 'necessary love'. It is *Dangerous Liaisons*
crossed with *Claire's Knee*. I had had a chat with Ben at lunch. I told him
how much I admired his performance in the film version of Pinter's *Betrayal*.
Purna, who was lunching with us, was awe-struck by Kingsley's presence,
bringing her, as it did in a twice-removed kind of way, into proximity with
her great compatriot, Ghandi.

Because the Italians have a tradition of dubbing, they find no difficulty in
including foreign actors in their films. De Niro in Bertolucci's *1900* comes
to mind. He and Depardieu are from the same Italian village, a Frenchman

and an American. An English equivalent, say set in Dorset, with De Niro going off to study at Oxford while Depardieu stayed and worked on the village farm, however well-dubbed, would seem risible. Italian films, because they are not tied down by language, are visually more liberated. Fellini once said to me, 'John, if the Americans ever discover dubbing, we are finished.' He was referring to the freedom the camera enjoys when there is not the burden of recording usable dialogue. It is a similar freedom to that which David Lean enjoyed when he memorized the dialogue and cast aside the sound-track.

Our day concluded with a 10.30 p.m. showing of *My Own Private Idaho* by Gus Van Sant, who made such a coruscating job of *Drugstore Cowboy*. The opening minutes were electrifying, a barrage of imagery that promised a kind of Joycean cinema. I loved its daring and wild ambition but it finally was so overloaded that it spun out of control, exploding in all directions. At its centre was a performance of astonishing maturity by River Phoenix that somehow imposed itself on the fragmentation and held it all together. There is something very fine about him, a purity, a special, rare spirit.

6 September, Venice

Another meeting of the jury, this time to assess the films so far. A power axis is forming between the forceful Mortiz de Hadeln, director of the Berlin Film Festival, and Michel Ciment. Oddly, they disagree about many of the films, but they combine to assert the rights and independence of the jury. There were rebellious murmurings about our president, Luigi Rondi, who rarely attends our screenings, but has his own, privately, in the tiny basement theatre. There is a sneaking suspicion that he does not actually see the films. We have all been warned of his great political power and how he will manipulate us all. He was a former director of the Festival before it was forced to close down by Italian directors' violent protests at its political bias.

Mortiz tried to catch Rondi out. He asked him what he thought about the rape of the little girl in the Polish film. There was no rape, of course.

'Why are you trying to trick me?' He smiled and explained wearily that his important political meetings prevented him from being with us. He raised his hands in supplication and smiled and smiled. Michel said we needed more contact with him.

By this time we were all suffering from the stifling heat in the room. Rondi had insisted that the air-conditioning be turned off and was wearing a heavy cardigan. 'I am an old man. I feel the cold.' He smiled sadly and folded his hands across his chest, as if arranging the dead body he might become if we insisted on lowering the temperature.

It was decided that each film would be voted on and if it received at least one positive vote it would be retained at this stage. There was little enthusiasm for the films so far, but a performance here, the photography there, saved some from extinction and at the end of the day only Chantal Ackerman's *Nuit et jour* was eliminated. She had buttonholed me several times, outraged that I saw her film with a simultaneous translation instead of with English subtitles, insisting that in this case the text *is* the film. However, not a single member of the jury, including the francophones, had a good word to say for it, so I shall spare myself a second viewing.

Ackerman worked with Warhol in New York and was influenced by his films made in real time. She herself shot a film about peeling potatoes which escaped my attention. This film is more structured, but, as if she is nervous of being accused of making a conventional film, she leaves out all the crucial emotional scenes in this story of two boys in love with the same girl. She makes her actors strike poses and tells us in narration what they are feeling. I can see that she is trying to avoid the banalities of a familiar love story, but she does so by holding them distastefully at arm's length.

Oja Kodar says her parents can hear the shelling and it gets louder each day. Outside the Festival building a young Yugoslav journalist told me that his friend, a young camerman, had been killed whilst filming the conflict. He said his friend had decided to work in films after seeing *Excalibur*.

We screened the now scratched 16mm print of *I Dreamt I Woke Up* in the small Volpi theatre, where the throw is short enough to make a halfway decent picture. I arranged this for the people who had come specially – Garech and Purna, Seamus Deasy and his wife, John Archer, Michel Ciment and Peter Rawley, an old friend and sometime agent. I also included Oshima since we were in the same boat, as it were. His film about his mother's life in Kyoto was surprisingly gentle and stately, a forgiving documentary from a man who had yearned for total revolution as the only remedy for Japan's oppressive ills.

This was the very first screening of my film. I felt less strain seeing myself and my most intimate world exposed than I normally do when showing a new film for the first time. This would seem to suggest that I am more jealous of my reputation as a film-maker than as a person. Of course, although I own up to many weaknesses in the film, much is still hidden. I am hard on myself, but not ferociously so.

7 September, Venice

Prospero's Books has been praised for its technical innovation. Greenaway worked in Tokyo with the High Definition company HDTV, which gave him access to all the electronic wizardry that is readily available once you get to video. He was able to do all the things we see on MTV, and he did. The result was disappointingly cluttered and banal. He deconstructs *The Tempest*, mangles it, mutilates it, and does what I would have thought impossible: removes all humanity from it.

The familiar pounding musical score, the heavily atmospheric sound effects, the overload of imagery, all suggest a quotation from *Macbeth*: 'a tale/Told by an idiot, full of sound and fury,/Signifying nothing.'

What is alarming about Greenaway is that the cruelty in his films – the sadism, the sex-hating, the food-hating, life-hating, child-hating, woman-hating, excrement-loving – finds such a joyous response in so many people.

I remember watching *The Exorcist* with an audience that revelled in the tortures inflicted on the possessed child. I wondered then if the evolutionary spirit's response to over-population was to instill a hatred of children. Or is it that cruelty is deep-seated in the human psyche and this kind of spectacle gives us the opportunity to indulge it?

Some years back when Simon Relph was running British Screen, he wrote asking my advice in assessing a Greenaway project, *The Belly of an Architect*. The fate of the film rested with him. Without British Screen's investment, it would not be made. Simon said he had a blind spot for Greenaway. He was therefore disqualifying himself and would go along with my view. I shall look out my letter when I get back, because what I remember saying about that film could apply to this one and the others that have preceded it.

Here it is:

6 February 1986

Dear Simon,

Oh dear, what to say, how to start? I was immensly impressed, oppressed by the script.

With *Draughtman's Contract* I was of the 'emperor's new clothes' school. Seeing *A Zed and Two Noughts*, followed by an erudite and detailed interpretation by Greenaway on stage at the NFT, I realized that his films are constructed on labyrinthine but nevertheless solid intellectual frameworks, and although little of this reaches the visceral surface, it gives his films this air of tremendous assurance. They are made with such unerring certainty that we are half-convinced that only our own inadequate intelligence prevents us from understanding. Having now read a Greenaway script, I can see how definitive he is. I am only surprised it did not arrive cut in tablets of stone. Does he never have any doubts? Most film-makers, most artists, have only an inkling of what their work is about at this stage. He is so overbearingly certain. The script is stifling. There is no room for actors to breathe, let alone breathe life into these venal characters whose every move and thought he ruthlessly dictates.

The script is an impressive literary document. He has massive ability. His films are visual, architectural, musical – but not cinematic. The sum of the parts is less than the whole. His precision and controlled effects make one long for the wild abandon of Ken Russell. The density of the thing is very wearisome.

There is his usual gallery of cold, cruel and predatory characters, but the story is much easier on the audience than the others and in Kracklite he suggests a much more human figure than he usually allows. Whereas the supporting players are treated with his customary contempt and disgust, Kracklite is vulnerable and appealing. Of course he is vain and greedy and probably a fraud, but how gratefully we cling to him in this icy desert of a story. Alas, Greenaway only invites us to feel for Kracklite so that we suffer all the more as the author remorselessly documents his humiliation, pain and degradation.

I have genuine admiration for Greenaway's prodigious skills, but I don't think he is a natural film-maker.

I would hate to have to make a decision on this. Most of the money has been found. How can you not go in? I can't see this doing better than *Draughtman's Contract*, which has just now broken even on a much smaller budget. You won't see the money back, and yet are there other scripts with better claims? If you forgive the pun, I suggest you go with your gut feeling.

Simon called me when he got my letter and said, 'You still haven't said yes or no.' I said that Greenaway had a vision, however bleak, and if you don't give money to him, who can you give it to? He gave it.

8 September, Venice

Spent a delightful dinner with my fellow juror, Silvia D'Amico Benedico, who produced *Dark Eyes*. We kept each other laughing by exchanging anecdotes about Marcello Mastroianni. She also talked about Nikita Mikhalkov, who directed *Dark Eyes* and whose film *Urga* we will see later in the competition.

Mikhalkov comes from a privileged family in Moscow and he and his half-brother Andrei Konchalovsky were allowed to come and go, visiting the West even during the most repressive times. They are resented and envied by many of their compatriots, especially today, because they were such darlings of the old regime. Silvia told me of her struggles to finance *Dark Eyes*. She put herself deeply into debt to make it. No one would distribute it. Then Marcello got the best actor prize at Cannes and suddenly they all loved it. Before she could seize the moment, the moment seized her. She was rushed to the hospital for open-heart surgery. She took the first lousy deal on offer for the film. None of this has soured her wickedly funny wit nor dented her charm.

Jim Belushi loves to play the ugly American. He pretends to be an unreconstructed jock. He does this to infuriate his wife, Marjorie. When he makes a sexist remark, she storms off and won't speak to him for several hours. It seems to be both serious and at the same time a game they play. They go out jogging together in the mornings and they meet fellow Americans, but seldom an Italian.

9 September, Venice

Pierre Edelman from CiBy 2000 is here. He told me how much everyone in his office loves *Broken Dream* and how happy he is that the company is making it. He apologized for *Chymical Wedding*, which he had also loved deeply. They had said they would make that too then suddenly went silent. Apparently they had balked at the sex scenes.

Three films yesterday.

Meeting Venus, in which the admirable Istvan Szabo has ventured into the English language and Puttnam has tried to put together a truly European movie. A cocktail of nationalities come together to put on *Tannhäuser* in Paris. Hungarian conductor and Swedish diva (Glenn Close) get off on the wrong foot, then, of course, fall in love. It has wonderful elements, but they never quite come together. It is about freedom and responsibility, about how democracy does not work in art, and how free love does not work in marriage. The themes are interesting. Although Puttnam's intent was to develop a pan-European film, Glenn Close's presence, the way everything dances to her tune, her rhythm, unbalances the piece and reminds us of the power the American distributors wield, even on a film like this.

A Divina Comédia by the eighty-year-old Portuguese director Manoel de Oliveira, is a playful and youthful conceit in which patients in an asylum imagine themselves to be characters from Dostoevsky, Christ, the Virgin Mary and sundry others: actors playing madmen playing roles. It is perhaps more of a theatrical than a cinematic idea, but the fact that everyone in the film is 'pretending' allows us to overcome the resistance we bring to every movie, the little voice in the head which says, 'You are an actor trying to be someone else. Convince me that you are that person.' It gave rise to some brilliant acting, and, confined as the film is, it gives a feeling of luxurious spaciousness, of the vast landscape of the human psyche.

In *Schrei aus Stein*, Werner Herzog takes his actors off to scale an impossible mountain in Patagonia. The climbing scenes are stupendous, but the actors cannot compete with the reality of the mountain. It is overwhelming. Only Brad Dourif and Donald Sutherland, with their quirky wit and outsized personalities, manage to survive the avalanche that Herzog contrives.

10 September, Venice

9 a.m. was rather early to be confronted by the opening scene of Derek Jarman's *Edward.II*, in which the king's lover makes his long opening speech sitting on a bed beside two brightly lit, naked men, who are copulating with considerable enthusiasm.

The superb acting and staging of the film is constantly undermined by the anachronistic scenes of homosexual propaganda that Jarman interpolates throughout the text. He does a good job of interpreting the play in homosexual terms, and does not need to wave banners in our faces. Jarman's heterophobia is forgiveable, given the anti-gay legislation in Britain, but what are we to make of an extra wearing a T-shirt which is emblazoned with the words QUEER AS FUCK? The credits read: 'Marlowe's Edward II *improved by* Derek Jarman'. The title of the published screenplay is *Queer Edward II*. It all smacks of gay naughtiness.

The film is full of energy, rage and invention. Jarman creates a richness of texture with minimal resources, and yet he wantonly mars what is otherwise a powerful piece of cinema.

Easily the best film so far is *Raise the Red Lantern* by Zhang Yimou. Exquisitely acted and shot, it tells the story of the four wives of an old master of the Chen clan. Although set in the 1920s, it is clearly an allegory of modern China. Each wife represents a period in contemporary Chinese history – the fourth being a rebellious young woman who is severely punished for daring to challenge the absolute authority of her remote and elderly husband. She goes mad, and a fifth wife, faceless and defeated, is brought into the household.

It is a superbly modulated and balanced movie, profoundly subversive yet beautiful and controlled. It does not have the spiritual grandeur of Chen Kaige's *Life on a String*, but, taken together, they represent a range and power that few, if any, other countries can match this year.

I met Zhang Yimou afterwards. When I saw him, I suddenly realized that he also acted in his films. He is delicate and shy. Talking through an interpreter, he said how relieved he was to talk to someone who was not a journalist. He told me that the film had not yet been seen by the government department. When it was, he would simply receive notification that it either could or could not be distributed. No explanation would be given. *Ju Dou* was banned even though its political content was much more oblique and concealed than *Raise the Red Lantern*'s, so it seems very unlikely that the Chinese will be allowed to see it. Although Chen Kaige and Zhang Yimou live and work in China, their work is exiled.

11 September, Venice

The Festival, which felt so thin early on, is ending in a rush of notable films. Skolimowski weighed in with *30 Door Key*, a stylistic exercise in absurdist comedy. That master of the absurd, Crispin Glover, is in it and I was happy to see him again. He arrived from LA to support the film. When he woke up yesterday, he called down to the front desk to ask the time. They told him it was six o'clock. However, when the faint light outside the window got darker rather than lighter he began to get suspicious. He called again. It was indeed six o'clock, but p.m., not a.m.. He had missed his day's interviews.

Terry Gilliam offered us *The Fisher King*. This is his attempt to do penance for the wild excesses of *Baron Münchhausen*. It is the Grail legend in modern New York. Terry does little more than tip his hat at the great themes the story throws up and it settles down to being a kind of neo-mythic buddy movie. His riotous imagination cannot be wholly held in check and it breaks out from time to time. He is an arsonist without matches, an anarchist trying to join the civil service.

As the lights went up after *Urga* by Nikita Mikhalkov, we, the jurors, exchanged looks of profound relief. Here was the Golden Lion. Set in Chinese Mongolia, it tells the tale of a Russian truck driver falling amongst a family of nomadic shepherds. It is hugely entertaining, with a gallery of finely observed characters, and it deals with the problems facing primal people in coming to terms with modern life – in this case, Communism.

The Russian juror Naum Kleiman has travelled widely in the West, but until now has never been allowed to bring his wife with him. This was her first trip outside the Soviet Union. We took her on a tour of Venice. She was lost in wonderment. Naum, whose erudition knows no limits, was such a knowledgeable guide that I was soon lost in wonder myself. Why would a Soviet Jew know the exact pecking order of the Apostles on the front of St Mark's Cathedral? He gave a self-deprecating shrug which seemed to say that this was the sort of knowledge that any educated person would surely have at his fingertips.

As we sat eating a *gelato*, we fell to talking about myth and cinema. Naum told me about some unpublished writings of Eisenstein's in which he addresses the subject and speculates that, for example, the detective story could correspond to one of man's earliest traumas. The child of a hunter–gatherer family would set out to find the anonymous marauder who had fathered him. The search, the tracking down of suspects in the detective story, might touch those atavistic needs and yearnings.

Eisenstein fell foul of his Communist masters because not all of his film theory coincided with Marxist orthodoxy. Was Lenin the true lost father that we all seek? Was he also the callous rapist who turned his back on us, his children? I began to see why this theory had remained unpublished.

12 September, Venice

By yesterday we had seen all of the films in the competition although the Festival does not conclude until Saturday. We got ahead of ourselves so that we could deliberate today in order to give the Festival organizers time to get the prize-winners back to Venice for the awards ceremony.

Jean-Luc Godard's *Allemagne neuf zero* at sixty-two minutes is jam-packed with more ideas and originality than all the other films put together. The narrative concerns a spy who has been placed as a mole in East Germany and never called upon to go into action. With the unification of Germany, he is redundant. Around this Godard spins various threads – Communism, capitalism, solitude, ecology – and together they become an extraordinary dissertation on our times. Godard is always pushing film beyond its limits and reminding us of how banal and conventional most films are.

The jurors were taken off in a launch called *Confusion* to Count Volpi's villa to deliberate. We sat under a Canaletto painting of Venice not too different from the view outside the window.

The count himself was absent. It turned out that he was with Belushi's wife in Venice, where he also has a palace. He has been entranced with her all week, and with Jim locked up in his villa, he was lunching her. I teased Jim about this and he pretended to be sick at the thought, but it was clearly all part of their marriage game.

After some foreplay, we began to make decisions. There was considerable consensus right away, except for Pilar Miro, the Spanish director and some-time Minister of Culture, who took her own rather eccentric course. Since she spoke only Spanish, she was rather cut off from the rest of us.

I expected *Urga* to be unanimous for the Golden Lion, but surprisingly, Naum Kleiman put up a spirited opposition to it. He said Mikhalkov is flashy and manipulative, that much of it was over-acted. The film sympathized with the peasant's desire to have another child, which was contrary to the welfare of China, and the military song that features importantly in the film celebrated Russian imperialism. Naum's choice was *Meeting Venus*. He felt Szabo was dealing with a topical and important subject, an East European artist trying to cope with Western systems.

Naum nevertheless accepted the verdict, and with a delighted smile said, 'It's wonderful to be able to be a minority!'

The Chinese film enjoyed the most support after *Urga* and we discussed how to reward it. There was strong support for giving it the jury prize, but since that prize is generally given to an avant-garde film not likely to be popular, it was considered that it might give the wrong impression of *Raise the Red Lantern*. The Godard was strongly promoted for this prize and Michel Ciment made a strong bid for Manoel de Oliveira. At eighty, he had never received a major award. We all admired his film, so we voted and he got it.

There were several contenders for best actress and each had her passionate supporters. Two of the Chinese actresses were contenders, the third and the fourth wives; Johanna der Steege, the Dutch actress, for her role in the Phillipe Garrel film *Je n'entends plus la guitarre*; and Tilda Swinton in *Edward II*. In the end the vote went to Tilda.

Our president, Luigi Rondi, whom we had been warned would manipulate the prizes according to his arcane political interests, exerted no pressure whatsoever, nor indeed did the Festival director, Biraghi. Only when it became clear that no Italian film would receive a prize did Rondi make a small plea asking us to help him, please do something. We found we could not do so, but a special Golden Lion was found for the great Volonte for his life's work. Rondi had to make do with that.

There was general agreement that the young River Phoenix was the outstanding actor of the competition.

The Garrel film was much admired. It is the anatomy of a love affair, very intense, naturalistic, almost without style, but it had a kind of brutal honesty in the way it confronts the enigma that is at the heart of every relationship between a man and a woman. Not my kind of film, but I admired it deeply and it stayed with me longer than most of the others.

We discussed it at dinner one night and I said that I thought it was about how a man destroys a woman by not loving her enough. Jim Belushi said he had seen it quite differently. It was about how a woman can completely screw up a guy. His wife gave him a daggers look and she cold-shouldered him for a full day. Just the mention of the film made him wince. He glanced out of the window, reminded that his wife was drinking champagne somewhere out there with Count Volpi.

Zhang Yimou, Phillipe Garrel and Terry Gilliam got the Silver Lions and Godard the Senate Prize. We were all sworn to secrecy: the official line was that no decision would be made until the next day.

14 September, Venice

We finally showed the 35mm print of *I Dreamt I Woke Up*. The quality was remarkably good and the reception was too. There was a crush to see it and two extra screenings were put on. *Le Monde* called it one of the highlights of the Festival.

Somebody leaked the results. Yesterday morning the Italian newspapers all printed a full list of the prizes. They got everything right except for one: they all gave the best actress prize to Glenn Close.

When the official list was released, David Puttnam told me that Glenn was devastated, since everyone had congratulated her for winning. He said that he was going to persuade her to present the best actress prize. Would I support the idea? I said that it would be both courageous and gracious and that I would urge the Festival and my fellow jurors to accept such a generous gesture.

The ceremony in St Mark's Square tonight was a fiasco. In that dramatic setting, they put on a kind of sub-Oscar show with dancers miming the history of the movies and other extravaganzas even less pertinent to the prize-giving. A man rushed on stage the minute the television broadcast began and attacked the compère. He was overpowered. By the end we all felt like doing the same.

The guests of honour were the foreign ministers of Italy and Germany. Oja Kodar was able to confront them. She said, 'My country is bleeding. What are you going to do about it?' They told her they had been discussing it all day. She had to make do with that.

Jim Belushi was to pick up Terry Gilliam's award. As we sat up on the platform looking down over the starched and bejewelled audience filling the square, Jim fretted nervously over what he should say. He said, 'C'mon John, gimme some lines. I'm an actor, I need lines.' Between us we contrived a few choice banalities and Jim started saying them over. We worked on emphasis, on pauses, on delivery. It was a mess. He just couldn't get it right. I was really worried for him. Finally, he had to go up there and do it. He was absolutely commanding, his timing perfect. Confident, assured. He's an actor.

In return for delivering Glenn Close, Puttnam obliged the Festival to show two clips from *Meeting Venus*, and to do a ten-minute interview with her on the stage. In place of a clip of the Oliveira film, the Festival mistakenly showed a clip from an Israeli film. The jury flailed its arms frantically, but the clip ran on. Silvia D'Amico Benedico was so disgusted with the proceedings that she kept trying to change the channel on the monitor to watch a film that was showing on another station. The show overran and no clips were shown from the four films winning major prizes. A casual viewer might have got the impression that *Meeting Venus* was the big hit of the Festival, whereas it won no prize at all. I am lost in admiration at David's skill in turning a reverse into a triumph.

There was a dinner at a magnificent palazzo on the Grand Canal. We were ferried there. There was a crush of people. The dining room looked beautiful, the chandeliers blazing with candles, but one look was enough for me to realize that the meal would take hours. We were leaving early in the morning. We, the jurors, decided to go back to the hotel.

The kitchens were closed. We managed to get some toasted sandwiches and wine and sat there in the huge, empty, marbled dining room. Various drunken malcontents, unhappy with our verdicts, came in and shouted at us, but we were happy in our fellowship. We had lived together for two weeks to the exclusion of our normal lives and we felt a special warmth for one another. We exchanged addresses. We laughed. We hugged.

It was all over.

Jim and Marjorie Belushi left hand in hand, all breaches healed.

15 September, Venice

Early departure on the hotel launch for the airport. A bemused, sleep-walking River Phoenix joined us on the boat. He had flown in the previous night to receive his award and he was already on his way back to Toronto, where *My Own Private Idaho* is playing in the Festival of Festivals. Michel Ciment had told us the story of his arrival in Venice. No one had met him at the airport and he had somehow managed to find his way to one of the hotels in Venice. He was checking in when Michel, walking through the lobby by chance on his way to the ferry to the Lido, spotted him. Michel assured him that he was meant to be staying at the Hotel Excelsior and took River with him.

River has always been my first choice for *Broken Dream*. I had brought a copy with me in case I had a chance to give it to him, and I did. We talked. He is honest and direct, open and vulnerable, yet there is an inner resolve and resoluteness which keeps him safe from the wiles of the world.

19 September, London

Sean Ryerson and I took an early flight to London, the Aer Lingus flight jammed with Irish businessmen downing a morning whiskey.

We met Claude Nedjar in David Norris's office. On and off David has been my lawyer for more than twenty years. He is one of those rare members of his profession who can always come up with ways of making things work rather than pointing out why they cannot – which is the doleful habit of most of his colleagues.

Back in 1978, Claude Nedjar introduced me to a French novel by Daniel Odier called *The Travels of John O'Flaherty*. It had an interesting central idea. I decided to make a screenplay. I had read Neil Jordan's short stories and a TV film-script he had written. I asked him to write with me. Claude and I became joint producers.

Neil and I soon left the book behind and set out on our own flight of fancy. We sat in an office at Ardmore Studios each day and wrote together, acting out the scenes. Out of it all came *Broken Dream*.

Now that I am reviving it, we have made a deal with Claude to buy his share of the project and pay off the author and publisher, even though there is scarcely any resemblance to the book any more, which Daniel Odier acknowledges. However, unless the title and copyright is free and clear, CiBy 2000 will not release funds to the picture. I was happy to see Claude and to contrive him a little windfall. He has had hard times and the money was welcome. Jeremy Thomas advanced the monies for all this, encouraged by CiBy 2000's passionate enthusiasm.

This is the first time in twenty years that I have not been my own producer. There is some comfort in having someone other than myself paying out this 'seed' money, which is always at risk and is lost if the project fails, yet unless you put out the cash to pay lawyers, prepare a budget, design the movie, etc., you have no hope of getting backing.

20 September

Alan Parker has a lacerating wit and the cartoons he used to publish in *Screen International* were snapshots of all that is absurd and pretentious about the film community. Yet his movies tend to be emphatically dramatic, to say the least. His friends have been saying for years that he should make a comedy, something he has not attempted since *Bugsy Malone*.

He has done it with *The Commitments*. It is the gritty, flip side of *Fame*, set in darkest Dublin.

The Dublin première was a national event. The cinema was swamped with press and television. The cast of unknown Dublin kids and their families were in the audience. It is the only time I have ever heard the casting director's credit greeted with cheers. There has never been such frenzied euphoria since Ireland scored against England in the European Nations Cup. Parker's skill in orchestrating this raw talent is prodigious.

25 September

My last meeting as a governor of the British Film Institute. After nine years the Minister of Arts and Libraries has decided not to reappoint me. These monthly meetings have generally been fascinating. The board consists of fourteen or so fine minds – educationalists, trade unionists, MPs, publishers, producers, TV executives. The expertise they bring from their various disciplines illuminates the issues and I often came away feeling that I had learnt something of the current political and social state of the nation.

Under Anthony Smith, the BFI expanded and burgeoned. His friendship with Paul Getty resulted in millions flowing into the coffers. Tony's avowed aim was to gain for the BFI esteem and status comparable to that enjoyed by the National Theatre or Covent Garden. They were heady days. Jeremy

Isaacs was running Channel Four and was one of our governors. He supported the BFI production board, whose films began to enjoy considerable success and the guarantee of a Channel Four airing.

Tony was a brilliant and passionate advocate of the BFI and he carried us all along with his ambitious masterplan. Yet National Film Theatre attendances slipped downwards each year, the Archive remained as inaccessible as ever, and the academics still dominated the Institute with their theoretical papers couched in impenetrable language. But these were simply further peaks that Tony Smith would scale when he got round to it. The combination of Tony's brilliance and Dickie Attenborough's charm in the chair fairly swept all before them during the expanding 1980s.

Things went sour when Tony failed to get Jeremy Isaacs's job at Channel Four when Jeremy left to run Covent Garden. Tony seemed to have the inside track, since Dickie was also Chairman of Channel Four, but Michael Grade pipped him at the last minute. Tony resigned and took the job of ruling an Oxford college.

Wilf Stevenson, who succeeded Tony, is a mild, thoughtful man who is perhaps better suited to these recessionary times. He does not dominate, as Tony did, but seeks consensus from the Board. This worked well enough until the appointment of Alexander Walker, the critic. Alex is extremely conscientious and has brought his rigorous critical mind to bear on the conduct of the Institute, but unfortunately he is so insistent and contentious that his long, confrontational diatribes have quite wrecked the balance of the meetings. Perhaps we were too comfortable. His points are often sound, but the pleasure went out when Alex came in.

I wrote back to the Minister reminding him that, apart from Dickie, I was the only film director on the board, and I hoped he would replace me with another. After all, without film directors, there would be no BFI.

4 October

David Lean's memorial service in St Paul's was so magnificently and expertly staged that many of us afterwards found we had had the same thought: the master had directed himself from the grave.

The great organ, the St Paul's choir, and a full orchestra opened up with 'Sunrise' from *Thus Spake Zarathustra*, forgiveably borrowed from the epic *œuvre* of Kubrick, a suitably cosmic comment on David's work and life. There were readings by John Mills, Peter O'Toole, Omar Sharif, Sarah Miles, Tom Courtney, and, most powerfully of all, by the actor George Correface, who was to play the title role in *Nostromo*, the last in the long line of Lean's leading men. He read the opening and conclusion of the script and did enough to convince us that David would have launched another career.

The readings, mostly from his films, were interspersed by soaring anthems from the choir and the secular film music of Maurice Jarre, who was conducting the orchestra himself. Melvyn Bragg gave a warm and loving account of David's work. As the torchbearer of the arts, Melvyn is destined to bury the men whose lives he celebrates. Robert Bolt limped bravely to the microphone and spoke with his stroke-impaired, computer-like voice, each word a staccato stab of pain. He said, 'David – I – am – here. Everything – I – know – about – film – you – taught – me.'

John Box, Lean's designer, spoke of David as a great architect – he compared him to Christopher Wren and his films to the cathedral in which we stood.

Even the sun broke free of a grey sky, just for a moment, and sent a shaft of light through the stained glass, like a benediction. I imagine David watching the rushes and saying, 'Bit over-the-top, that shaft of light. Oh, bugger it, leave it in, it works.'

6 October

Just returned from a weekend in Brittany.

A château in the middle of the Forest of Brocelliande houses an Arthurian centre. To celebrate the tenth anniversary of *Excalibur* they have mounted an exhibition of artefacts. I lent them the Grail and Excalibur, and some items of armour from the film.

I was greeted by bards and harpists, Druids and archers. Sooner or later they all asked me the same question: 'Don't you hate Paris?' When I said no, I felt that I had failed the Breton litmus test.

Over the last ten years *Excalibur* has been watched over and over again by the Bretons and has become more like a religious ceremony than a movie. As they showed me their megaliths, and sacred and ancient oaks, they watched me carefully for my reactions, hanging on my words. They expected revelations, and I am afraid I disappointed them. They were charming and generous, but some of the wackier people reminded me of the findings of the Celtic exhibition in Venice: Brittany is one of the dying fringes of that civilization.

12 October

Spent this last week with Tony Pratt, designing the sets for *Broken Dream*. Phillipe Rousselot came for the last three days. We had to invent an architecture for the film. We started by thinking in terms of German Expressionist film sets, with forced perspectives and leaning buildings. We added in some Gaudí. It looked too theatrical. We gradually evolved a style which is heavy and monumental, somewhat oppressive, yet not definable as belonging to any period. We want to express a world eroding. By showing this massive architecture being eaten away at the edges, we make that point strongly. The heaviness also contrasts with the lightness of Ben and Nell (the main characters), as they gradually achieve weightlessness.

We worked through all the special effects sequences and made rough storyboards which Tony will draw up in more detail next week so that we can go over them step by step with the computer-effects people. That meeting will take place when I return from my casting trip to Los Angeles.

17 October, London

Jeremy arranged for me to meet Yves Attal in London for lunch. I went over for the day. Attal is a lawyer who has represented Wim Wenders among others and has now joined CiBy 2000. I described the film, how it would look. He seemed guarded. Jeremy told me he had just joined the company and was feeling his way. He raised the question of making the film an Anglo-French co-production. I did my best to be positive about this, but I groaned within. It is so restrictive and artificial. We already had Rousselot, who is French, and intended to use the Eclair lab in Paris, which would help. I said we could do the sound mixing in Paris, the music recording, and possibly find a French composer. We would need at least one French actor in a leading role, and I guessed it would have to be Nell. I had intended to cast the family around River Phoenix if he agrees to do the film, using American actors so that they would have a common accent. The co-production would require all cast and crew to be either French or British with two exceptions, of which River Phoenix would be one, so that idea would have to be sacrificed.

I asked Attal about his position in the company. He looked uneasy. He was unsure of how responsibility divided up between himself and Jean-Claude Fleury, who has been running the company under Bouygues. Pierre Edelman, whom I met in Venice, floats between these two. Bouygues is renowned for his policy of divide and rule.

Bouygues is said to be the richest man in France. Apart from building new cities and the channel tunnel, he also owns TF1, the first television station in France. Attal told me that Bouygues had considered buying a Hollywood studio – Paramount was a possibility – but after looking at it carefully he decided it would be more interesting to build his own.

He went after top film-makers, promising Bertolucci (and Jeremy) $50 million to make *Buddha*, announcing similar deals with David Lynch, Spike Lee, Jane Campion, the Coen brothers, and Wim Wenders. He intends to make a European studio to rival the Americans. Besides financing these films, he will also put up the money for prints and ads, aggressively marketing his films and keeping control over them.

When I heard all of this, I almost fell on my knees and kissed Bouygues's surrogate's feet. How long have we awaited such a man. Not wishing to appear too eager, I restrained this impulse and merely nodded my approval.

21 October

Back in Los Angeles for three days of casting. Down to Malibu for lunch with Bob Chartoff. Burgess Meredith came. I have been thinking of him as Old Ben, but he is over eighty and has had a series of set-backs: a gall-bladder removed, then he had a fall and broke his pelvis. He looked sprightly, no trace of a limp, his wit and humour intact, but his face is drawn, there are the lineaments of past pain. He arrived with Barbara Carrera, a one-time Bond girl who now has the Duke of Northumberland in tow, an affable fellow, who was bemused and captivated by Los Angeles. Burgess showed us a wonderful propaganda film he had directed during the war, instructing GIs on how to behave in England.

As arranged, I called River Phoenix when I got in and he came to see me last night. We had a long talk about the script. His close circle of father, mother, girlfriend had all read it and approved. He showed considerable maturity. He wanted to consider it carefully, all the implications. His face is on magazine covers everywhere. He is currently shooting a studio picture called *Sneakers*, which has a starry cast including Robert Redford.

I met River's father afterwards. He has a farm in Costa Rica growing organic vegetables for the local people to compensate, in some small measure, for the pollution and destruction wreaked upon them by us. There is an air of goodness about the Phoenix clan that is wonderfully free of piety.

24 October

Breakfast yesterday with Jeff Berg. He is head of ICM, one of the top three agencies. His view was that the film business was in deep crisis. Attendances have fallen, while film costs have ballooned. Most of the major studios are saddled with huge debts. It is going to get worse, he said. The market will not support pictures with these huge budgets. 'Well,' I said, 'how can they reduce costs when you agents insist on your stars getting paid 5, 10, even $15 million a throw?' Jeff said the stars would give the studios a break when the studio executives cut their own huge salaries. Meanwhile he was conducting a Draconian cost-cutting programme at the agency. I saw this in practice when he left me to pick up the bill.

Today's breakfast was with my old pal Mike Medavoy, now running TriStar for the Sony company. I went up to his house on the very peak of Beverly Hills with views across Los Angeles on one side, and over the San Bernadino valley on the other. The house is enormous, just completed. The walls display his very fine art collection and the screening room with its sliding walls and state-of-the-art equipment in enviable. Banks of the latest Sony equipment fill the closets. I said I hoped Blake was right, that the road of excess leads to the palace of wisdom.

Mike has two big and expensive pictures opening at Christmas, Spielberg's *Hook* and *Bugsy*, starring Warren Beatty, directed by Barry Levinson. He looked remarkably relaxed about it, although I imagine his future hangs on how they perform. When I chided him about these bloated budgets, he said the problem that exercised him was the mounting cost of marketing. He said it now costs up to $4 million to put a campaign together – just making trailers, designing posters, financing press junkets, screenings, etc. The marketing costs come on top of that. To open a picture across the US, TV advertising can now run to $15 million and in some cases as much as $30 million.

I have met some of the best young actors in LA over the past three days, casting for the roles of Nell and Chuck. You learn a lot about a script from actors. I asked them to talk about the story and the characters. Most of them had no difficulty in entering this invented world. The story appeared to fill a need in them, a spiritual yearning. My fear that actors, particularly American actors rooted in naturalism, would find it difficult to surrender to the logic of dream, proved unfounded. The kind of remark I expected, 'Well, I guess you have to figure out a way to play it,' never materialized.

I had seen Armin Mueller-Stahl in *Music Box* and *Avalon*, and of course in the Fassbinder films. I wanted to meet him to discuss the part of Ainscott, who is the engine of the story, the drive. He came into the room, his pale blue eyes smiling. He said, 'It is one of the best scripts I ever read. I understand it totally. I understand you totally. If you want me, I am yours.' An actor's flattery is a debased coinage, but there was something about this man that convinced me of his sincerity, and if he was not sincere then he is a great actor – which is even better. We chatted amiably like old friends. At one point he leaned forward and said, 'I was not honest when I said this is one of the best scripts I ever read. It is *the* best. I thought if I said it straight away it would be too much.'

25 October, Salado, Texas

The Dream Symposium was a reluctant chore. But in this strange little town in Texas, great men have gathered from all over to speak about dreams. Harry Wilmer, the organizer of this annual event, looks so much like Jung it is disconcerting. I travelled from the airport with the man who discovered Rapid

Eye Movement, Dr Dement. Another man with burning eyes has come up
with Lucid Dreams, a technique which allows us to be more conscious of
our dreams, their content and meaning. My contribution related dreaming to
the experience of watching movies. What I discovered was that these men in
their diverse ways were involved in adventuring into the nightly theatre of
dreams, a place that could, if fully understood and controlled, supersede
movies. There is fascinating research being done on shared dreams. Another
man told me of his work in proving by experiment Jung's theory that we can
experience dreams which contain detailed information that belongs to other
cultures unknown to us, that through dreams the great repository of the
collective unconscious is available to us.

Twenty miles from here, a few days ago, a man drove his pick-up truck
through the window of a restaurant and shot dead more than twenty people.

26 October, New York

Stopped over on the way back to London to meet two actresses for the part
of Nell: Emily Lloyd and Julie Delpy. They are poles apart yet both could
play it in very different ways. How casting defines a movie.

Delpy is exquisite, ethereal, with a bruised delicacy. I had seen her in
Tavernier's *The Passion of Beatrice* and had been impressed. I was entranced
by her. She has the most beautiful colouring and her face is expressive even
when hardly moving. Emily is comic and irreverent, a mimic, a clown. I would
have cast her as the older sister in *Hope and Glory*, but she was only fifteen
at the time. I already had several children in the cast. The restrictions on
actors who are under sixteen are properly severe, so I reluctantly let her go.

She is currently in a Woody Allen picture playing a snobbish Upper East-
side intellectual, a character so remote from her own that I begged her to do
the accent for me. It was astonishing. She transformed before my eyes: accent,
attitude, appearance. Yet somehow, she lacks the spiritual grace of Delpy,
and I am sure CiBy 2000 would be delighted with a French actress in the
role. It would probably clinch the co-production.

28 October

Of all the flights I took between Dublin, London, LA, Houston, Austin, New
York, London, not one of them was on time. JFK airport in New York was
closed by fog and they bussed us to Newark Airport. I had picked up *The
Devil's Candy* by Julie Salomon and I buried myself in it during the painful
journey. It is the story of the making of *The Bonfire of the Vanities*, a hugely
expensive picture that was a disastrous failure at the box office. Peter Guber
bought the book when he was still a producer at Warners before taking over

Columbia for Sony. They got nervous when they realized that all the characters were deeply unsympathetic. Hollywood lore insists that you must have a hero you can root for. Guber's solution was to cast Tom Hanks as Sherman McCoy, the venal bond trader who personifies the greedy 1980s. Hank's nice-guy personality would make Sherman sympathetic, Guber reasoned. The obvious fact that it also grotesquely undermines the central idea of the piece was never faced up to.

Warners executives sought to assuage their anxieties by resorting to further casting absurdities. Bruce Willis was given the role of the seedy English reporter in a further attempt to 'buy' a hit by throwing in another 'popular' star. Finally, the Jewish judge was played by Morgan Freeman, a black actor, because Warners were afraid of the accusation of racism. Mega-budgets come with a huge burden of fear, and in most people fear paralyses judgement.

The Warners executives were crawling all over Brian de Palma from the outset. Two of them, Lucy Fisher and Mark Canton, turned up in New York and were offended when de Palma refused to allow them to be present at his rehearsals. That shocked me more than anything in the book. Filming by its nature is a somewhat public activity. Rehearsal is the intensely private time between director and actor when they can take risks, make fools of themselves, experiment. An executive who wants to crash a rehearsal is crudely ignorant of the movie-making process. My heart went out to de Palma. Every wound and cut he took, I bled for him.

David Lean told me of how he dealt with studio executives when they visited the set. He would greet them warmly and politely, give them a tour of the set, introduce them to all the actors. He would send for a cup of tea and sit down with them to chat. Eventually it would dawn on them that David did not intend to resume shooting until they left. The large crew, hundreds of extras all waited patiently. Making mental calculations about the cost of their visit in lost time, the executives would suddenly discover that they had to leave immediately. 'Must you really go so soon?' David would say to their backs as they scurried away.

29 October

Whilst I was away Tony Pratt has drawn up the storyboards for the special effects sequences. There are some four hundred drawings in all. We spent the whole of today with the computer people going through each effect in detail. The computer can handle conventional optical-effects work like marrying up two images, blue screen work, etc., faster and better. But it offers a much wider range of tricks, and any technique it has acquired and learnt it can reapply. It is very good at distorting objects, making them elongate or twist into other shapes. It can put in shadows, alter colours, change shapes.

However, anything that has not been done before is painstakingly slow. The sort of transformations that occur in *Terminator 2* are achieved by marrying a live image with a computer-generated image which is the equivalent of animation – frame by frame painting.

30 October

Jeremy tells me that CiBy 2000 are now saying that an Anglo-French co-production is a condition of the deal.

Tony Pratt will come to Ireland this week and we will concentrate on developing models of the major sets. We have made a deal to take over the whole of Ardmore Studios, or at least the three major stages. There are six large sets to be built, so each stage will have to be built on, struck, and re-built. We have to work out a shooting schedule which allows us the necessary construction time for each. So, as usual, we will be obliged to shoot the film completely out of sequence.

1 November

Jeremy has finally got a date for me to meet with Bouygues in Paris: 13 November. Attal and Fleury are now saying that the deal is subject to Bouygues's approval. Jeremy and I had been under the impression that the deal was approved already. They had accepted our budget of $16 million. I called Fleury, who said Bouygues was irrational and fickle and his mind changed like the wind. Not very reassuring.

Jeremy says CiBy 2000 are now complaining that the budget is too high and that they hate the idea of Julie Delpy. They say she is temperamental, that people detest working with her and that all her films have been flops. I am shocked. I thought they would be delighted that I want to use a French actress whose lovely, vulnerable face adorns every magazine you pick up. I spoke to Bertrand Tavernier about her and he gave her a rave review. The Schlondorff film in which she stars with Sam Shepherd had just opened to poor business in Paris. If CiBy 2000 want to be a major studio, they are certainly picking up the worst habits of their Hollywood models.

13 November, Paris

Fleury and Attal attended our meeting with Bouygues. I gave a passionate account of the film during which Bouygues nodded off to sleep for a few moments. Even when awake he seemed vague. This film company is a toy for him and he plays with our lives.

At a separate meeting afterwards, Fleury said they would finance the picture but only up to $12.5 milion. He suggested that we could achieve this if Jeremy and I took no fees. We pointed out that even if we did, we would still have a shortfall of $2.5 million.

Their opposition to Julie Delpy was quite virulent. They had suggested that I meet Vanessa Paradis, a young pop star who had made a successful movie in France and was now the new Chanel girl. An advertising campaign was afoot that would make her face famous across the world. She came in to see me at Jeremy's hotel. She has a sweet child-like face, unformed yet wanton. We chatted for a few minutes and I asked her to read the script.

Sensing a cooling off at CiBy 2000, Jeremy has given the script to John Heyman. He and his partner Chris Blackwell of Island Records have offered to put up the finance, so we have a fall-back position. At least we hope so.

14 November, London

Jeremy stayed on in Paris to take another meeting with Bouygues, this time with Bertolucci, who was to report on the progress of the Buddha project. I would have loved to listen in on that.

I spent the day with Tony Pratt. Sid Nightingale, the construction manager who did *Hope and Glory* with us, came in to budget the various sets and to give time estimates on each of them. Tony and I spent most of the day juggling with the schedule.

Jeremy got back from Paris this evening and immediately drove to Newbury to see Chris Blackwell. He wanted to pump him up before our meeting with John Heyman tomorrow. He called me late and said, 'Do you think Vanessa Paradis is a possibility?' I said I was willing to test her. He said that, perhaps rashly, he had mentioned her to Blackwell, who had got very excited. He thinks she will be a big star in the pop world.

15 November, London

We met John Heyman this evening at the Dorchester. John is intelligent, urbane and Byzantine. I was impressed by his thorough knowledge and understanding of the script, which we discussed at length. His main concern was that it should get a PG rating in the States. I gave him comfort on that. Finally, he said he would read it again the following day and call us. Despite his enthusiasm, he somehow evaded making a commitment.

16 November, London

Jeremy left for Japan without having heard back from Heyman. I called Heyman at the Dorchester. He had lost his wallet and all his credit cards and was so distraught he had been unable to concentrate on the script. I sensed that Heyman without his credit cards was Samson without his hair.

I saw *Toto the Hero*, the first film of the Belgian ex-circus clown Jaco van Dormael. What a brilliant début. He tells the story with the camera. His compression and ellipses and clever visual transitions make it one of the most cinematic movies in a long time. The story spans a lifetime and kaleidoscopic events with such lightness and grace that you want to get up and cheer. It is in every sense a big picture, yet was clearly made with a modest budget, and from the credits it was apparent that the finance was gathered from all over Europe.

I Dreamt I Woke Up was shown at the London Film Festival and I answered questions afterwards. The first thing someone said was 'Can we come visit you? It looks like such a paradise!' Then someone asked, 'Are you more comfortable in your own skin now that you have made this film?' I replied that at this moment, confronting this audience after revealing myself on film, I felt like jumping out of my skin. A middle-aged woman asked why they don't show films like this in her local cinema. I said thank God they don't. That got a big laugh.

19 November

Jeremy called from Tokyo. The good news was that he had secured a Japanese tax shelter deal which would be worth 25 per cent of the budget. Heyman was hedging, saying that he wanted to get a US distribution deal before committing. Jeremy offered him the tax shelter. He promised to get back to us.

Pierre Edelman called to say that Vanessa Paradis was crazy about my script. This got everybody excited at CiBy 2000. It occurred to me that with the tax deal in place, CiBy 2000's $12.5 million would now be enough to get by on. I said to Edelman that I would test Paradis as I intended also to test Delpy.

Jeremy spoke to Edelman and said he would make a deal with them if CiBy 2000 came through with the money before Heyman.

26 November, Berlin

I am here to see Armin Mueller-Stahl for the part of Ainscott.

Are those smiling, china-blue eyes of Armin's true or do they flatter to deceive? He is a joyous person, open and free. He lives the life of the artist, loving music above all. He writes, he paints, he acts, he plays the violin. They are all one to him. His spirit is a warm thing. He is happy, content, pleased. Why does such contentment seem suspect? Why do gloom and despair ring more true? Perhaps because they are a closer reflection of the world as it is. Yet he suffered under the Communist regime. He was persecuted for opposing the government in East Germany. He describes himself as a clown. I believe that. And a clown has tears. Yet still I wonder if he is not too benign for Ainscott. Certainly he will make him real, but does the German accent have too many connotations for a character mesmerizing a community? We had dinner together at the Paris Bar after reading some scenes in the hotel.

Meanwhile Jeremy insists that we have a firm deal with Heyman. He has been saying that for two weeks, yet he refuses to allow us to take on crew. If he was sure, he would forge ahead. We are stalled. Tony is not allowed to employ draughtsmen to prepare the plans for construction, which should start before Christmas if we are to hold the schedule. We can only get the Olympia Theatre in Dublin for a fixed period. The exterior scenes must be shot before the leaves come on the trees. Worst of all, we cannot close deals on the actors.

I spoke with Iris Burton, River's formidable agent, last night. He has many tempting and lucrative offers. I fear we may lose him. If we do, the project will collapse. I managed to smooth her feathers, which Sean had ruffled in his attempt to beat down her price for River. We are living on the edge. I told her Jeremy would call her today to make the deal.

Watching CNN this morning as the grey dawn light seeped into a cold Berlin, I see that *The Addams Family* had a huge opening in the US: $24 million. Scorsese's *Cape Fear*, which did $10 million last weekend, astonishingly maintained this figure. That was all it needed. A couple of movies the audience wants to see. The gloom has lifted. Hollywood is euphoric. Yet the deeper malaise remains. Orion, a company that has tried harder more than most to make better films, is so mired in debt that even two major hits, *Silence of the Lambs* and *Dances with Wolves*, failed to save it. It was so pressed that it was forced into a fire sale of its unreleased movies. It sold *The Addams Family* to Paramount for a knockdown $21 million, less than it took in its first weekend.

Reading Richard Ellmann's book on W. B. Yeats. He makes much of the division between the mystical dreamer and the man of action who tried to forge a new Ireland. Yeats was aware of the divide. A voice in his mind constantly called for him to 'hammer your ideas into a unity'. I share those separate urges: to dream and to act. Making movies provides the unity, I suppose. Yet my belief in the sovereignty of the imagination has tempted me to disengage from political and social issues. It is time I hammered my ideas into a unity.

27 November, Paris

Vanessa Paradis came to see me yesterday as arranged. Next door to the Lancaster Hotel, a mob of teenagers besieged the rock group New Kids on the Block. She came in distraught. 'They chased me,' she said. 'They hate me.' I asked her who her fans were if teenagers did not like her. 'Others,' she said with a shrug. She confessed that she was committed to making an album in the States, then a tour and that she would not be free for a year and a half. This was a great relief. Jeremy had pressed me to consider her, because she is Polydor's hottest new pop star and that links her to Chris Blackwell, Heyman's partner. She is on the front and back covers of French *Vogue*. She is hot and she is completely unsuitable for Nell. This was empha- sized when Julie Delpy came in. She read for me. Her ephemeral beauty, spirituality and skill gave Nell the radiance that she needs.

Jeremy called. The deal with Heyman is finally made. He will put up $15 million, which means Jeremy and I must defer fees. We have a good chance of recovering our position from the Japanese or Irish tax shelters, but who knows? At least we are doing it. At last I feel a lessening of anxiety. We can go into action.

1 December, London

Stopped off in London on my way back from Paris to meet Jeremy and his lawyer Julian Dickens. David Norris came with me and we hammered out a deal appropriate to the new circumstances. Deferring our fees does not bring the budget down to $15 million, so other cuts are necessary. Jeremy expressed his concern that we were stretched in every department and that if we slip up anywhere, we have no margin for error.

We went to Pinewood and worked with Tony. He had developed the major set of the first town, which includes the theatre façade. The model looked magnificent. The architecture was other-worldly, yet solid, heavy. Alas, we have comparatively little action on the set and so it is an obvious place to make savings. Sadly, we ripped it apart and devised something simpler.

It was Jeremy's idea to reduce this set; it will save £150,000, as well as relieving some of the pressure which has built up because of the delays. It will take less time to build and less time to make the drawings.

Phil Stokes called yesterday. If we cannot employ him soon, he will be forced to take another job. He has spent his own money developing and testing the various special effects we need. He was very excited about an experiment he conducted yesterday. By feeding water into a jet engine, he was able to vaporize it and create a mist that covered an area 40 metres deep and 200 metres wide. This opens up marvellous possibilities for our fog sequences. No one has been able to make artificial mist on a grand scale before.

4 December

For three weeks John Heyman has been saying, 'Yes, I am doing it. Give me a couple more days.' But for several days Jeremy has been unable to reach him. Jeremy says his own resources are now exhausted. He is halting the production as from today.

5 December

I have spent the day calling people to tell them the news. Tony Pratt's contract has been terminated. Phillipe Rousselot was shocked. There is money owing. Sean Ryerson has not been paid for three months' work. The worst hit is Phil Stokes who, based on our assurances that the picture was 'go', has bought a £12,000 truck, the two jet engines, as well as other items amounting to £30,000. I spoke to Armin Mueller-Stahl and Julie Delpy, and their agents. Ron Davis, who was to have edited the film, was terribly disappointed.

River and his agent, Iris Burton, were very supportive. They urged me to keep trying and promised to 'hang in'.

I sent Jeremy a memo itemizing the sums owed to various people, pointing out that they were people who trusted me as I had trusted him. If he wouldn't or couldn't pay them, I felt obliged to do so. He said he would do what he could, but it was not possible for him to pay all debts.

I am still hoping Heyman will come through, and I am going to try other avenues, but the finality of the situation came home to me when Sean was forced to release the Olympia Theatre. Without it, our whole schedule collapses.

6 December

I called Jeremy and was surprised to discover that he had gone off to Rome. I tracked him down there eventually. I said we should try Canale Plus. He said, 'Why not?' I called. They were interested, and I couriered the script over.

I spoke to Mike Medavoy tonight, asked him to read it, and sent it off to him. He liked the idea of River Phoenix. If he wants it, he will want all territories, which will end all this uncertainty and horsetrading. Whether Mike will be able to put his mind to it is another matter. The future of his company is riding on the openings next week of *Hook* and *Bugsy*. I can imagine the atmosphere at TriStar. Reactions from press screenings will be filtering back, sending ripples of fear or elation through offices too paralysed with anticipation to think of much else.

7 December

I was delighted that *Toto the Hero* ran away with several prizes at the European Film Awards. Ken Loach's *Riff Raff* was European Film of the Year. Successful on the continent, it has had only a miserly release in the UK, its home territory.

12 December

No word yet from Canale Plus or Mike Medavoy.

Jeremy finally reached John Heyman and said, 'John, you left me exposed. We had a deal.' Heyman answered, 'Give me until 6 January.' How much better is a kind 'No' than a cruel 'Yes'.

Sarah Radcliffe, who produced *My Beautiful Laundrette* and *A World Apart* and other estimable movies, called, having heard of my problems. She hoped I might now be available to direct *Galapagos*, a script that William Boyd wrote some years back. I told Sarah that I had read it at the time. I was attracted to the idea of characters who are disillusioned with society and choose to live on a remote island, rejecting not only the conventions but also the comforts of civilization. The theme of modern man searching for harmony with nature but confronted with its brute reality is one I have pursued before in *Deliverance*, in *The Emerald Forest*, in *Hell in the Pacific*. The problem in this case is that the characters are pathologically disturbed before they arrive on the island of Galapagos (the very name is resonant with the ruthless demands of natural selection). I don't subscribe to the conventional wisdom that movie protagonists must be sympathetic, but these are simply repulsive.

Sarah asked if she could help with *Broken Dream*. Her company, Working Title, has been taken over by PolyGram, who also purchased Palace Pictures the other day, leaving Jeremy and Puttnam as the only independent production entities in the UK. She told me that PolyGram had instructed their new captive producers to go after pictures in the $15–20 million range. It never ceases to surprise me that, however bad things get, a new player will appear, and hope leaps into our broken hearts once more. I sent the script round right away.

I spoke to Peter Rawley last night in LA. I was anxious to hear how *Hook* had opened. They are all depending on Spielberg to rescue the industry from recession. Peter said that it had opened well but not very well. He had not seen it, but reviews were mixed. People were saying that the film is very good but it is not *ET*. That is very bad news, particularly for Mike Medavoy and, by extension, for us.

Peter went on to say that, according to recent research, the core audience in the States, the 30 million or so regular movie-goers, are staying away from cinemas, choosing to watch movies in other ways, mostly on video, I suppose. I said that I thought business was looking up with *The Addams Family*'s huge opening. He told me that it had dropped off by 50 per cent and that the studio had spent $37 million advertising it. *Cape Fear* and *Beauty and the Beast* had similar precipitous drops. 'You have chosen a very difficult moment to re-finance your film,' he said.

15 December

The days are slipping away and our chances of reviving *Broken Dream* diminish. No word from Canale Plus, Sarah Radcliffe, or Medavoy.

16 December, London

David Deutsch produced my first film, gave me my first break, as he did for so many others. His death gathered us together and we paid him tribute tonight. He was generous and kind and brought joy into many lives. Alan Bates gave a reading. Freddie Raphael and Michael Winner spoke; all were deeply moved. I said to Freddie, 'What greater achievement can there be than a life that inspired such affection from so many?' Each of us had found that David's presence had consistently lit up our lives. He never spoke of his own misfortunes, nor complained of the cruel suffering he had to endure in the last months of his life.

David's father, Oscar Deutsch, founded the Odeon circuit, his initials forming the first letters of the name. David told me that when he was at Oxford, Odeon architecture was reviled as the worst kind of kitsch, so he kept very quiet about the fact that his mother designed many of those interiors. More recently the Odeon style came back into fashion and was much admired. At last David was able to proudly reveal his mother's part in it.

20 December, London

I bumped into Greta Scacchi in the King's Road. 'I hear Jeanette Winterson turned down your offer for *The Passion*.' I said that was indeed the case. 'She turned me down too,' said Greta. 'I was desperate to do the role.' She hesitated, then added, 'If you had made it, would you have cast me?' 'Of course, Greta.' She went off feeling much better about the whole thing.

24 December

This weekend *Hook* dropped 35 per cent from its already modest opening, and Jeff Berg tells me the experts predict it is unlikely to reach $75 million at the box office. No picture of mine has ever made that figure, yet for *Hook* it is a disaster. *Bugsy* also opened wide this last weekend and it apparently did not perform well even with the boost of having won best picture, director and screenplay at the LA critics awards. Mike Medavoy must be shattered. Jeff Berg finally reached him, gaining the impression he had not yet read *Broken Dream*. However, Mike said there was considerable enthusiasm for the script in the company. Jonathan Darby, an assistant of Mike's, duly called and confirmed that interest, yet they seem some way from a commitment.

Peter Rawley called to say that in the present climate the studios are saying 'no' to everything. The pictures that are being made are getting their budgets slashed. He said that actors who were getting $1–2 million dollars are now being offered $500,000, take it or leave it. Poor things.

I have now resigned myself to postponing the picture until September of next year. With a six-month gap, maybe I'll try to do a small picture in between, on the lines of *I Dreamt I Woke Up*.

There has been no word from Jeremy Thomas for some time, but he called today – from Australia!

27 December

Coming to the end of this journal and, reading it over, I am conscious that I have left a lot of loose ends dangling, but that just happens to be the way things are, for the real world does tend to lack dramatic shape. Perhaps that is why it is so hard to find endings for movies. Imposing solutions on the messy business of life often feels forced. The studios are always urging us to make endings that are 'uplifting', but, as Orson Welles said, 'Happy endings are only possible if you don't tell the rest of the story.' Sam Fuller's advice was more practical: 'Spend your money on the ending and shoot it early in the schedule. If you wait till the end, the money has usually run out and you are too exhausted to get it right.' That might also apply to the larger world. As we sink into a deepening economic recession, money seems to be running out and our leaders look exhausted. Nobody can think of a plot twist that will make everything come right in the end. Politicians, commentators and economists have taken to talking about 'possible scenarios', and, given the momentous problems that beset our battered little planet, none of them can come up with a script that would get past the lowliest reader in a Hollywood studio. The trivial tribulations of a film director as set out in this diary are certainly small beer when seen in the wider context.

So, what of the future? Next year will be difficult, but it will surely be only a brief stumble in the all-conquering advance of the moving image. High-definition television will bring more vivid images into the home. Omnimax and Virtual Reality will strive to match the veracity of the human eye. The camera has tamed our planet, domesticated its dangers and wonders, diminished its mysteries. F. Scott Fitzgerald wrote, 'The movies have taken away our dreams. Of all betrayals, this is the worst.' For we have been everywhere, seen everything. There is no experience that we can approach in innocence. We have lived it all out at the movies. We have made love in every possible way, died a thousand different deaths. We have scaled all the mountains, dived in the deepest oceans, closely observed all the creatures of the earth. T. S. Eliot, reaching for the remotest form of life as a metaphor for his degradation, said, 'I should have been a pair of ragged claws scuttling across the floors of silent seas.' What's the big deal, Tom? We've been there already.

Movie-makers search frantically for unused locations, for corners of the earth that have never been seen on film, only to discover a piece of gaffer-tape or, the ethnographical mark of moving-image culture, the polystyrene cup. We are second-hand people. How often, in emotional situations, do we say, 'it was like a bad movie'?

When Buñuel was preparing *The Discreet Charm of the Bourgeoisie*, he chose a tree-lined avenue for the recurring shot of his characters traipsing endlessly down it. The avenue was strangely stranded in open country and it perfectly suggested the idea of these people coming from nowhere and going nowhere. Buñuel's assistant said, 'You can't use that road. It's been in at least ten other movies.' 'Ten other movies?' said Buñuel, impressed. 'Then it must be good.'

Buñuel's image will always be with me, but who remembers the other ten movies? Only the artist can transform the physical world, can pierce the veil, can uncover mysteries that lie hidden beneath those pretty pictures. Only *Life on a String* did that for me this year.

Broken Dream is about how an old illusionist discovers the ultimate trick – to make objects disappear. He teaches it to his son, and when the boy has grown strong in it, the old man asks his son to make his body disappear. He wants to follow the objects across, for the present world is fading away, coming to an end. Once he is on the other side, the old man hopes to make a bridge so that the other characters can cross too. When we probe deep enough, our achingly beautiful and sorrowful world is made up, finally, of subatomic particles moving randomly in vast empty spaces. What we perceive, what the camera records, are certain mathematical arrangements of these particles which may, in truth, have no existence at all, but be merely echoes or shadows of their non-selves. So could not the imagination construct another world out of these ghostly fragments? *Broken Dream* is about making another reality, another world, out of magic, out of imagination. I have the movie in my head. With a lot of work and money, other people could see it too.

I suppose I will have to go off to Los Angeles in the new year and try my luck, but I have to face up to the possibility that it will not be made at all. It would then join *The Chymical Wedding* in my private movie theatre of the mind. Unmade movies at least have a kind of purity, but *Final Analysis* was a movie I started and which was made by someone else. I am curious to see it. There have been rumours that it previewed poorly. It was to have opened at Christmas but failed to put in an appearance. A friend of mine was driving past Warners the other day and he saw the huge billboard for *Final Analysis* being painted out.

I once went into the film vaults at Warners. I was looking for a piece of negative from *Deliverance* which they had lost. There was one area which was shuttered off with steel mesh and its doors firmly padlocked. 'Could it be in there?' I asked. The Keeper of the Vault drew me away. 'No one goes in there,' he said. Then he whispered in my ear the dread truth: 'That's where they keep the unreleased movies.' I stared in horror at the mountains of mute cans. 'Goes right back to the beginnings of the studio,' he added. We hurried away as if the devil was at our tail.

I saw *Hearts of Darkness* the other day. It is a record of the making of *Apocalypse Now* and it documents Coppola's agonies in the face of overwhelming difficulties. He had the jungle. He had Brando. He had his own money at risk. Making that marvellous movie against those odds was one of the mightiest victories in the history of film. To achieve it he had a whole arsenal of equipment and armies of technicians at his disposal, and he needed them all. And yet, surprisingly, at the conclusion of the film he predicted that, with the availability of cheap video cameras, one day soon a fat girl in Kansas would start making miraculous movies in her back yard and that film would thus find its Mozart. *I Dreamt I Woke Up* was a film made in my back yard and it still cost £100,000. Remember, Francis, even Mozart needed an orchestra. I am afraid the fat girl will end up taking the Greyhound bus to Burbank and lining up with the rest of us at Warner Bros looking for money.

4 January 1992

Whoops! The Christmas/New Year box office in the US broke all records. *Hook* has made a valiant recovery, confounding the doom-sayers. Jeff Berg says that despair has given way to euphoria at the studios. 'Come out and grab some while it lasts.'

I'm on my way, Jeff.

2   The Burning Question:
Absolute Freedom?

It is often said that film is the art of the possible. Budget limitations, our concern for the audience, for the financiers, and for the critics shape and define the movies we make.

But suppose the situation was otherwise. Suppose a film-maker had an unlimited budget, and no obligation even to distribute the completed film. What would he or she do with this freedom?

We are seeing at the moment the dilemma of Eastern Europe, where the collapse of the state subsidy structure has forced film-makers to confront the whole question of artistic freedom. Before the collapse of Communism, film finance was provided by the state, but they were restricted in what they could say. Now they have freedom of expression, but are constrained by the demands of the market. As Milos Forman has said about the difference between working in Czechoslovakia and in the United States, 'In Eastern Europe it is like being in a zoo – you are kept in a cage, but you have a roof over your head and someone feeds you every day; in the US it is the jungle – you are free to go where you like, but everyone is trying to kill you.'

Does being freed from the cage, or protected from the jungle, freeze the imagination or set it free?

We asked a number of directors from all over the world the following question: If you were given an unlimited budget, and were under no obligation to distribute it, what film would you make?

The response was . . .

Arthur Penn

Not unlike the prisoner long confined to a solitary cell, when confronted by your postulation of a film with unlimited budget and no necessity of distribution – the door of the cell flung open and freedom offered – I cling to my tiny, familiar prison space. My imagination refuses to venture forth to freedom.

Vague voices: 'tennis without a net', 'the art of the impossible', 'set out to make a masterpiece and halfway through all you want is to finish'.

But wait. If I goad it and shame it, my imagination finally slips into the light and produces a vague image of a film.

It is a film about the end of the first millennium of the Christian era, AD 1000. Widespread fears of the End of the World and the Last Judgement abound. Desperate efforts made to cleanse souls and expunge records. New religious intensity burns fiercely. Destroy any infidels that come to hand. Pilgrimages to the highest mountains in order to be 'the first'.

And then the day, and the day, and the day and then the day ends.

Oh well. We have another thousand years. What shall we do with them while we wait? Perhaps we have failed in our zeal. Let's kill more infidels.

'Knights Ho! Let's have a crusade! OK, all you guys in armour up on those horses. No, no kids, we don't want any kids now. OK, lower Sir Knight on to his steed! No! Tell those kids if they behave themselves they can have their own crusade, but they have to behave! All right, forward! We ride east! No, east!'

OK, so we lost the crusades, but wait till the next to last reel when we have the Gulf War. We'll get back at those guys. This movie goes on until we win – or lose!

Listen, Boorman and Donohue, you were the ones who gave us licence to make a film of unlimited budget and no obligation to distribute. In me it produces a movie without end. I can't stand the freedom.

No, give the obligation to wrap an actor by a certain date, a time to finish, an insistence of choices. 'Wait for this light and those clouds to clear or use that time to devote to a fragile scene yet to be shot' – that decision makes my heart beat faster and my armpits damp.

I can suffer the fools and their finances. Give me choices to make and I can begin to force a film into existence; carve out of chaos some vestige of order and allow it to declare its form.

I need restraint, limits; above all choices.

We all want more time and money and 'freedom', but give me unlimited quantities of any, and I sneak back into my cell and blink the harsh light out.

My movie goes away.

Samuel Fuller

| *The Lusty Days* | | *San Juan* |
| Romantic action-comedy | or | Action-comedy |

Jane Campion

With my unlimited budget and obligation-free distribution I would explore portraiture. First, a self-portrait; then, if I enjoyed doing that and thought it revealing and curious, I might move on to others. I'm mostly interested in what's a Human, and what sort of one I am – for starters.

Finally, I would finish with an adaptation – first for the stage – of *A Portrait of a Lady*, then do a film version. I'd do it as a play first because I think it's a very performance-intelligent novel and I'd like to get a sense of its overall dramatic strength and delicacy, as well as a feel for length and dramatic adaptation. I'm in love with novels. I particularly like the last third of *A Portrait of a Lady*. I am chastened, however, as many adaptations don't thrill me.

Costa-Gavras

In such Draconian conditions, it is, I am sure, impossible to be able to choose a subject or to direct a film.

Krzysztof Kieślowski

I don't believe in absolute freedom. In practice it is impossible, philosophically unacceptable. We direct ourselves to get freedom and every time we realize we can't reach it. And, looking at it in this way, the goal is not as important as the means of attaining it: it is not possible – thank God! – to achieve our goal. So it is obvious that I am favourably disposed to compromise. And not because it is useful. First of all, because I don't know the answers, and in making films I ask questions. Questions and doubts, lack of self-confidence, curiosity and amazement that everything goes on in a natural way – all this puts me in the position of an observer and a listener. I change my script very often – the scenes, dialogues or situations – because I can see that people around me have better ideas, more intelligent solutions. It doesn't disturb me that these are other people's ideas. When I have accepted and chosen them, they become mine.

As a film director I am realistic. I am using the world of events and the world of thoughts, and I treat them equally. I am also realistic in my approach to the work. I respect my producer, money and, above all, my viewer. Not just because I have to. I do so because I want to. In my opinion, the production of a film – however costly – has its own morality. And I am trying to obey this morality, because I want to obey. A cup of coffee may cost 1½ dollars, may cost 3 or 5 dollars, but when it costs 120 dollars, drinking this coffee is immoral. It is exactly the same in the production of films.

The film I want to make is the film I am able to make. There are no others. I don't think of other films. I don't have a million viewers waiting at the entrance of the cinema, but I need to feel that someone needs me for something. And even if I make films – like all my colleagues – for myself,

I'm looking all the time for somebody who tells me, like a fifteen-year-old girl in France, 'I saw your *Double Life of Veronique*.' Then I want to see it several more times. For the first time in my life I have seen and I have felt that there is something like 'soul'. So, if I were not concerned about this girl's opinion, there would be no reason to take the camera out of its box.

Claude Miller

Ulysses by James Joyce.

Francesco Rosi

Orlando Furioso by Ariosto.

Kevin Reynolds

I have always been fascinated with war as a human creation and how each generation perpetuates it. In particular, I am fascinated with the scale and tragedy of the Second World War. I think in centuries to come the Second World War will take on the epic proportions of the Trojan War or the Crusades and I would love to do the quintessential Second World War movie as I think it would be portrayed, say, 500 years from now.

I would take one character – a young American paratrooper – and watch him leave home, train, cross an ocean for the first time and then experience the entire conflict through his eyes. It would be almost surreal in style and choreographed to the achingly poignant music of Shostakovich's 7th, 8th and 9th Symphonies. It would take months to shoot and cost fifty or sixty million dollars.

Denys Arcand

Before shooting anything I would need to do some research. In fact, a great amount of research. This research would imply months – make that years – of skiing in the Alps, the Rockies and the Andes. Then I would have to do some scuba-diving in the Red Sea, near the coast of Belize and in the Philippines. I would also need membership privileges at Wimbledon and a box at Salzburg. I would have to be permanently accompanied by a Thai masseuse, an Italian mezzo and several other stunning beauties. A private aeroplane would probably be required, and a yacht would be nice also. At this moment, I cannot reveal the exact nature of the research itself, but since the film is not going to be distributed and the budget is unlimited, why are you worrying?

Istvan Szabo

I would most like to make a film of the story of my family during the last 150 years. Their fate shows exactly the birth, development and systematic destruction of Central Europe's bourgeoisie and intelligentsia by the twentieth-century dictatorships.

Magical love and career stories reveal changing morals, desires, passions and purposes under the various social systems.

Ken Russell

A film called 'Space Gospel'.

I wrote it in collaboration with Derek Jarman, revealing the New Testament as Amazing Science Fiction.

Sydney Pollack

It will perhaps seem strange for someone who usually makes big-budgeted, large studio films to say that it would be impossible for him to make a film with an unlimited budget. Frustrated as I may be with whatever limitations there are, it is, for me, those very limitations that serve initially to point me in a direction to solve the creative problem. I'm afraid I would find my imagination not up to the challenge of working with no limits whatsoever.

Mike Figgis

Unlimited budget? What a terrifying idea. Big budget equals large crew equals a sea of unknown faces on a never-ending pay cheque equals loss of artistic control because it is hard to exchange intimate ideas with strangers. It is hard enough to relate to a small crew.

It has been my observation that small projects are harder to finance and distribute than larger ones.

Unlimited budget? OK, very low. Enough to pay a small, dedicated crew and some unknown actors. I'd probably shoot Super 16mm.

No obligation to distribute? This is a tough one. I'd see no point in making a film that wouldn't be seen.

As I move from project to project the truth becomes clouded. There is a seemingly logical idea that each film should cost more than the one before. In fact, there is no real connection between the ability to say something with a camera and the idea of unlimited budget.

Louis Malle

Pretty much what I am doing now. Unlimited budget would give me the opportunity to reshoot everything I've done if I didn't like it.

Ettore Scola

I've made low-budget films and ones with high budgets, but I am not concerned with cost: my imagination is not fired up nor dampened down by the financial aspects of film-making. At this moment, if I had an unlimited budget, I might use it for many 'small' films.

Vincent Ward

Would an unlimited budget and no obligation to distribute the film freeze my imagination or set it free? (Your very question leaves me writer's-blocked! But this, I suspect, has much to do with a fear of hexing any project truly close to my heart.)

I'd love to make *Apocalypse Now 2* (and call it *Apocalypse Later*). Or do one hundred episodes of *One Hundred Years of Solitude* – and make it in Virtual Reality (especially the scene where everybody in the village loses their memory). But most of all, I want to make *Perfume* – in Odorama.

Paul Verhoeven

Art is communication. Without distribution – without an audience – any form of art is senseless.

An audience is necessary, but that should not be translated into 'concern for the audience'. I've never felt any concern for the audience, which has sometimes pissed off the audience, but that's communication too. Budget restrictions can be a bit of a strain, but generally speaking a movie gets the budget that it deserves – the remaining restrictions induce creativity.

So: an unlimited budget is as much nonsense as a symphony of ten hours. How much art can we stand?

I strongly feel that in due time you can make any movie you want for a realistic budget – minus 10 per cent.

Michael Verhoeven

As I was never in the situation to really do a movie like I want – because of constant lack of money – I would feel free free!

And I would do my next film as always . . .

David Byrne

The way in which the question is phrased forces one to imagine something out of the ordinary: a very expensive film that the public never sees. I guess these things exist. I imagine a documentary on atrocities 'produced' by Hitler and Goebbels. A very boring epic mini-series on atomic testing produced by the United States Department of Defense (we've seen the standard stock-shot of a building being blown away and 'observers' watching a Nevada test . . . but there is lots, lots more . . . and worse). Obscure medical tests and clinical films. Industrial films. Huge productions shown only to potential investors and stockbrokers.

But what would *I* do?

For me, the constraints have always been an essential element in the creative process. Whether those constraints are budgetary or my own limitations, it doesn't matter. They force one to make something where there was nothing. The limitations become advantages. An itch that must be scratched.

And, although we constantly push against those constraints, and complain and feel put upon, most mega-budget spectacles (but not all) impress us only with their audacity.

I have avoided the question.

Zhang Yimou

I would like to make a film about the Yellow River – about the people who live and work on it. It would take me at least ten years to make it. I have no idea how long the film would be, probably as long as the Yellow River.

Gus Van Sant

My relation to budget is a funny one, in that the less money that I have, the more creative I have to get to overcome limitations. Actually, the limitations themselves make a film look a particular way. So far the budgets that I've had have been enough to do what I want to do. I imagine that if I were given an unlimited budget, and was under no obligation to distribute it, I would get horribly out of control and make a mess of things, then try to buy my way out of my mistakes.

Richard Lowenstein

All forms of creative expression involve a degree of compromise. The mere process of bringing an ethereal thought process into the physical world must involve some degree of compromise, whatever the medium might be.

Film, along with most art-forms, is unshakeably bonded to the desire to communicate, the desire to touch another person in some way. This bond rigidly fuses the need to distribute to the need to create.

These days creative elements involving cast, script, music, subject matter and the like tend to be influenced, if not controlled, by those who hold the purse strings and those who control the distribution outlets.

Freedom from the constraints of distribution is, therefore, more importantly a freedom from the bureaucratic vagaries of certain funding bodies and distribution companies.

Liberation from this would, indeed, be a liberation of profound proportions.

The removal of budget restrictions, however, is an invitation to egomania. A budget has a responsibility not only to the script, the film and the creative talent involved in the production, but also to the state of the society around us. The budget has a moral responsibility not only to reflect what the script, film-maker and crew are attempting to do, but to also reduce the level of compromise to a reasonable level.

The most obvious advantage would be the availability of adequate amounts of time for the actual processes of the film-making. Acting, lighting, camera, sound and script development all tend to suffer in the low-budget area of film-making.

So, to answer the question – without distributors or budget restrictions, my themes and ideas wouldn't change, it's just the ability to bring them out into the real world with a minimum amount of compromise that would be improved.

Paolo and Vittorio Taviani

Unlimited freedom of choice can paralyse the ability to choose. Often limitation is a spur to the imagination. But, playing along with your impossible game, here is our impossible desire:

To have enough capital to secure the services of the team – actors, technicians, etc. – for two years. This would allow us to shoot at our leisure; to rethink every detail from one shot to the next, like our master Charlie Chaplin; to look at the film a year after it has been finished and reshoot anything that falls short of perfection.

This is our impossible desire . . . Yet the film that is closest to our hearts is *San Michele aveva un gallo*, which we shot in four weeks, with 14,000 metres of film.

Terry Gilliam

I consider myself one of those fortunate film-makers who have never been given all the money they want to put their ideas on film. I have always preferred to work within financial limitations. I realize this sounds like rubbish coming from the maker of *The Adventures of Baron Münchausen*, but it's true.

From the beginning, I have been convinced that I have always been saved from mediocrity by lack of money. When we embarked on *Monty Python and the Holy Grail*, we planned to make a 'real' Knights of the Round Table film. We were keen to be proper film-makers, showing that we, too, could make the kind of epics we had grown up watching – *Ivanhoe, Robin Hood, Camelot* – with knights swashbuckling around the place on great steaming chargers. But, because we didn't have the cash for a spectacle on that scale, we had to get rid of the horses and, in their place, substitute coconuts, banged together by each knight's over-worked page, clip-clopping behind his master who, in turn, pretended to be riding an imaginary horse in the way children do. With that one desperate leap, the film took off into its own world, freeing us from the need to compete with other medieval epics on their terms, allowing us to create our own twisted version of the Middle Ages. I'm certain that with horses and our inexperience we would have become bogged down in logistics and the need for a 'normal' reality and would have produced a less unique and funny film.

Budgetary limitations also helped make *Brazil* far more intriguing and disturbing than it would otherwise have been. We had to try to create another world by adapting existing objects we could buy cheaply, instead of designing our ideal world and then building it. With 'found' objects there was always an element of surprise and a constant need to adapt preconceived ideas. Familiar objects took on new shapes and meaning. The world became a distortion of our present world, not some distant place which could be brushed aside easily as a fantasy. Because of a lack of loot we used posters to create the world beyond the immediate view of the camera. We could imply what else was out there without having to show it.

A kind of claustrophobia could be maintained while still creating the feel of a complete world. With sufficient money I would have built incredible flying machines, extraordinary trains, fantastic boats which would have looked wonderful but, in the process, would have distracted from the atmosphere that proved to be so critical to the effect of the film.

The Adventures of Baron Münchausen was different from my other films in that, for the first time, I was working with a producer who claimed he would provide everything I ever wanted. The fact that he couldn't and didn't created a living hell. I was, and still am, very literal about taking people at their word and holding them to their promises. However, when, as is inevitable in these situations, the shit hit the fan, we were forced to close down while Charles McKeown and I attempted to trim the script. The pain was quite unbearable at the time but, when you are forced to destroy your work in an attempt to save it, certain creative magic occurs.

Originally, the moon sequence involved thousands of giant characters all with detachable heads. It was conceived as a Cecil B. DeMille extravaganza with great crowds, much singing and dancing and feasting – all during an eclipse of the moon. The yearly eclipse provided a chance for everyone to forget everything and start again with a clean mental slate. Unfortunately, the celebration resulted in a lot of heads becoming separated from their bodies and then being unable to remember where they belonged. The sequence ended in a grandiose, outrageously spectacular slapstick chase with the Baron and friends riding and attempting to control a giant palace guard's headless body as the eclipse and the King pursue them.

Attempting to keep the film alive, we cut the moon's population down to two, King and Queen. In doing so, it concentrated our attention on the detachable head phenomenon and resulted in a very bizarrely literal interpretation of the problems of Cartesian mind/body duality. What was originally a lot of ideas jumbled together in a slightly rambling, but spectacular, sequence became one very clear and much funnier idea that was exactly to the point, and far more original.

You might ask, 'Why didn't we see these "better" solutions when we were writing the script?' Answer: 'Because we didn't have to.' There was no pressure to limit our imaginations. We were creating a world where anything was possible. Our imaginations soared, but not necessarily towards the best possible film. That's why I'm happy trying to work within a budget.

With all my films, but in particular *Brazil* and *Münchausen*, I have been able to work completely free from restrictions at the script stage. It is only the reality of making the films within financial restrictions that creates the catalyst that triggered some of our most creative work. It also provides the excuses for why the films aren't perfect.

Total freedom would put an unbearable onus on me to make perfect films and that, in turn, would freeze me creatively. Backed up against a financial wall, I can dare to take outrageous chances and daring leaps that are far too intimidating when all the money in the world is available. I need a budget to fight against: it makes my imagination work twice as hard.

3   Film Fiction:
More Factual than Facts
Samuel Fuller

I'm no debunker. I love myths and legends that began in the Old Testament, hurdled Greek and Roman mythology and still keep us in wonderland with fairy tales. Then came the movies and opened up the gates for the animated cartoon – making even a tale like *Snow White* come to life.

That's the magic of film. Film, of course, is all make-believe. Or is it? How much truth is there in fact? How much falsehood in fiction? A newspaper lives on facts. A movie lives on fiction. There is a big difference. Fact is open to all – but a fact may be truth to one person and a lie to another.

Fiction has no boundaries, no law, no rules. Fiction is entertainment. And movie fiction is king of all entertainment because it can bring you tales of artists, writers, poets, inventors, explorers that lift you out of your seat with action you cannot see in any other media of communication.

Movies are so powerful they can change the law.

And I'll tell you one that did.

For many years America was aware of the beatings and crippling of inmates in prisons. The awareness wasn't strong enough to keep Americans from sleeping nights. Newspapers exposed the floggings; the readers reacted but then turned the page to another story, and the inhuman treatment of prisoners was forgotten.

In 1932 the movie *I Am a Fugitive from a Chain Gang* hit the screens of America. Starring Paul Muni as the fugitive, and directed by Mervyn LeRoy, this fiction story was loosely based on a real prisoner who escaped from a chain gang, but was recaptured and clubbed and flogged until he escaped again. This time he disappeared.

A familiar story of mentally warped guards getting a kick out of beating the hell out of any prisoner they felt like abusing.

The movie, however, had one advantage over guards, warden and even newspapers irate about such medieval tortures in their modern penal institutions. That advantage was the camera.

That advantage was fiction. Every instant of that fiction up there on the screen you saw very clearly. Because it was all visual, you got to know Muni; you not only saw but felt his strength, weakness, courage, anger, helplessness. And what you saw was so emotional, it shocked you.

But hold on. That's only the beginning of the fiction of a movie.

We are flogged with Muni, bleed with Muni, feel pain with every blow on his head and back. We have become Muni because camera close-ups can do that. We crouch with Muni at every sound. We wimper with him as no one treats our bleeding, bruised backs.

We escape, run. Where? Every second we might be caught. And the more we are Muni, the more the fiction of brutality in the movie becomes factual. Why? Because we are hit with hammer-blows of emotion.

We have gone through such an inhuman ordeal that all we can do is write to the warden, the governor and the newspapers.

And we did. Thousands of letters. Thousands of letters of anger and shock to the White House.

The people who saw that movie made Georgia outlaw the chain gangs in their prisons. The warden was discharged. God knows what happened to the governor.

As Hippolito, Cardinal D'Este wrote in the early sixteenth century, 'If it's not true, it is well invented.'

4   The Early Life
of a Screenwriter
Emeric Pressburger

edited by Kevin Macdonald

Introduction   Kevin Macdonald

When he was in his late seventies and early eighties I used to visit my grandfather, Emeric Pressburger, two or three times a year at his ancient, oak-beamed, thatched cottage in Suffolk. His short, grey-haired figure would come to the door, welcome me in and immediately show me to the lunch table – it didn't seem to matter what time of day it was – and Emeric would busy himself as the 'wizard' (Michael Powell's nickname for his collaborator) of his tiny kitchen.

It was always the same. As soon as I saw the first course I would wish I hadn't had any breakfast. And when I saw the second I wished I hadn't eaten at all the day before. The meal was gargantuan and Hungarian, and usually went something like this: slices of boiled tongue and foie gras to start with, then slabs of pork, fried potatoes, cucumber salad and – only right at the end when you were dying of thirst – a litre of ice-cold, specially imported Czechoslovakian beer. Pudding was a complete ritual of bloating: a cavernous pot of chestnut purée and whipped cream, followed by bowls of coffee you could float a brick on.

After lunch we would retire to the living-room-cum-study, where Emeric's enormous work table was piled high with notes, manuscripts, tins of boiled sweets, office gadgets, yellowing news-clippings and, lost among it all, his streamlined green Hermes typewriter.

'Vas it enough?' he would ask peevishly.

Apart from a saunter round the garden and maybe a trip to feed his dependants, the goldfish, there was nothing to do for the rest of the day but talk; or rather for him to talk and for me to listen. Slowly, meticulously, as was his way with everything, he chose his words, as though a wrong move would detonate a hidden mine. All Hungarians have strong accents – apparently they even have different-shaped palates from the rest of us – but Emeric's was thicker than crude oil. All Ws were pronounced as V (as in 'vy?' – the favourite word of many Hungarians) while perversely, some Vs were pronounced W (as in 'warious persons'). 'The' was 'De', or something close, and Rs were slightly rolled. Additionally, his grammar was definitely imaginative – 'if I vould be derr now, I vould have done warious things differently' is a representative sentence.

Emeric was essentially a storyteller, not a conversationalist, and he would keep you entertained for hours. There were anecdotes and stories about his films, about restaurants (which also featured heavily in the other categories, of course), about gardening, about his goldfish and about football (mostly Arsenal). The impression I got from them was that he had an endless string of eccentric friends with unpronounceable Eastern European names. There was the friend who ate an entire champagne glass for a bet, the cousin who landed an aeroplane on Budapest's central avenue, and the head waiter in Vienna who addressed him by name after thirty years' absence from his restaurant. But the best stories, and the ones he enjoyed telling the most, were about his days as a poverty-stricken down-and-out in Weimar Berlin, and how he got his first break in films. It was the period of his life that always stayed with him most vividly.

When he died in 1988, among the stacks of paper and gadgets on his desk, I found some notes that he had been making, who knows when, of those same stories. This article is based on the notes augmented by my own memories. I hope that I have retained some of his conversational tone, though of course I cannot reproduce the gentle deliberateness of his voice or that most Hungarian of English accents, the idiosyncrasies for which I remember him most.

In 1902 Imre (Emeric) Pressburger was born in the Hungarian town of Miskolc. At the end of the First World War he and his family found their corner of Hungary swallowed up by neighbouring Romania. Thus began a pattern of alienation that was to last the remainder of Pressburger's life. Forbidden to return to Hungary for higher education and reluctant to study in Romania, Pressburger travelled to Prague to attend technical college. After two years he moved to a similar institution in Stuttgart. In 1926 the death of his father forced him to discontinue his studies and return home to Romania. An attempt to set up a radio station failed dismally, and when he found himself liable for military service in what he considered a foreign army, he decided to leave the country for good.

The Early Life of a Screenwriter

What was there for me in Romania? I was burying myself there. I decided to go to Berlin, my German was good, and it seemed sensible that if you wanted to make a go of it in a foreign country you should go to its capital. I packed up my books and a few other possessions, bought a railway ticket and bade farewell to my mother.

The journey took for ever. We waited a whole day in Vienna. Germany had changed since my last visit, things were terribly expensive, and everything looked run-down. I left my books in the left-luggage and that was the last I

Emeric Pressburger in his thatched cottage in Suffolk

saw of them – I could never afford to get them out again. Every day the cost mounted and my meagre supply of money dwindled. I found a cheap boarding house in the Gartenhaus run by a Czech woman and her daughter. One of the other guests came to sleep with me on the first night, a very nice girl. The landlady made a terrible fuss and told me that I was lowering the tone of the establishment. I told her that it wasn't my fault, the girl had come to me. She looked me up and down and said, 'Impossible.'

Within a few days it became obvious that I was not going to be able to pay my rent. I gave two weeks' notice and the landlady once more became terribly upset, saying that I ought to give four weeks' notice and that I was only acting out of spite. She didn't believe me when I said I wouldn't be able to pay after a month. I felt very depressed about the whole situation – in Berlin with no money and no prospect of a job, and an abrasive landlady to boot. The only positive aspect of those days was a bitter-sweet encounter with a lovely girl who lived on the opposite corner. I waited outside her door for hours and she came out several times to walk the dog, but I never had the courage to talk to her.

When the fortnight was up I left the room, with the landlady's protestations ringing in my ears. I didn't know where I was going to sleep and the landlady had kept all my belongings as some kind of ransom. My few remaining possessions were stuffed into a bulging attaché case; I think there was a spare shirt and a lot of useless junk. For a period I was absolutely miserable and slept on park benches and in shop doorways. My only income came from a few translations that I did for a fellow Hungarian called Ujhelyi Nandor. I suppose I earned a mark or two.

After some time my cousin Bondi turned up, doubtless on the run from the Hungarian law after some escapade – once, a few years previously he had stolen a plane and landed it on the central avenue of Budapest – that was the kind of adventure Bondi got up to – and it had earned him the label of the family scoundrel. His father was a wealthy factory owner and so of course he could afford a room. Once or twice he allowed me to sleep on his floor. This was a frightful ordeal: I had to be quiet as a mouse, for fear of arousing the suspicions of his landlady, and hide in the cupboard in the morning when she brought him his coffee and toast.

I was often very hungry in those days and used to stand outside the most expensive restaurants and cafés looking at the food, dreaming of a time when I would be rich enough to go into one of those places and eat as much as I wanted. It was a fairly difficult period, but altogether it sounds worse to read about than it actually was to experience. I spent my time mainly in the park, the Tiergarten, where I met some very interesting characters. There was a chap who could whistle double tones, and there was Treffer, a man with a very sweet smile who had sent his war decorations to Mrs Roosevelt in exchange for an entry permit to the USA; unfortunately she sent them back saying that she had no right to help him. Treffer was a passionate ballroom dancer and I was a passionate watcher of pretty girls. So, as often as we could afford, we went to the Palais am Zoo to hear an Italian big band with a very good clarinettist, and to dance. Although I know how to dance I have never really mastered it, and modern dancing is something beyond my abilities. I am also terribly shy. I find it unbearably uncomfortable to ask a girl to dance. However, I always admired the snooty, well-made-up creatures who wouldn't even deign to talk to me. Still, to be a foreigner in those days was a great thing with the girls. To read a foreign newspaper in a Berlin café had almost as much cachet as to own a car.

One day I heard of an Austro-Hungarian charity organization which maintained a refuge, a home for ex-citizens of the ex-monarchy, somewhere on the Friedrichstrasse. Such information circulated among us tramps now and again: some of it proved to be accurate, some inaccurate. On this occasion the information was accurate. The board of directors of the organization met regularly in a flat on the Budapesterstrasse, so there I went. I was received by a young secretary, a Hungarian student called Imre Revesz. He was a pleasant fellow and told me to sit and wait until the members of the board, particularly one illustrious banker, had arrived. I sat watching waiters carrying large trays covered in sandwiches and other delicacies through the ante-room where I was waiting. I was, of course, very hungry, and I remember again that desperate longing to gorge myself on food, to quell my appetite – the appetite of several hungry wolves. At last the important banker arrived. He was informed of my case and I was ushered into the plush offices. I can't remember what I was asked and what I told them, but they seemed to be rather impressed. I must have told them that I played the violin but that I had no instrument at that time, for a few days later I was informed by Revesz that the organization was going to buy me a violin.

They also provided more immediate help. I was given a chit which allowed me to have a bed at the Friedrichstrasse home for a whole week. Nobody enquired how I was going to get there, although it was some two miles away, even if you walked through the park. Although I had about thirty pfennigs (enough for a single bus fare), not wanting to spend good money on such luxuries I set out to walk there. It must have been 8.30 in the evening when I found it. I rang the bell and a retired Prussian sergeant (at least he looked like one) opened the door. When I told him that I had come for a bed he bawled me out with his regulations, which laid down that no lodger was allowed to enter later than 8.00 p.m., and that I should return with my chit in the morning. He slammed the door in my face. I was blind with anger. I kicked the door and hammered against it as hard as I could (which wasn't very hard), but there was no reply.

Now it was the time to spend my thirty pfennigs. I went to the nearby station and from there telephoned the association. I got through to Revesz and he called the president, who couldn't believe his ears. He told me to go right back to the home and by the time I got there he would have spoken to the sergeant. I did as instructed, and this time I was admitted, though one does not need a rich imagination to guess the kind of reception I was given. But the main thing for me was that I was admitted.

I was shown to a room where eight beds stood. Seven of them were already occupied. My neighbour was a Hungarian and he started to tell me why the association did as it did. Apparently many poverty-stricken people passed through Berlin who had once been citizens of the dual monarchy. Seeking hand-outs, they used to lay siege to the homes of their well-to-do ex-compatriots, whose names and addresses could be bought for cash from those who had already harvested the crop. The association was a necessary self-defence. My companion himself had just come from Paris, where, he said, there was a mounting hatred of Hungarians due to one Graf Festetich, who, replete with misplaced patriotism and unable to find a way of actually helping his own country, had decided to ruin the French economy by flooding the country with counterfeit francs. Ridiculous stuff, but serious enough for France to expel all Hungarians from the country who were not vital to the economy. Of course the poor and helpless were kicked out first.

I drifted off to a warm and comfortable sleep, but in the early hours of the morning I was woken by a scraping sound coming from my neighbour's bed. I asked what he was doing. In whispers he told me that he was scraping his violin clean. Some Frenchman, in search of revenge, had shat on it and the poor Hungarian had felt embarrassed to clean it in front of the others.

I stayed on at the home for about three weeks, in spite of the general rule that no one should stay longer than one. In order to encourage the inmates to work, one of the rules of the establishment was that everyone had to leave by 6 a.m. At 5.30 we were given some brown fluid, which they imaginatively called coffee, a large piece of bread and some margarine. And then: 'Raus!' Naturally, it was impossible to obtain work so we cruised up and down the streets, sat in parks, perfectly content in the knowledge that we had somewhere to return to in the evenings, and feeling that we belonged somewhere.

Towards the end of the week I received a summons to appear once more at the association's headquarters on the Budapesterstrasse. Revesz gave me a violin and told me some splendid news: the director of the association himself had found me a job. And what a job it was! From the following day onwards I would play as a holiday substitute in the Capitol Cinema orchestra under Schmidt-Gentner! The Capitol was one of the most elegant cinemas in the west end of Berlin. The biggest independent, it was famed throughout the country for its orchestra of about forty musicians. And I was to be one of them!

The following morning I arrived at the cinema and introduced myself to the shrewd conductor, who nodded but said nothing and watched the leader of the orchestra show me to my place. Now, I happened to be quite a good violinist. I had played in my home town's symphony orchestra, had formed my own quartet during my student days, in both Prague and Stuttgart, and I had been quite a success in Weimar. However, I had had no violin for about three years, and he who calls himself a violinist and has not played the instrument for three years must either be a megalomaniac or just plain crazy. I had said nothing of this when they gave me the violin; it would have been crazy to put such a good job in jeopardy. I thought, 'I'll get permission to stay at home for a few days to recondition myself by practising.' Although I had these noble intentions I never had the opportunity of carrying them out. The accompaniment of silent films in a large cinema with a sizeable orchestra had grown out of all proportion and could be inordinately complex. The score we were to play had been cobbled together by the conductor from innumerable bits of existing scores according to well-known markings. Well known to the others, not to me. I got into trouble during the rehearsals on that account and because of this the conductor began to listen to me playing. Then, quite suddenly, he stopped the whole orchestra and said, 'You! New boy! Alone!' At that moment and for a long time afterwards I thought how cruel it was of him to show me off in front of the whole orchestra. But of course he was right. His job was to produce a good orchestra and a fine sound. I played my little piece atrociously and was dismissed on the spot.

I went straight to the Budapesterstrasse to tell of my failure and hand back my violin. I tried to explain, but had the impression that no one understood. I saw on their faces as they looked at each other an expression which said, 'What did I tell you? That'll teach you to trust these chaps – vagabonds, the lot of them.' I was allowed to stay on at the home for another week and then it was back to the streets. Still, I said to myself, you had almost a fortnight with a bed and those large hunks of bread with margarine, and, after all, spring is only a few months away. On top of this, miracle of miracles, I had twelve marks in my pocket, the day's pay for my inglorious performance at the Capitol. With this I could have a tiny cabin at the Salvation Army in their huge dormitory, and when my fortune had sunk to a couple of marks I could sleep on a rope. 'Sleeping on a rope' was a service offered by second-class pubs after they had closed to normal customers for the night. You sat in a row of chairs in front of which a rope had been strung, so that you could lean on the rope and support your head while sleeping. Sleeping on the rope had its climax in the morning when the time came to be rid of us sleepers. The cleaner, or the publican himself, came and cut the rope and we fell forwards, dazed, angry and helpless, to the onlookers' mirth. Strangely, there were always onlookers, probably they too had to pay for the pleasure of the entertainment. I didn't really mind that, though. It was the Salvation Army lot that I detested. I disliked their holy talk, their charity-minded bearing. I often pleaded with them to let me stay overnight when I had nothing, or not quite enough for a bed, but they were pitiless. They chased away anyone who did not possess the few coins necessary. I have never forgiven them to this day.

One day my good friend Treffer told me his great secret. He was a secret author. He gave me his collected – handwritten – works and I read them all. I was appalled; he really had no talent and no idea. I was certain that, although I had never tried, I could write far superior material. The idea grew on me and I decided to become a writer. I wrote furiously and everywhere: in stations, on park benches and, mainly, in post offices. In warm post offices I wrote on the back of telegram forms and sent my handwritten efforts to newspapers and magazines. I gave my address poste restante and started keeping files (in my already stuffed attaché case) of all my short stories. Within a few months I knew that the *Vossische Zeitung* took twenty-three days to read and send back my stuff, the *Berliner Illustrierte* four weeks, the *Münchener* a few days less, the *Frankfurter Zeitung* only two weeks. In all those months only one of my stories got lost and was not returned to me, and even this one turned up eventually; I had sent the *BZ am Mittag* two stories and, true to form, after twenty days I received the usual slip which said: 'We regret that we cannot make use of your two short stories entitled "The Street" and "Auf Reisen" ("Travelling"), and we are sending them back to you together with our thanks.' When I saw that only one of the stories had in fact been returned I wasn't even angry. I had plenty of time and I started the following morning to copy the story out again. By lunchtime, or rather, the time when other people had their lunches, I had another copy, probably better than the one the paper had lost.

Now in those days I was somewhat accustomed to miracles. For instance, one day, in the early morning, as I was at a brand-new post office on the Lietzenburger Strasse I watched a well-dressed lady buy some stamps, and saw that somehow she let all the change, several marks, fall on to the stone floor. I shall never forget the sight of those coins rolling along the floor in every direction and the exciting metallic noise they made as they hit the cold stone; but, apart from myself, nobody in the post office seemed to have heard or seen anything. When the lady left I got down on the floor and picked up every single coin and nobody even questioned me, not even my own conscience.

On another occasion a more godly miracle befell me. On the coldest nights it was unbearably uncomfortable to sleep in the station, let alone on a park bench. On one particularly bitter night I hatched a desperate plan. I knew of a synagogue (the famous one on Fasanenstrasse) which had, in the courtyard of the main building, a small prayer hall where the few who never missed the early-morning prayers could assemble. Above it there was a library with a reading room attached which closed at 10 p.m. – later than any other reading room in town, and it was well heated: an ideal place to sleep. All I had to do was to hide in the attic until the man whose job it was to lock the place up had left; then I could descend to the reading room and stretch out on one of the padded benches and sleep while the central heating blazed all night. To make my plan foolproof I would rise at about 7.30, join the praying few downstairs, and leave the premises when they did.

At about five minutes to closing time I left the reading room and tiptoed up the stairs that led to the attic. I waited. I heard the reading room personnel leave and knew that, except for the guard who would lock up, I was the only person in the building. Suddenly I had a doubt. The guard had only to step round the corner on the landing and he would discover me. So, as softly as a thief, I descended to the first floor and went into one of the lavatory cabins. There I sat in the dark and waited. It didn't take long, perhaps half an hour, before the guard came. There were four cabins. I sat in the third. I could see the light of his flashlight, he opened one cabin, then another, then he stopped. I knew (as I knew when Bondi's landlady stood in front of the cupboard, with me inside) that he felt something was wrong, but he didn't care to, or didn't dare to, open the next door and find out what it was. He went away. When I heard him locking the door below I walked into the reading room and looked out of the large windows which faced on to the railway tracks that ran into the Zoologischer Garten station. Then I chose a bench and lay down to enjoy the warmth and cleanliness of the place.

I slept in fits. I had no watch but didn't worry: the famous Gedachtniskirche was only 200 yards away and you could hear the clock strike every quarter of an hour. I knew that at 7.30 I had to descend and join the prayers below, so, when I thought the time had come to count the strokes of the clock I began to listen. I heard the clock strike, I heard the quarter, the half, the three-quarters, but each time when the hour was struck a train thundered into or out of the station below. I began to worry; I couldn't go down before the service had started – that would be fatal – nor could I afford to miss the service, and it only lasted about fifteen minutes. I started to listen to every noise that came from below. At a Jewish service the faithful chant their prayers aloud and I hoped to catch a phrase of this chant. I lay down on the floor and strained my ears. I couldn't hear a thing. Whenever the clock struck outside I ran to the window and opened it, only to find that the station noise was too great and completely drowned out the chimes. I began to despair. It was dark outside at 7.30 in the winter, so I had no clue at all what the time was. Then, as though my prayers had been answered, I heard clearly from below the congregation's chanting. No train came to drown it; I didn't have to stick my ear to the floor, it came as clear as day. I opened the door and still heard the chanting. I quickly descended the stairs. In the prayer hall there were only two people. They couldn't have been chanting, the service couldn't have started: a Jewish service needs at least twelve people, to form a quorum. The two greeted me with smiles. Now there were three; only nine more to come.

So, as you can see, I was not entirely unused to miracles in those days. But it was a few months later, at the end of March, that the biggest miracle of all occurred. That particular March was much better than most; the snow had melted and occasionally a pale sun warmed our limbs. I knew of a nice little café – the Café Am Knee – where, for twenty pfennigs one could get a glass of hot milk. In German cafés sugar and water always went with your order. Water was served, according to ancient custom, one glass with each order, and the sugar lay on the table, free for anybody and in unrestricted quantities. Every customer like myself knew that if you ordered a glass of hot milk you could fill it up to the brim with so many lumps of sugar that the whole thing became solid, you could eat it with your spoon, and it represented the best value for twenty pfennigs that you could get anywhere. Of course, sitting in the pale sun just outside the café with a copy of the first edition of the evening paper – the *BZ am Mittag* – which also cost twenty pfennigs, was not a proposition to be sneezed at either. Still, the mental picture of that pulpy, sugary hot milk won the day. I went inside, gave my order, loaded my glass with lumps of sugar and sat back to enjoy my surroundings, happy to do nothing but scoop a spoonful of that heavenly stuff into my mouth from time to time. Perhaps half an hour later a newspaper vendor came in and some people bought papers. It sometimes happened that customers (millionaires, no doubt) bought the midday paper, ran through it in no time and went, leaving twenty pfennigs' worth of newspaper on the table. You had to keep a look-out and grab it before the waitress got her hands on it. A man at the next table bought a paper, glanced at the headlines and turned the page. I was contemplating whether he was one of those types who didn't take his paper with him when I glanced at the page he was now reading. There – my heart stopped still – there, was my short story, 'Auf Reisen', printed in the paper. My name after the title and words – my words! – in column after column. I had to close my eyes – I couldn't bare the blinding aura of it.

Immediately, I dashed out of the café and hurried towards the Ullstein building, where the paper had its offices, to tell one of the cashiers the wonderful news and ask for my honorarium. The cashier began to tell me that they always paid a few days after printing, then he stopped and looked at me, realizing that I was a somewhat out-of-the-ordinary case. He told me to sit down and went off in search of his superior. Wanting to create a good impression, I did not sit down: my trousers were worn so thin at the knees that you could see straight through them when I sat down; standing they appeared quite all right. When the cashier returned he brought with him eighty marks, in crisp new notes. Never before and never since have I earned that much.

And this was the story they printed:

'Auf Reisen' ('Travelling') *BZ am Mittag*, 28 March 1928

At that time a village stood on the site of this town, the mail coach was running instead of the fast train and my grandfather was travelling instead of me. A young lady and an old man were sitting opposite him. The man was snoring, drawing deep, heavy breaths. A signet ring glittered on one of his fat fingers. The lady was reading poetry. Grandfather did not take his eyes off them; he wanted to fix this image of them in his head, an image which seemed of little significance, but which for him was to become the beginning of a veritable adventure. Such an image could be elaborated upon, embroidered with fantasy and then dreamed of. At least until the next coach station. Suddenly a tear fell on to the book. There was no mistake; the beautiful lady was crying. The man next to her was still snoring, the wheels were rolling joyfully along the road, the sun was shining, and Grandfather still had a long way to go before becoming Grandfather. He leant forwards and asked her quietly if she was not feeling well. The lady did not answer, but simply took out a handkerchief. Trembling, she clumsily wiped her nose with it and released a stifled sob, a tiny sluice into the ocean.

'Is there anything I can do for you?' Had Grandfather had two lives he would gladly have sacrificed one of them for her. At last she raised her eyes and, in a scarcely audible whisper, she said, 'I'm so unhappy.'

The horses' hooves thundered over a wooden bridge and the first house of a village appeared. The coach would be stopping in a few minutes.

'Come with me,' Grandfather begged her. 'We could leave the coach without being noticed.'

She said neither yes nor no, but the two of them got out in front of the post-office building. Another coach, which was travelling north, was ready to go and soon its wheels were rolling for a second time over the little bridge.

The old man with the signet ring was travelling in the carriage going south. He began to snore again, even louder this time, so that the two students who got in at the next station had to wake him. The first one asked, 'Did we disturb your sleep?'

'Heavens!' the old man rubbed his eyes. 'Where's the young lady?' The students roared with laughter and looked under the bench. 'My, you did sleep well!' said one of them. 'There's nothing better than a good dream,' said the other.

The old man cursed, flung open the door, leapt from the carriage and found himself standing in the middle of a dusty street in a place he didn't know, a cloud of dust behind him and in front of him the village which is now the town towards which I am heading today.

The telegraph poles were hurtling by outside and the young woman to whom I was telling this story looked at me enquiringly, while the fast train hurried rhythmically across the plain.

'So what happened in the end? What became of the runaways and the poor old husband?'

'Nothing special. The lady became my grandmother.'

'And the husband?'

'But, my dear, he was her father. The young girl was a sentimental thing.'

The woman laughed. 'So this will be the first time that you have visited that town?'

'That's right.'

'What time do we arrive there?'

'In about half an hour.'

'Aren't you frightened that something similar might happen to you?'

'My dear, unfortunately the circumstances today are entirely different. Your companion is not asleep and you are not reading poetry.'

'But my husband is in the restaurant car,' she smiled.

'. . . and these days one doesn't read much poetry.' I finished off the sentence and then kissed her on the lips, and then again, as if to make a colon. Outside it was getting dark.

'How quickly it gets dark in the summer,' I said, 'and how long your husband is away.'

She looked at me whimsically. 'The train will be stopping soon, history could repeat itself.'

'I doubt that, my dear. These days we may well travel faster but we act more slowly.'

She did not look angry in the slightest. 'So that our story will have an ending,' she said, 'I've lied to you about having a husband. He's my lover.'

'I thought so. Women deceive their husbands much more readily. We've been travelling together for the whole day and you didn't so much as look at me before I began telling my story.'

'Your grandfather's story,' she corrected me.

'No, no, it's really my own story. A well-tried and tested story.'

The brakes were bearing down upon the wheels and I lifted my suitcase from the rack.

'And what about the town?' she asked.

'I tell this story about every town.'

'What a strange person you are!' she laughed. 'When you get back to Berlin, give me a ring.'

I told her that I would take down her phone number immediately, but I didn't do it. I didn't want to alert my wife to my travelling adventures.

I can't remember now what I did with my new-found wealth. I probably bought a paper and went to a restaurant, but I certainly looked at some 'To Let' ads that very afternoon, since the same evening I took a room, in Halensee. The flat belonged to a taxi driver and looked out on to a Garten-haus. From my room I could see, every night, a pretty girl doing gymnastics in the nude in the house opposite. But she had young men with motor cars as her boyfriends, and I could not compete with that. I was allowed to use the bathroom and spent long hours in it, after my landlord and landlady had gone to bed, as if I wished to bathe off all the dirt I had assembled over the past year and a half. She was a dear soul, the landlady, very fat and very jolly, a typical Berliner. She could (and would) roast wonderful belly of pork for me when I bought a piece, and she would pull my leg about my love life, while her husband, who had the solemn hearing and air of discontent of taxi-drivers everywhere, looked on disapprovingly.

The day after my story was published I decided to call on the editor-in-chief of the *BZ am Mittag*, to introduce myself to him and thank him personally. His secretary persuaded me that it was the literary editor whom I ought to visit and directed me to his office. The literary editor was called Norbert Falk and he had red hair that looked like a wig. He received me kindly and listened curiously when I told him that I had just come to introduce myself to him formally. He watched me, obviously thinking that he had never met a young fool quite so foolish as this one. Then he said, 'Instead of coming here, wasting my time and yours, you should have sent some more stories.' I opened my grimy old attaché case and spread out my collected works. From time to time he printed them and I got tremendous amounts of money (or so it seemed to me), not quite eighty marks, but not much less. Certainly, I became one of those very few young writers who could make a living on what they wrote.

For some time afterwards I continued to write short stories, but really my heart was lost to films, and had been for a long time. Talkies had just started (*The Singing Fool* had begun its run in Berlin), so I decided to start an offensive against the script department at UFA, the best known of the German production companies, and the biggest in Europe. I sent them what I thought, in my innocence, was a wonderful film story. It would be wrong to say, 'Then I waited and waited' – I had no time for that. I wrote and wrote, furiously. I sat in parks – the weather slid slowly into spring – I had got so used to working in parks that I could do more work there than anywhere else.

I paused in my scriptwriting only to give thought to the theory of film; I was a pensive young man in those days. There were few books to learn theory from and anyway I couldn't afford to buy them, so I concluded that I would have to tackle the subject on my own. I often came to conclusions similar to that: when I had no crossword puzzles to solve, I always found making them just as amusing as solving them. I finished the first chapter of my theory of film and called it 'The Subject', and decided that I would see what the experts thought of it. I copied it out in a neat long hand and sent it to the trade journal of the German-speaking film world, the *Film Kurier*. In my accompanying letter I said nothing about who I was; I simply stated that I had the intention of writing a series of articles on every aspect of film-making – this being the first part, the others would be on 'Writing a Film Script', 'Acting' and 'Directing'. I asked whether they would be interested in printing them.

A week later I received a reply. Certainly, they wrote, they would be very interested and wanted the remaining articles by return post. So there was nothing else to do but to write them. They were printed too, in four parts, just as I wrote them. And that, apart from my day in the Capitol Theatre orchestra, was my first contact with the world of film – as an expert in acting, film-writing, editing and producing, who had never seen a script, met an actor or set foot in a studio.

Four weeks to the day after sending my first story to UFA, I decided to call at the film company's head office in the Kochstrasse, to enquire about its fate. UFA had a large dramaturgy department with about eight employees who did nothing but sift and read and send back manuscripts. They didn't keep me long, and a rather luscious looking lady of about twenty-eight or twenty-nine came to ask me what I wanted. I told her about my story and she asked me how long ago I had sent it. 'Exactly four weeks ago,' I said. She shook her head, 'It takes four weeks for them to read and send the stuff back,' she replied. 'Don't you ever keep anything?' I asked. 'Not really,' she said. 'Occasionally we keep one, the odd one, for a week or two longer, but – and I've been here over four years – we get an average of eighty manuscripts every week and UFA has never bought a single one of them.' She smiled, I sighed and said, 'I'll call again in a fortnight.' She assured me that by that time the manuscript was sure to have surfaced. She would look for it personally, and it was highly improbable that their foolproof filing system could go wrong in any way.

I did as I was told and returned a fortnight later. Frau Lulky (that was the luscious lady's name) was in a fluster. She had indeed found my manuscript. It turned out that one of the readers had passed it on to a dramaturge and he had handed it (miracle of miracles!) to the chief of the department, Fritz Podehl. Perhaps I would be good enough to contact him in a week or two? I promised I would.

The occasional short stories in the paper were a great help, but they were a most irregular income. I would sell two in one month and then not sell anything at all the next. When I couldn't pay my rent and felt I was cheating my nice taxi-driver and his jolly wife, I felt ashamed and came home late so that I wouldn't meet them, taking a bath in silence, hanging a rag from the taps so that they wouldn't make any noise when they dripped – like a thief who binds cloth to his feet when stealing about the house.

I got into the habit of frequenting a fashionable café on the Kurfürstendamm, sitting on the terrace and writing and writing. I think I suffered from over-concentration when I was working and needed something to draw part of the intensity of concentration from my work. I watched people coming and going quite oblivious of them, always writing more and more. The few people I met in the café, the regulars, soon became used to my hypnotic state, and

The offices of UFA (Universum-Film A-G)

didn't try and disturb me when I was working. I remember a painter called Scheurmann who had a studio higher up the Kurfürstendamm, with a pleasant wife and a pretty daughter of about seventeen. One afternoon the painter's wife arrived at the café without her husband or daughter. I saw her coming and noticed her sitting down at my table – I probably even greeted her distractedly. She took off her coat, laid it aside and then suddenly screamed and started to bash at me with her newspaper. Fortunately her husband arrived and he, together with the blows and the general merriment, brought me out of my trance. It transpired that when she had sat down and taken off her coat she had suddenly realized she was clad in nothing but her pants! People had gasped, and she had directed all her embarrassed fury at me for not warning her immediately when she began removing her coat. I swore to her that I hadn't noticed anything was wrong – certainly nothing so extraordinary. This made her even more furious.

The Scheurmanns were lovely people, artists as they are described in books, and I was soon forgiven my inobservance. I was really quite fond of them and, for some reason, they adored me. I was invited frequently to the studio, to eat my fill and talk about the world. The daughter, I believe, fell in love with me, yet I was quite oblivious to this – for I too had fallen in love, but with another girl. She was one of the great loves of my life and her name was Traute. I met her through Lord Klein, a commercial traveller who to us represented worldliness, elegance and ease. When I say 'us' I mean a small group of young Hungarians who, it seemed, never had anything to do, and sat about all day in the cafés of Berlin.

One afternoon Lord Klein told me that he had just returned from Czechoslovakia (a former Hungarian territory), where he could travel about without restrictions (which ordinary ex-Hungarian citizens could not). He spoke the language and had been doing excellent business. During the trip he had visited the town of Zilina for the first time and had taken a room in the main hotel. On arriving in his room he had phoned downstairs and told the lovely red-headed telephonist that he was having some trouble with his phone and needed her immediate assistance. She came, he kissed her and a few minutes later they were in bed, both forgetting the telephone. Some time later she opened her pretty eyes, looked at the ceiling and, half to herself and half to the lord, she said, 'It's very strange this. The majority of the guests treat me like a lady – rightly so – but when a Hungarian arrives in the hotel, after the shortest possible time, he somehow manages, under a web of deceit, to trick me into his room and before I can say "knife", I'm in his bed. How do you explain it?' Lord Klein remained silent for a moment, weighing up the pros and cons of betraying his countrymen. Finally, he couldn't resist the temptation. 'You see,' he confessed, thus debunking the origins of a legend, 'in the men's lavatory, scribbled on the wall in Hungarian, it says: "The red-headed telephonist can't resist making love." '

I have never forgotten this – not because it is an unforgettable story, but because at that moment I saw the most lovely girl arrive in the café. Lord Klein rose and, telling me he had an appointment with her, left me. I watched her as he walked towards her and the memory has stuck in my mind; she wore a full, dark taffeta skirt, a white silk shirt and a heavy, tight black leather belt over her tiny waist. She and Lord Klein seemed so worldly together, as though they belonged to a different world from common people like myself. They sat down at a table some distance away and I saw the lord make a remark about me to her, and she glanced over at me and smiled. A few minutes later the lord paid his bill and they rose. She smiled at me again without provocation and her companion, being behind her, could not see it. He touched her on the arm and then strode over to me, 'I have a business appointment,' he explained. 'I wonder if Traute could sit with you for a bit?'

I stammered something, got up and followed him over to where she stood. Lord Klein introduced me to her and winked at me. 'Don't get impatient – it might take some time,' he whispered. I assured him that I had plenty of patience.

We sat down together and started to talk – about what, I can't remember, but I will never forget the terror I felt when I suddenly realized that I didn't have enough money to pay for anything she might order. The waitress came, recognized her as a customer who had already ordered something at another table and brought over her old drink – much to my relief. The most significant part of the afternoon was that Lord Klein never returned, and when Traute and I eventually parted I had her telephone number. I would like to have phoned her that very evening, but even if I had scraped together the few coins necessary for the phone call I could never have afforded to take her out. So I waited for better times.

About this time I received a note from Revesz at the association, saying that he had found a job for me. The next day I went to see him and he told me about the job. It was with a Hungarian building contractor who managed about a dozen apartment houses for their foreign owners. I was required to look after the accounts, collect the rent, deal with complaints and relieve him of his troublesome tenants. I had never had anything to do with house management, and until quite recently I had had no experience of renting a room either, but, he said, that didn't come into it at all. I only had to write into a ledger when a tenant sent in his rent and write threatening letters to those that failed to do so. There was nothing more to it, he assured me. But of course there was.

First of all, the history of these rental properties was of some interest. During the great German inflation several foreigners bought up a lot of property in Berlin at dirt-cheap rates. After the currency had been stabilized the government and tenants, quite understandably, began to turn their attention to these properties. Special taxes were introduced, tenants demanded repairs to be carried out by the absentee landlords, who were never seen and whose sole aim was to squeeze as much profit as possible out of their properties. The atmosphere between owners, authorities and tenants got worse and worse, and in a couple of years most of the houses had been resold. However, when I became a 'house agent's clerk', this sort of business still existed and was in its most sordid final throes. Everything about it was corrupt, and I was constantly being offered bribes by crooked builders, or getting into squabbles over the rent.

I sat in an office with a young female secretary called Fräulein Dahne, and in the next room two young Hungarian civil engineers worked, one called Antos and the other with a name I forget. Anyway, Antos was the more interesting of the two: a young man whose great hobby and passion happened to be railway timetables. One could ask him, 'Antos, how would I get from Berlin to Shanghai by rail?' and he would ask, 'Which day of the week would you start?' He explained that some trains were not running on certain days and when you told him your proposed day of travel he would start belching out information like a computer. He knew everything; you could even choose cheaper trains if you had not sufficient means for the fast connections, and he was always up-to-date. He was also a magnificent mathematician, and I would love to know what he ended up doing with his life. However, the most powerful personality in the office was our boss's housekeeper, a jovial woman of about forty, full of fun and unrepressed eroticism. She never talked about anything but sex, encouraging me and Fräulein Dahne to make love there in the office – though we never did – and teasing Antos about his conservative views on sex. She would also report all the intricacies of our boss's sex-life in the most lurid detail, making us roar with laughter.

When my father had died in 1926, my mother had gone to live on her own with childhood friends in Hungary. She was always longing to be with me, to look after me, not realizing that children grow up and are better off not being looked after. But I was longing to make her happy and, as soon as I had saved a little money, I sent her the fare and took a little furnished flat in Anspacherstrasse (just around the corner from the department store in Tauentzienstrasse) in one of those Berlin specialities, the Gartenhaus. Here we lived together and I told her about Traute. She listened to me somewhat frightened. I could read in her eyes what she was thinking: 'I have just found him, only to lose him to someone called Traute, whom I had never even heard of until a few days ago.' As my financial prosperity improved I saw Traute often. I learnt that her parents owned a bakery shop and she often sat in the shop at the cash desk, but I gathered she found this a little degrading. I took her out, once to a dancing place, but I could never master the intricacies of the tango or the foxtrot. The tango 'I Kiss Your Little Hand, Madam' was new then and everybody sang it. In one of these dance places we met Lord Klein. He was with one of his innumerable young ladies and we chatted most amiably, thus sealing the peace between us (which had never really been broken), the lord never mentioning the right of conquest.

One Sunday Traute and I went on a picnic. We took a train travelling, I think, due north, got off at a small station and walked. Traute suddenly looked like a very young girl. She wore glasses and, this time, a tweed skirt with a thick pullover. She had brought sandwiches, two thermos flasks (one with hot coffee, the other with cold tea laced with rum) and pastries from her parents' shop. I had brought a rug and plenty of good spirits. We found a lake, walked along the bank, running about like school children, ate everything, lay in the soft grass and rolled on to the rug, making love again and again – arm around arm, legs around legs. The day drifted into evening. I had never before been so in love. As we sat in the train again her head fell on my shoulder, her light-brown hair brushing my face. I didn't dare move, thinking she had fallen asleep. Then I heard her whispering something so softly I couldn't quite catch it. I whispered back, 'What?' Again she murmured something, moving closer to me, and now I caught what she said: 'I'm going to die.' She turned her head slowly so that I could see her face. Her lips were smiling, but her eyes were swimming in tears.

One evening Traute came to visit us for dinner so that she could meet my mother. Anxious to like her, and anxious to please me, my mother cooked dinner (she was a wonderful cook) while I surveyed the place with a critical eye, covering up darned patches in the table cloth with cruets and an ashtray, moving the chairs to cover a stain in the carpet and saying a quick prayer that the two women in my life would like one another as much as I liked them. They didn't converse much, since my mother spoke poor German and because she wanted me to be alone with Traute; she spent most of the evening in the kitchen. I told Traute that Mother always worried about her cooking: never about the quality – she was like all true artists, absolutely confident about that – but about the quantity. If the food was all gobbled up, she was convinced there hadn't been enough. If the guests left something over, she was still worried it had not been enough. After dinner I took Traute home and then sat with my mother on her bed, holding her hand. She said little, just squeezed my hand as though she felt she were losing me.

The following day Traute had no time to see me. Her mother was ill, she said, and so she had to look after the shop. But when I phoned her about lunchtime, her mother answered the phone and told me that Traute was not in and had gone out for a while. I spoke to her the next evening and she sounded gay, singing bits of a popular song down the phone, teasing me, telling me not to be so serious all the time, so impatient, so tense. One ought to be lighthearted, live for the day, she said. Don't always try and plan into the distant future. I never saw her again. At first I thought she had been surprised by our poverty; now I'm convinced it was because, as she had said on the train, she was sure she was going to die. I used to lie in wait in the dead of night, standing in doorways from which I could see her flat, above the bakery, watching the chimney smoking, observing men in white carrying freshly baked bread into and out of the shop, lurking there until a taxi arrived, with her inside it, always very late, sometimes after three in the morning, always a man with her who kissed her goodbye, rarely the same man twice. Once I recognized the lord bringing her home. I would walk back to my tiny flat with a poisoned heart, angry, jealous and helpless. I phoned Lord Klein that very night. He was a little cross at being woken in the middle of the night. He told me that Traute knew that I waited in doorways for her return at night. He said that he wanted to talk to me about her. I said I would come straight over, but he persuaded me that the next day at twelve in the Café Reimann would do.

I lied at the office, saying that I had to pay a visit to a troublesome tenant. Lord Klein came late. He had had a very difficult middle-aged virgin to look after. She was very rich and wanted to marry him, but that wasn't what he wanted at all. Then, at last, the conversation turned to Traute. 'I have nothing to do with her,' he insisted. 'She is very sick – tuberculosis. I hope you've never kissed her on the mouth. Have you?' I told him that I had and that I didn't care – I would even like to kiss her again. He tried to persuade me to go to a doctor at once, but I wouldn't hear of such nonsense. He told me that she never kissed anyone on the lips any more – perhaps on the cheek. Klein then tried to change the subject. He said he would introduce me to a very nice girl, the brooding sort, just how I liked them. I told him I only liked Traute. He told me that I would soon forget her. Time would heal, so why not help it along? I felt sick and had to go to the lavatory, where I vomited for half an hour.

I tried telephoning her frequently after that, but she never answered the phone and instructed her mother to say she was not in when I called. Now, I would like to think that she did not want to take any risks on my behalf, that she didn't trust herself to resist the temptation when she was with me – but really I don't know why she left me in the cold. Some time later, when I had had my first success in films, I called her again, with a tremendous yearning to share in my good fortune with her. I spoke to her mother, who cried as she told me that Traute was staying in a sanatorium, not far from Berlin. I asked for the address, but she said her daughter refused to have visitors. She promised to take some flowers from me and tell me about Traute's progress if I telephoned from time to time. When, a few months later, I bought my first car, longing to show it to her, I phoned her mother once more, determined to worm the address out of her. She told me the name of the cemetery. Traute had died the week before.

But all that was in the future as I called again at UFA for my appointment with Herr Podehl. He was a splendid man, genuinely anxious to do a good job and a true friend of writers. He fought for them and for their work, supporting them when they were ground up in the huge mills of the organization. He liked me, I believe, and I certainly took to him at once. He explained, with a total lack of condescension, how production worked at UFA. There were six production units, each with a leader, and they chose and developed about twelve subjects a year, from each of which about half were actually made. It was the dramaturgy department which found subjects, wrote treatments, doctored scripts and made contact with writers, before handing the material on to the production units. Herr Podehl said that he had liked my story and had circulated it among some of the production heads, but he couldn't generate a lasting interest in it. I immediately opened my battered attaché case and handed him another treatment.

A fortnight later he contacted me again to say that he liked this one too, but that, again, the production chiefs had been lukewarm. When a third story met the same fate I was again summoned to Podehl's office, and he admitted that he was a little worried by the situation. 'You have brought me three decent stories. I encouraged you, and yet you haven't earned a thing from us yet. So, if you want to do it, take a look at this book. If you like it, write me a short film treatment. That would be a commission, of course. I can pay 200 marks.' I took the book from him and left the office, trying not to appear too eager, although I knew, and he probably did as well, that it wasn't a case of liking it, or even reading it – I would do it.

When I had completed my assignment I took the treatment to Podehl and he seemed pleased with it. But I don't think he ever imagined it would get made into a film. It was one of those dud properties which every film company has which are given out to young writers just to let them practise and earn a little money. My mother couldn't believe her eyes when I showed her that handful of crisp, new ten-mark notes, and she shook her head in awe and disbelief when I said, 'Mother, I'm going to leave my job as a house agent's clerk. I'm going to be an author.' 'Don't rush it, darling,' she pleaded. 'Don't throw away a good job, a lasting job.' But I had already made up my mind.

The next time I went to see Herr Podehl he told me that he had still had no luck with my stories. However, a new young director working in Bruno Duday's production group had been very interested in one of them called *Mondnacht* ('A Moonlit Night'), a clever romantic trifle about the power of the moon over the lives of ordinary Berlin folk:

'One should not think that the moon only sets the huge ocean in motion. It also stirs up the smallest droplets, causes them to foam up and crash against each other as it whips up the waves. Under the influence of the moon people become irritable, women seem more attractive than usual, and small events take on the significance of fateful omens. The sea of feelings rises ever higher. This is when people say, 'It is time for the high tide to come in.'

Playing on this moonlit night are:

The banker, Maidoerfer, who was waiting for his latest lover,
His chauffeur, Mr Hedeman, who wanted to go out with his friend today,
Whose sister is the maid of Maidoerfer's who lost the fifty-mark note.
Miss Kranich is one of the banker's former lovers and she should have received the note,
Which her brother, Mr Kranich, found.
Mr Finder, a labourer, arranged to go out with the chauffeur and
Miss Finder is his elegant sister and the banker's newest lover.
A Full Moon also plays,
And the Night, And the Spring, And the City,
And the Uncertainty, which hangs in the air.

That was the introduction. Anyway, Podehl wanted me to go and see this new director who had been under contract for months but who had not yet found a subject which he found sympathetic. I found the director in his office, quite depressed. His first film had been an avant-garde success called *Menschen am Sonntag* ('People on Sunday'), a short, silent documentary-style film about the ordinary adventures of four ordinary working-class Berliners. UFA had hired him on the strength of it and now he couldn't find anything to follow it up with. Did I have any ideas? I told him that I did, and rushed straight home. Of course, I hadn't had any ideas when I was in his office, but by the time I arrived home I had the whole story mapped out in my head. I stayed up all night typing and retyping, and first thing in the morning I went to see the director. I waited in his office as he read the treatment, and when he had finished he looked at me and said, 'This is my next film.' I was overjoyed, stunned speechless. In his autobiography Robert Siodmak, for that was the director, says that I started to cry. I don't remember that, but it is quite possible.

To write the script I was given a collaborator by Herr Podehl, a wonderful lady called Irma von Cube, an experienced writer who would teach me how to write in the proper style. The film was called *Abschied* ('Farewell') and was set in a boarding house of the type I knew well. It was about ordinary Berliners and the tragic misunderstanding which splits up two young lovers. The great invention in it, and what Siodmak particularly loved, was that it was a film that took place in real time. It was a two-hour film and concerned itself with two hours in the life of the boarding house.

The critics loved it, the ordinary people shunned it, but on the strength of it I was employed by the mighty edifice of UFA, as *Lektor und Dramaturg*. I was given my own little office, and on my first day there I bought a camera – being an UFA employee you got terrific discounts at the camera shops – and photographed myself at work. And that was how I got started in films.

Emeric Pressburger went on to become one of UFA's most respected writers, making at least eleven films in a little over two years. Apart from scripting Siodmak's first feature he also made three films with Rheinhold Schunzel, UFA's most popular director, collaborated on Max Ophul's first film, I'd Rather Have Cod-liver Oil *and made a film in his native Hungary. At the beginning of 1933 Hitler's rise to power drove him from the country. He fled to France and there continued to write, scripting at least five films in two years. In 1935 he arrived in England and in 1938 met Michael Powell, with whom he was to collaborate for the rest of his life. Together they wrote, produced and directed, under the banner of the Archers, some of the best and most original films in British cinema history, including,* The Spy in Black, 49th Parallel *(for which he won an Oscar),* The Life and Death of Colonel Blimp, Black Narcissus, The Red Shoes *(the biggest-grossing film in British cinema history) and* The Tales of Hoffman. *In the 1960s he returned to prose writing and published two novels. In 1981 he was awarded a fellowship of BAFTA and in 1983 became one of the first six fellows of the British Film Institute. He died in 1988.*

[This extract has been taken from the forthcoming biography of Emeric Pressburger by Kevin Macdonald.]

'My first day at UFA I bought a camera and photographed myself at work'

Pressburger's UFA pass

Pressburger writing *Abschied* with Irma von Cube

Abschied (1930), directed by Robert Siodmak

5   Demme on Demme

The following piece has been compiled from two interviews which David Thompson had with Jonathan Demme. The first was done for BBC television in November 1989. The second was done in London at the National Film Theatre in 1989. The section on Silence of the Lambs *has been taken from an interview conducted by Saskia Baron for the BBC's* Late Show *in May 1991.*

INTERVIEWER: *You were born in Long Island, but at the age of fifteen you moved to Miami. What was the contrast between those two places?*

JONATHAN DEMME: The biggest contrast was moving from an area where kids couldn't drive to an area where kids could, and your life explodes in a certain way under those circumstances. But in New York living on Long Island was very lonely, and moving to Florida was kind of getting out of the suburbs, getting out of a metropolitan situation into big, big spaces and kids that drank beer and drove cars and talked with funny accents – it was a very exciting kind of thing to have happen to you at that age.

INT: *And originally you were set on a veterinary course?*

JD: Yes. I very much wanted to be a veterinarian and had worked in animal hospitals from the age of ten or eleven. I would go and wipe down tables between doggies and kitties for the vets. I was obsessed with being a vet, everything was geared towards that, and by the time I was in high school I had become a really excellent kennel man and veterinary assistant and could do amazing things.

What happened is – it's a simple, sad story – after high school, I saved up enough money to go to college for a year. So I went, and then encountered college chemistry and I had a complete inability to master the most fundamental kind of chemistry, and within two days I was miles behind everybody else. I was sitting there listening to them talk this foreign language and realized that medicine wasn't for me. But I wanted to stick out the term because I had put so much money into it, and also I was a movie junkie at that stage of the game – I had been for quite some time.

INT: *What sort of movies were you seeing then?*

JD: Actually, that was a cusp in my life. Up to then I was seeing popular American movies of all kinds, and at college it was my first chance to see

Jonathan Demme

things like Bergman movies, Truffaut movies. That was eye-opening for me. I remember the excitement I experienced the first time I saw *Shoot the Piano Player*. It was probably the first movie of my life I had seen with subtitles, and I realized there was a whole other kind of excitement and fun you could have watching movies. There's this moment in *Shoot the Piano Player* where Charles Aznavour tells the hoods, 'If I'm lying to you, may my mother drop dead,' and the film cuts to his mother dropping dead! I'd never seen this sort of thing in American movies, and it was really great.

I had noticed that our college newspaper didn't have a film critic, and I felt that perhaps if I could be the film critic I could see the movies for free, because I certainly couldn't afford to go and see them on my budget at that stage of the game. They didn't have one, so they said, 'Well, give us a sample of your views.' I was so excited about getting this job, but I couldn't even afford to go to a movie, so I said, 'OK, I'll go and see *Wrong Arm of the Law*, which is playing at the State Theatre now.' Then I went racing to the library, pulled out all the magazines, saw what the critics had had to say about *Wrong Arm of the Law*, formed an impression of the film, wrote a review, took it back, they accepted it, and I became a film critic at college.

INT: *And it was being a film critic that got you your introduction into the movie business.*

JD: Yes, it's true. Once you start going to movies for free, it's hard to start paying for them. After I left college, I came across a little newspaper back home in Miami called the *Coral Gables Times*. It was a shopping bi-weekly, but they didn't have a film critic and were willing to let me write reviews for them, so I started doing that. At that time my dad was working for the Fountainbleau Hotel, and he met the amazing movie mogul Joseph E. Levine, who had done *Hercules, A Bridge Too Far*, any number of films. He was very, very active – especially in the 1960s and early 1970s. My father mentioned to Mr Levine, the great mogul, that his son was a film critic, so Levine said, 'Well, I must meet him. Bring him to my houseboat,' which was down in the canal across from the hotel. I came along – my dad had told me to bring some of my reviews – so I did, and there was Levine, and – yes – it was a pink houseboat, and – yes – he had a cigar a foot long. There was another producer there with a gigantic cigar, and they got out the scrapbook and started flipping through these reviews. They got to one I'd written of the movie *Zulu*, which I'd had very strong feelings about and written an especially positive review. '*Zulu*, ah!' He started reading it and: 'My God . . . brilliant . . . marvellous.' He looked up at me and took the cigar and, jabbing me in the chest, said, 'You've got great taste, kid. Do you want to come and work for me?' He actually offered me a job as a publicity writer and I said, 'Yes, I do,' and he said, 'Where do you want to work? New York, London or Rome?' So I said – and this was pretty hot for a Miami kid, you know – I said, 'I'll start

Charles Aznavour in *Shoot the Piano Player*

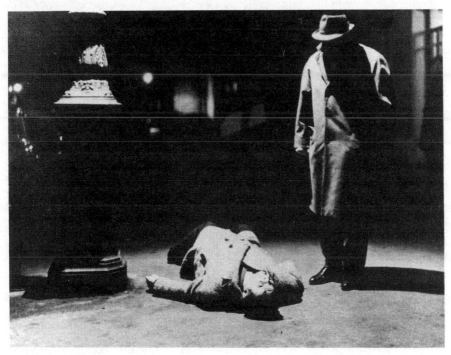

Shoot the Piano Player (1960)

off in New York.' Modestly. So I went and did my military service – quick –
and I called up afterwards and there was, indeed, a job available, and I went
up and took it.

INT: *And this also brought you to London, eventually, in the late 1960s.*

JD: Yes. I came to London in 1968, having had a variety of publicity jobs.
There was a production company that was making television commercials,
but wanted to get into film production, and because I was a publicist with
United Artists they thought that I might somehow be able to help them get
movies financed in England. They weren't experienced at that sort of thing,
but I took the job and came over to London. I was not very good at selling
commercial directors; I couldn't do a thing. I had a lot of great lunches, but
it didn't work out. So I started writing some movie reviews for a couple of
periodicals – I was pretty much of a drop-out at that time. It was the heavy
days of the Vietnam war. I was really happy not to be living in America, a
country I had grown to hate at that time, in many ways. While I was in
London Roger Corman came over to Ireland to make a film called *Von
Richtofen and Brown*, and I got a call from my old friends at United Artists to
see if I'd be the unit publicist on the film. So I come over to Ireland from
London to be interviewed for the job, and, as fate would have it, he was just
forming New World Pictures, his big production distribution company. He
interviewed me for the publicity job and said, 'OK, you can have the job and,
by the way, do you like motorcycle movies?' I said, 'Yes, especially your *Wild
Angels*,' and he said, 'Well, good, because I'm desperate for screenplay writers.
I'm over here in Ireland for the next several months, and would you write a
motorcycle movie for me?' So I said, 'Sure.'

I then went to a gifted friend of mine, a guy named Joe Viola, who was
directing commercials here in London and who's a great storyteller, and said,
'Joe, we have the chance to write a script. What do you think?' and he said,
'Absolutely.'

We had heard that some of the better motorcycle movies had been based
on some of the Japanese samurai films – for example, *Seven Samurai*, which
had become *The Magnificent Seven*, became *The Savage Seven* directed by
Richard Rush; and, of course, *Yojimbo* had become *For a Few Dollars More*,
which in turn became some other terrific motorcycle movies. So we went to
Rashomon – because there's a murder and a lot of sword-fighting and abuse
to women, which was very popular in movies in those days, and unfortunately
remains that way. We did a motorcycle version of *Rashomon* and Roger read
the script, and said, 'OK, the knifing is great, the rape is great, but lose this
varying points-of-view thing, fill in the gaps.' He was off to the Middle East
to try to put some production deals together. 'I'll be back in four weeks. Have
a script ready for me and maybe, you know, it'll be made.'

We met him at the London Hilton a month later, having written our sleazified motorcycle *Rashomon* and we handed it to him in the lobby of the hotel. He said, 'Wait a minute, guys. I'll read it right now, come into the bar and have a drink.' That was strange, sitting at a table with a guy who's reading your script while you make small talk with your partner. He read it and looked at us and said, 'OK, this isn't bad. It needs a lot of rewriting, but it's not bad. Joe, you direct commercials, so why don't you direct this film? Jonathan, you've been trying to produce commercials, why don't you produce this film? Be in Los Angeles in six weeks.' So that was it. Suddenly we were film-makers and we went over and did some rewriting and made the film – which we made for $120,000 – and we kept working for him.

INT: *The second film you did*, The Hot Box – *you got to do some directing on that, didn't you?*

JD: We were over in the Philippines – on one of the more remote islands, Negros – and we had all the problems that that bigger movie, *Apocalypse Now*, later had: we had monsoons, endless disasters; we got very behind schedule and it became necessary to catch up, to have some second-unit work, which is when a smaller team goes out and gets shots that don't involve dialogue.

I went racing off to the local cinema because I suddenly realized, 'Well, I've always loved movies, but how exactly do you make them?' There was an Italian movie playing at the tiny little cinema on the island, the Doomegeti Theatre – a remake of a Brazilian classic *Conga Shiero*, directed by a guy named Giovanni Fado. It was exceptionally well done. I scribbled shots down and went out with the second unit the next day and stole some of Giovanni Fado's shots, set them up in the same way, and just fell in love with the process.

I had really discovered something. I thought, 'There's a way of actually earning a living doing this. I want to go for it.' So when we got back to Los Angeles I asked Roger if he'd give me a shot at directing and he said, 'Sure, write up a women's prison movie and we'll take a look at it,' and that, for my sins, became *Caged Heat*.

INT: Caged Heat *is your first collaboration with Tak Fujimoto, who is the director of photography on a lot of your movies. Over the years you've gathered together a group of people you work with quite regularly now.*

JD: Well, when you work with someone who's very gifted in their area, as Tak Fujimoto is with lighting and camera, and you don't alienate them on your first experience with them, of course you want to continue it. I tried very hard to get people who are more gifted in their area than I would ever hope to be – on an ideal level – and that extends to both sides of the camera. For me, that's the key to good directing: hire eminently gifted people and let them pursue what they do.

I think Tak's a great cameraman. I never discuss the lighting with Tak at all because I know, first of all, his ideas would be far richer than mine;

Caged Heat (1974)

Caged Heat

second, I wouldn't understand what he was talking about. And there's another thing – when you start shooting a movie, you work so hard every day, you're up at the crack of dawn, you shoot all day, then you have to go to dailies; one of the excitements for me, one of the things that lets me end the day on a high note, is seeing what Tak did on film. So I just let him take care of that and by now he has evolved a camera approach that works for me in a very good way, that he endorses, so we don't even discuss shots any more. I watch rehearsals through my view-finder and, at a certain point, I notice that Tak has put some marks down on the floor, so that means a shot has developed, and the actors get their make-up on and he lights it up and then we start shooting.

INT: *In* Caged Heat *the lead actress, Erica Gavin, is well known for being in Russ Meyer films; so too is Charles Napier, who's turned up in virtually all your movies.*

JD: As I said, the time I spent in the cinema on the island of Negros was very significant. It was also when I saw my first Russ Meyer movie – *Cherry, Harry and Raquel.* Charles Napier played Harry. I just thought, 'This guy is an incredible actor.' Even while making a Russ Meyer film, he delivered this extraordinary performance.

One way of strengthening your film is to find people – actors – who really impress you. When you're working with Corman, you have to look for inexpensive actors, so I thought, 'He's making Russ Meyer movies, we can certainly afford him.' I called Charles. He was in the next film I did, we became very good friends and we've worked together ever since.

I keep waiting for Chuck Napier to become a really big movie actor, but it seems so far it's been slightly out of his reach. He played Sylvester Stallone's nemesis in *Rambo 2*, but he still hasn't gone into a regular working thing with the majors. I hope that happens. I think he's one of America's finest actors.

INT: *So working with Roger Corman was obviously a key experience in your life.*

JD: When we went to work for Roger Corman, it was incredibly exciting for someone who had loved movies as much as I had all my life to be, believe it or not, making one. What I didn't realize at the time was that I was also receiving an excellent education in film-making – maybe the best that was available in America at that time, or even today. Those of us who have worked with him call it the Roger Corman School of Film Technique. Not only are you given the responsibility to make a picture, but you're being fairly besieged by Roger's various aesthetics: on a visual level, what makes a good-looking picture; on a content level, the old Corman formula, which was that your film should have a lot of action, it should have a lot of humour in it, it should have considerable nudity in it – and by that he didn't mean male nudity, either – and a subtle social message – preferably from a leftist perspective. And he felt that the titles of the films should somehow try to encapsulate all

Roger Corman

these ingredients. The subtlety of the sexual content was something he always tried to bring to bear in films like *Angels Hard as They Come.*

It was a great experience. Having made sure that you accepted the rules of how to make a Corman movie, Roger then gave you an enormous amount of freedom to go ahead and do it. It wasn't until you started diverging from the formula, or from the approach, or – God forbid – went a moment over schedule, that you heard from him. And, of course, if you did stray from any of the pre-agreed conventions of making Corman movies, then you heard from him in no uncertain terms.

Beyond that, Corman is a great guy. It was incredible to be able to hear so much stuff from him and spend time with him. He's one of my favourite people.

INT: *You did your next film for Corman,* Crazy Mama, *at the very last minute, didn't you?*

JD: Yes. I was working on the script for *Fighting Mad* at the time and was very excited about it, and Roger was preparing to make *Crazy Mama* with Shirley Clarke directing. Shirley Clarke had made a number of underground films, was clearly a film-maker to be reckoned with and maybe, in his mind, one desirous of a chance to do something in Hollywood – as though he was Hollywood, which he wasn't. But Shirley Clarke did start the movie – not during shooting, in pre-production – and then they had a falling-out about something, and she chose to walk out; but they had the cast booked and a release date set in about three months. That's how Roger would finance all these pictures in those days: he would go to the exhibitors with a title and he'd say, 'OK, we're going to make *Crazy Mama*, and it'll be ready in June, and who wants to show it?' Because *Big Bad Mama* would have been a great success as well as *Bloody Mama*, he would get an enormous amount of advances – or enormous proportionate to the budgets he shot on – and with the money in hand he would then go ahead and make the film, so there was a no-loss situation. Sometimes he'd go out with a title to the exhibitors that wouldn't get made; maybe a cycle would go too far or what have you, and he'd say we're going to have this film ready in July, and if he couldn't get the advances, then a few weeks later it would be cancelled, 'because a few people had problems with it'.

But he had to deliver on *Crazy Mama* and he called me for what was supposed to be a script meeting about *Fighting Mad*, which I'd been working very hard on – researching and hoping to get an approval on the script, so we could start casting it and get ready to make it. He called me into this script meeting and said, 'OK, *Fighting Mad* is shelved, but you're directing *Crazy Mama* next week, and, in fact, you have a casting session for some of the smaller parts in one hour.' You know, when you're a director, you're always fighting for control of your film: control in casting, control of the script, control of the key creative elements, so that you can make the best film you're capable of making, because later, if it's poorly received, you're going to take a lot of heat, and you want to cover yourself as strongly as possible. Now he's telling me that I'm going to direct a movie that I've never even read the script of. I said, 'Roger, it's not possible. First of all, I thought we were going forward on *Fighting Mad* – I've got this brand-new script, it's imminent. It solves all the problems that you found the last time – you're going to love it. So thanks anyway, find someone else for *Crazy Mama*, but let us carry on with *Fighting Mad*.' He said, 'Jonathan, you don't get it. There never will be a *Fighting Mad* unless you direct *Crazy Mama*, and you've got to go to this casting meeting in one hour. I suggest you have a quick bite and get up there.' I said, 'Look, I've got to read the script.'

And that's what happened. I told him, 'You know, Roger, I will do this because you literally leave me no choice. Besides, I like you so much. You're obviously in a jam here, I want to help you out, but I know this is going to end poorly. I know this, you can't jump in this fast on a movie, make it in three weeks, and then have two weeks for the editing, mix it in one day and hope for a good picture. It's going to be a mess, you're going to perceive it as a mess, you're going to get mad at me.' He said, 'Not at all, not at all, it's great of you to go for it. You're going to do a fine job, go ahead.'

We made the film and all the actors hated the script – with good reason: it was lousy. It had a couple of good scenes in it, but it left a lot to be desired. It was one of those awful situations where you're trying to write it while you're shooting it. It also got shot too fast. The film was supposed to end in a bloody shoot-out where this family of women end in a bloody finale like in *Bloody Mama* and *Big Bad Mama*. This was the girl-gang genre. The grandmother, the mother, the great-grandmother, the daughter, the pregnant daughter – everyone was supposed to get shot. At this point I was starting to get a little distressed about the need for this kind of violence in those films, and wishing it could be different.

Also, another thing Corman had said from the start was: 'You've got to make the audience like your characters or they won't like the movie. You've got to really struggle to make people get involved in your characters and like them, so they'll share the experience of the movie with them, and they'll care about them, and care about the movie.' He even said – and it's probably true – 'Your villain has to be the most fascinating, if not likeable, person in the piece. Notice how *Psycho* worked so effectively. Really pay attention to these things.'

And now here we are with this *Crazy Mama* movie, where you have to like this family of women, and you have to experience all these things with them, including getting killed in a bloody fusillade at the end. I thought, 'Well, this is really going against Roger's primary rule. I'm fed up with these bloody shoot-outs, and I don't think it's the right way to end this film.' So when we got to the shoot-out scene, all the cops were now shooting each other. The women all escaped and drove away. Roger saw it and said, 'My God, there's no ending here. This is an outrage! What are you going to do? That was an expensive scene. We rented a country club for a day, for heaven's sake. We can't go back there.'

A lot of thought went into this thing and we came up with this cute little tag at the end of it. I sort of liked the idea that you may not get gunned down in America for trying to rob people and get rich, but, what's worse, you may wind up never quite making it – so we showed them in their little hot-dog stand five years later, still desperately trying to make money. But Roger was furious at me. He thought I had totally ruined the movie, that this would be the first *Mama* film to lose money because it hadn't delivered all the elements. He was right, incidentally, it was the first to not make money, and he cancelled *Fighting Mad*. He said, 'You know, I thought you showed a little promise when you made *Caged Heat*, but this is a miserable mess. Forget it, forget *Fighting Mad*.'

So I went home – but first I said, 'I told you so.' At home I thought, 'This is such a terrible thing to have happened.' I knew that the movie would not be good, and I had warned him, and sure enough here we are. So I wrote him a letter.

There were a million things that were crazy about *Crazy Mama* – one was that the movie was being produced by Corman's wife, Julie Corman, who was eight and a half months pregnant when we started shooting, which was understandably occupying her thoughts. Yet she was doing a tremendously intense job of producing a movie. When we shot our big car-chase scene in the park, we had an ambulance standing by, as you always do for action scenes in case one of the drivers gets hurt flipping their car over. We had three units working that day; I was in one place, the art director was somewhere else with a camera team, somebody else was elsewhere in the park. At a certain point we heard this siren start up and go roaring away and we thought, 'Oh, my God, somebody's got hurt.' We went racing over to the meeting area and the ambulance was gone. Who was it? What had happened? They said, 'Oh, it's Julie – she's in labour.'

So that happened. There was all kinds of chaos. But the great thing about Roger – there are many great things about him – but one is that when I wrote him a letter explaining what had happened and saying finally, 'You know, you shouldn't be cancelling this film,' I got a phone call from him the next day: 'Well, I'm still pissed off at you because I still think you could have made a better movie, but you're right about a number of things, and so we'll go ahead with *Fighting Mad*.' I've been very grateful to him for that.

INT: *Moving on to* Citizens Band – *which I suppose is your first major movie – how did that come about?*

JD: It came about, on the one hand, because I was friends with the producer's wife. Sheree Latimer had been in the Corman movies, and she was a very good actress. We had a group of people who knew each other and hung out together. Then Sheree married Freddie Fields, a movie producer, and she was constantly putting in a good word for me. Freddie was searching for a director for *Citizens Band*, so Sheree showed him *Fighting Mad*, which was also a rural film with some family scenes in it. So I think that's how I got to his attention.

More critically, the script for *Citizens Band* was turned down by dozens of directors; they had sent it to all the good directors, and everybody had passed on it. At a certain point, Sheree's campaigning for me finally got me a meeting, and I think that Freddie, who, as an agent – as a super-agent of people like Steve McQueen, Barbra Streisand and Judy Garland, to name but a few – had gotten used to power and the exercise of power in his work. When he met me, I came on like a very pleasant person (which I try to be most of the time) and also I was someone looking for a real opportunity to get out of the Corman mode and do a studio movie; I think he'd found someone who he thought was very controllable. So he picked me for it.

We made the film and I was getting more and more excited by this idea of less editing, of editing in the camera – as so many of the films that I'd admired over the years had done, without my even realizing it.

In fact, I met Bernardo Bertolucci just before I started directing *Caged Heat*. The one question he asked this new director – me – about the movie was: 'Are you going to use a lot of long takes?' – actually, he said 'long shots', but I wasn't sure if he meant wide shots, or what have you. I said, 'Well, what do you mean?' and he said, 'You know, are you going to design shots that won't require any editing?' I thought to myself, 'God, I would love to try for that,' but it's a very scary thing as a director, especially when you're starting out, to dare to do that, because if the shots don't work, then you're going to be in trouble in the cutting room. I tried a little bit of that stuff on *Caged Heat*, very much motivated by Bernardo's question, because I respect that so much in other film-makers' work, and I wanted it to be part of my work one day. But I wasn't going to rush it.

INT: *The film had a very good critical reception, but not a great public one.*

JD: It was an unqualified disaster at the box office – one of the most poorly received movies, in terms of business, released that year. People stayed away in droves, as the saying goes. In some theatres, only two people showed up its first weekend. The movie was quickly yanked.

One of the things that I loved about the script of *Citizens Band* was that it in no way relied on action, which was very happy-making for me because that

Peter Fonda in *Fighting Mad* (1976)

Rural life in *Fighting Mad*

Citizens Band (1977)

Paul Le Mat, Candy Clark and Roberts Blossom in *Citizens Band*

was one of my least favourite kinds of scenes to do. The more I directed, the more I was interested in character and behaviour. So this was amazing: a script with no action scenes, which was unlikely because with CBs you'd think it would be chock-full of the kind of scenes that made *Smokey and the Bandit* such an enormous hit. There were no cop encounters, no car chases. It was just these terrific characters talking to each other on their CB radios for an hour and a half. And perhaps that's the problem with the movie – you've either got to be open to that or not, and if you're not open to it, there's the slimmest of chances that you're going to enjoy the picture. But, if you are open to it, I think the script is so witty and the cast is so wonderful that you're in for a surprising movie experience, because the very thing that would seem to put you off – no action, all talk – is an enormous strength and value.

INT: *I guess you were particularly pleased with the casting of the film.*

JD: Yes. Because it was the first movie I did for a proper studio, *Citizens Band* was the first time I had the budget to work with, for argument's sake, the better actors. I exploited that opportunity to the maximum and feel that we were lucky in getting a great, great cast together for that movie.

INT: *But the ensuing year was pretty tough for you, wasn't it?*

JD: Each time you do a film you hope to expand your area of possible employers, you hope that someone else somewhere will see and like your film, and maybe you'll start getting scripts from another source. That had been happening a tiny little bit. I had been getting feelers at the time of *Citizens Band*, but not many. Afterwards, because it had been critically well received, despite being a miserable flop at the box office, I'd hoped that it would expand my contacts. But no one sent me anything. Then I'd go to my agent, because I was about to lose my apartment and was, literally, flat broke, and I'd say, 'OK, OK, we couldn't get any series TV, what about the game shows? Maybe I can bring a little something . . .' 'No, no, no.' Finally I was saying, 'OK, the *Evening News*, anything.'

But luckily Peter Falk, somehow or other, saw *Citizens Band* and liked it and invited me to come and do an episode of *Columbo*. It was absolutely a life-saver: it saved the apartment, it gave me a little bit of confidence back, and it was terrific working with Peter Falk.

INT: *Your next film,* Last Embrace *– wasn't that a script that had done the rounds?*

JD: No, that had made less rounds, although it probably would have eventually made as many rounds as *Citizens Band*. There were some people who had liked *Citizens Band*, some producer who knew it, so they sent *Last Embrace* to me and I loved the idea of doing a film that had the potential of being an Alfred Hitchcock-style thriller. By that I mean that kind of Hitchcockian sense of suspense and complexity of character, as well as narrative.

Also, I very much liked that it gave me an opportunity in an entertainment

Janet Margolin and Roy Scheider in *Last Embrace* (1979)

A Hitchcockian moment in *Last Embrace*

vein, to reveal something extraordinary about history. In this instance, it was
the existence of a string of whore-houses supplied by white slavers and run
by people within the Jewish church. Nobody knew about this. It was just part
of the organized corruption that many people of different faiths had been
able to do in New York, and this was strong stuff. I also felt that, if we could
get Roy Scheider for it, it would be great. I had liked him a lot in some of
his previous movies and thought that he could be the Bogart of the 1980s.

We went to work on the script. It was a flawed script, and we tried very
hard to fix it. More than anything the experience helped me realize: don't go
into a movie unless you believe in the script, because if you don't believe it,
how can anyone else believe it?

In the end, it's a movie that I consider – and I'm not alone in this – deeply,
deeply flawed in many ways, although I also think it has some values. But I
did it because I love that kind of picture, and I hate the idea of doing films
that are similar. I think it's important, creatively, to do something as different
as possible from what you did the last time. It keeps you from falling into
certain ways that seem to work and then doing them over and over again.

INT: *What about* Melvin and Howard *and the casting discussions on that?*

JD: I felt that Paul Le Mat would be a really fantastic Melvin. I had had a
great time working with him on *Citizens Band* and thought that Paul had an
unusually intense ability to communicate the ideas of the script to the other
actors – in character, of course – and, by extension, to the audience. Paul
had a kind of guileless, sincere innocence about him, an unspoiltness as an
actor and as a person, and I felt that it would be wonderful to bring that to
the part of Melvin.

My sense of Melvin – on the basis of Bo Goldman's script – was that he
was a beautiful naif, in the best sense of the word. So it was very important
for me to have Paul in the part. I also wanted to hire Roberts Blossom, who
plays Le Mat's father in *Citizens Band*, to play Howard Hughes. Because
Hughes was such an inscrutable character in popular American mythology –
you almost have to call it that even though he existed – I felt it would be
good to have an actor who nobody had any preconceptions about. So I was
very keen on Roberts Blossom. Meanwhile, Universal wanted Jason Robards
to play the part. A deal was struck: they said you can have Le Mat, if you'll
go with Jason Robards. And it worked out very well indeed. I'm delighted
that it happened that way. I think that Jason was beautiful in the part, and
also was a wonderful man to work with.

INT: *You must have been pleased with the Oscar nominations.*

JD: I thought that everybody's work was absolutely outstanding: Bo Goldman's
script, Jason Robards's performance, Mary Steenburgen's performance, which
was amazing. If, indeed, there is any logic to what Oscars are all about, then
they certainly deserved the nominations. But it was surprising that such an

Jonathan Demme shooting *Melvin and Howard* (1980)

Howard (Jason Robards) and Melvin (Paul Le Mat)

Linda (Mary Steenburgen) and Mr Love (Bob Ridge) on the game show

outside, off-the-wall kind of movie could receive three Oscar nominations. I loved that.

INT: *The game-show sequence in* Melvin and Howard *is very closely based, I believe, on a real game show.*

JD: It was *Let's Make a Deal* – a gigantically successful popular show. The host was a fellow named Monty Hall. When Bo Goldman wrote the screenplay he tried to base it as much as possible on fact, so he wrote *Let's Make a Deal* and Monty Hall into the script. *Let's Make a Deal* had gone off the air about a year before we started shooting. Monty Hall was then a real-estate entrepreneur, a multi-millionaire and didn't need TV, but apparently he missed it because when we contacted him about playing himself in the movie, he said, 'Yes, absolutely.'

This sequence was going to be the first scene that we were scheduled to shoot in the movie. About a week before we were supposed to shoot it, Monty finally got around to reading the script and there were some things that he took exception to, so he pulled out. We had to scramble in about a week's time and come up with an idea for a show that would achieve the same thing as *Let's Make a Deal*. We had to get a set together for whatever that would be, and we had to cast somebody – a brand-new character. I was thrilled in retrospect that it happened. Our great production designer Toby Rafleson was poised to do anything, and we decided to make a show that was a combination of *Let's Make a Deal* and *The Gong Show*. On *The Gong Show* you had to do a talent act, whereas on *Let's Make a Deal* you just had to wear a funny costume – so it gave us a chance to do both. Bob Ridge, who plays Mr Love, our game-show host, was a friend of mine with a great improvisational gift, and we literally improvised an enormous amount of the show. I was very happy with the way it turned out.

INT: *What particularly strikes me about that sequence is not only the tackiness of the whole show, but also the pleasure and real spirit behind the people involved. There seems to be something there that's become your strength: your sympathy for people in Middle America.*

JD: In the kind of society that we have in America, there are an enormous amount of people whose dreams are flung in their face every day – in the media, when they drive to work or when they're looking for a job. The ability to make that leap and get in touch with them is incredibly difficult. If you go to any of these game shows where people can literally have their life changed for them – absurdly enough, by picking the right gate, or what have you – it's difficult not to feel tremendous sympathy for that situation and really hope that someone is going to get a shot at improving things.

INT: *After* Melvin and Howard *there was* Swing Shift, *and then your golden period, I suppose, with your company Clinica Estetico and the David Byrne collaborations, starting with* Stop Making Sense.

JD: About six months before we actually made the movie, I went and saw the Talking Heads concert. I had been a fan of theirs for a number of years, but hadn't seen them perform in about five years. I was really staggered by the way they had grown, performance-wise. I'd been aware of how the music had been growing because I had listened to all their records, but I was astonished to see how the four statue-like performers who I once knew as the Talking Heads had turned into these great, free-spirited entertainers, and had involved all these other wonderful musicians. I thought it was a great show.

I was living in London during the heyday of the great rock shows and, in my view, had seen it all, but the Talking Heads – many years later – suddenly blew all that away. I thought, 'This is a movie waiting to be filmed.' It looked to me as if David Byrne changed character, as opposed to just singing different songs; the lighting concept was endlessly opening up and fascinating; I loved the way the show illustrated the growth of the band: he comes out alone and, one by one, the other members come out. So I contacted Byrne through a mutual friend, suggested the idea to him. He went, 'OK,' and a couple of weeks later they came back with the money.

INT: *What about the decisions you made about the way the film was going to look?*
JD: I thought that if, indeed, the goal here is to make the movie-goer get as excited by the film as I got excited by the concert – and that was the goal – then this has got to be a completely no-frills experience and nothing should intrude on the cumulative growth of excitement that the show itself has. So the idea of doing any kind of interviews with the musicians or any glimpses of back-stage life would have been completely contrary to the goal of the piece.

We shot a lot of audience reactions because, as with all good musical experiences, the audience's participation, the audience's response, is very much a part of the whole. And we had really good footage of the audience having all the appropriate reactions. But we found in the editing that every time we cut to the audience, it dissipated the build that we had working for us in the show itself. The process dictated that we should never cut to the audience until the very last minutes of the movie; we hoped that by cutting to the audience then we would, maybe, involve the movie audience. We also felt it was dangerous to cut away to an audience in a musical film because you're reminding the movie audience that the experience was not originally for them – it is for these yahoos who are jumping up and down and being really great on camera. So, preserving that sense of 'This is for you' reinforced our desire not to cut away to the concert audience.

In the end, it was such a great thing to be able to go out there with David Byrne and those guys and, in a very free atmosphere, make *Stop Making Sense*, where nobody had any concerns other than making the best possible film. That was really invigorating, and brought me back in touch with a lot of the

David Byrne performing in *Stop Making Sense* (1984)

things that had come to be the joy of the work for me, which more than anything is collaboration, working with gifted people and seeing the exciting results you get. So that was really terrific, and when we went and did *Something Wild* we pumped it all up again and said, 'OK, let's start from scratch now!'

INT: *Something Wild seems to be part of a group of films that dealt with comedy and nightmare at the same time. Why do you think that was?*

JD: When *Something Wild* came out I noticed that it got linked up with a couple of other films – one was *Blue Velvet*. They were very different from each other in a number of ways. But I know this mixture of violence was born of some eruption of what lurks below the American Dream. It was just a coincidence in terms of there being a little group of movies that did that.

INT: *What especially excited you about doing the script?*

JD: When you're reading scripts, trying very hard to find something you want to make a movie of, you read bad script after bad script, with the occasional almost-slightly-promising script thrown in. It's impossible to describe how tough it is to find a good screenplay – something you can read and think, 'Yes, this can be a good movie. Here is a story well told, that can really come to life on the screen.' And that's what happened, for me, when I read E. Max Fry's screenplay of *Something Wild*. I didn't recognize these characters from any other movies I had seen. It kept surprising you at every twist and turn, and there was this theme of the flipside of putting on your neat suits and committing a certain kind of financial violence as a successful yuppie in a corporation. The dark side of that is a guy like Ray Liotta, who resorts to a more fundamental kind of violence to solve his problems and to get ahead. I liked this collision and I liked what the script said about violence – how once you start going down that path it's going to be where you wind up, and you're going to take many unfortunate people with you. I felt it had a powerful, as well as pertinent, thing to say in the midst of a great yarn. That's why I liked it.

INT: *The film also provided another opportunity to work with David Byrne. How important is music to you when you're putting a film together?*

JD: In editing when you start putting music on the picture, the one thing I can say for sure about it, on a personal level, is that it's one of the most enjoyable moments of film-making. It synthesizes, in a way, the potential of this multi-media medium, which has so many different kinds of creative activity going on: visually, sound-wise, acting-wise. As in life, whatever piece of music you put behind a scene you've shot, it's going to feel a different way. That's something we all know about. We come home and we're in the need for a certain kind of music, depending on what kind of day we've had. And, yes, it alters our mood. So, given this mood-altering potential of music, it becomes a great source of fun, as well as a chance to make a scene that works OK work a whole lot better – to bring out the point of a scene that

Jonathan Demme with Jeff Daniels and Melanie Griffith on location on *Something Wild* (1987)

The aftermath of violence: Jeff Daniels in *Something Wild*

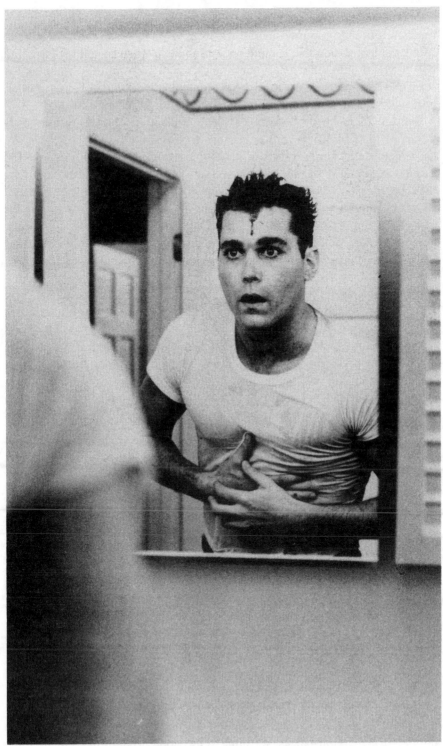

The aftermath of violence: Ray Liotta in *Something Wild*

you haven't really captured in the shooting of it, to excite the audience, to create the impression that something is happening when something isn't, and also to create little emotional touchstones which you can draw upon as the story changes – so that the music that seemed so innocent and sweet earlier, in new circumstances brings on a whole other set of feelings.

Because so much of *Something Wild* took place in cars where everybody listens to their radio, the music became an especially lush opportunity. We used reggae a lot because part of the theme of *Something Wild* was how Jeff Daniels is, literally, waking up and seeing things for the first time in a long time because he's been such a shut-down, bone-headed yuppie. For me, showing America to an exotic kind of music – reggae – helped to sell the idea of this new look at things. As far as David Byrne is concerned, obviously, because I know him, I can't help but think: wouldn't it be great to have some David Byrne music in this movie because he's one of the great composers of our time. But a busy man. So I appealed to him on the level of: 'Why don't you write a song for you and Celia Cruz?' (Celia Cruz is one of his great idols). That pushed the right button and David came up with the opening song.

When it came to *Married to the Mob*, I didn't dream of asking him to score it – he was working on a script for a new film, he was doing the score for a Robert Wilson play, he's doing this, he's doing that. But I did invite him to a screening. He took a look at it and asked what was I going to do about the music. 'Maybe I'll try a couple of things for you,' he said. It developed into an entire score which was, again, very much to the benefit of the movie.

INT: *What attracted you to* Married to the Mob?

JD: I am very concerned with themes and psychological subtext in movies, but the thing that attracted me to *Married to the Mob* was the complete absence of themes and subtext, on one level. I liked the idea of trying to do a movie that was a complete escapist fantasy, which didn't pretend it had anything profound to say about anything. It was fun to do, and very cathartic, revivifying.

INT: *Do you really mean it when you say* Married to the Mob *has nothing profound to say?*

JD: Well, since you're asking the question, I should be honest. The subtle social message of *Married to the Mob* is that people of different races especially, and people in general, can benefit by reaching out to other people, and by being reached out to in turn.

Let's face it, *Married to the Mob* is a blatant attempt at a full-tilt, crassly commercial entertainment – let's make no bones about that. Nevertheless, I did hope that if people liked the picture, part of their experience would be seeing this white person leave their comfortable, suburban, fully equipped home and become an absolute outsider – Angela moves into profoundly more difficult living circumstances, surrounded by people who, through their ethnic definition or what have you, are relegated to a certain outsider status. Without beating it on the head, the audience sees: well, what do you know, down there people are people. When someone gives her a chance at a job and sticks by her, because she's blessed with the absence of a racial distinction – she doesn't like people on the basis of what race they are – she's available to be reached out to. The fact that she's not a racialist proves to be an asset down there and helps her to get started on a new and positive path.

OK, that's probably corny, and it's not very well executed, but I feel it's as important an arena of thinking as exists in the world today. I mean, it's killing our society in a zillion ways, and it's so hard to not get sucked into the awfulness and the violence of racism, whether as an observer or a participant. Even when doing escapist movies like *Married to the Mob* you desperately want to try to get something positive, informationally, in there. I hope I can attack that sort of theme in a less hidden way in the future.

INT: *In some ways Angela's discovery of other races seems a reflection of your own love of black music and culture – and, of course, Haiti.*

JD: I have an intense interest in Haiti. I took a trip there and was so taken with the people and their struggle to achieve a democracy that I went back and made a documentary shortly after for Channel Four. I formed a lot of friendships and interests that will last me the rest of my life. This may have something to do with the fact that America is a country with an incredible diversity of cultural input. In our schools and in our communities – and by 'our' I mean white guys like me – we're taught all about our European heritage and our European roots. We honour them and are fascinated by them, but this is also a country with profound African roots. In recent years I've been a lot more interested in that and I've gained a lot more insights and truths about people from the African roots than from the old European ones.

Haiti was the first black republic in 1804, when they kicked the last Europeans out, so there's something extraordinary going on down there and I can't help but be drawn to it.

INT: *What about the casting of* Married to the Mob? *Was Michelle Pfeiffer your first choice?*

JD: The casting of the Angela character was the easiest it's ever been for me because, after I read the script which Orion had sent me, I called Mike Medavoy and said, 'This script is terrific, let's do it.' He said, 'Great! What do you think of Michelle Pfeiffer?' And I said, 'Good idea!' We sent her a script and she loved it and jumped in. I had come to know her on John Landis's film *Into the Night*, where I did an acting cameo. I got involved with the film because I was acquainted with John Landis, and it was one of his conceits in making the movie to hire twenty directors to do these cameos.

It was a terrific opportunity for me to try to get the actor's perspective on things, not so much from a creative point of view, but just the sheer terror

The outsider: Michelle Pfeiffer in *Married to the Mob* (1988)

The new Mafia don: Dean Stockwell in *Married to the Mob*

involved in getting into an outfit and suddenly having a camera looking at you.

That's how I came to know what a very intelligent, nice person Michelle Pfeiffer is. And because I met her under those circumstances, I had her in mind as someone who would be good to work with one day.

INT: *What about Dean Stockwell?*

JD: Well, he stole the part from somebody else whom I had in mind and I was on my way out to California to meet with. When I got off the plane, I picked up the trade paper, *Daily Variety*, and saw this huge photo of Dean Stockwell that had been placed in the paper by a new agency he had signed up with. I was looking at it and thought, 'That guy looks like the new Mafia don. Who is it? My God, it's Dean Stockwell, who was so great in *Blue Velvet* and in so many other things.' So I did a right turn and met with Dean. He liked it and came on board.

INT: *In some ways* Married to the Mob *seems a throwback to the Corman period in the way it was made, and the speed of it.*

JD: I hope that *Married to the Mob* has a lot of the elements and feeling of a Corman movie, because that means our aggressive attempt to entertain is coming across.

I feel that all films are exploitation films. To one degree or another, almost all films finally adhere to the Corman policy. So many of them do have an enormous amount of action; the sex is there; the laughs are there; and sometimes, to some degree, the social statement is there as well. The *Godfather* films are the most expensive Roger Corman films ever made. And I think that everyone's trying to exploit that formula, one way or another. But most people are less candid about it than Roger is.

So, if *Married to the Mob* feels like a Corman movie, I'm delighted.

INT: Married to the Mob *is a gangster movie. Has that always been a popular genre for you?*

JD: I have loved gangster movies ever since I started going to the pictures. That meant films like *The Big Heat*, Phil Karlson movies like *The Phenix City Story*. Gangster movies are such wonderful role-models for kids seeking a masculine identity. I say that sarcastically, because of course they're terrible role-models, but you don't know that when you're eight, nine, ten, eleven, twelve – you go, 'Yes, I wanna behave like that, I wanna talk tough and shove grapefruit in people's faces, and shoot them.' I just enjoyed those films, and that's where the distinction is for me in *Married to the Mob* – I like to think of it as a gangster picture, not as any kind of Mafia picture. If you're making a Mafia movie, it wouldn't be a comedy because it's a pretty despicable subject.

INT: *What about the final credit sequence?*

JD: Under the end credits there are a lot of shots that aren't in the movie.

There's a couple of reasons for that. The main reason is, hopefully, it's fun to see stuff that wasn't in the movie when the movie's over. Another reason is that we had to take so many scenes out of the film. We had a three-hour cut, and for a movie that's supposed to be, at the most, an hour and fifty minutes, it wasn't playing very good. I mean, the scenes were good and the actors were good, but it took far too long to get from A to Z. We had to start pulling out not only the stuff that was shaky, but some really nice scenes, and in doing so some of the actors' parts were reduced to almost zero, especially my dear friend Chris Issak, who will be a terrific actor if he does enough movies, and who was excited about playing this hit-man. Boom – his scenes came flying out, and for many, many other people as well. To put them in at the end of the film was a clumsy effort to reassure the Chris Issaks of the film: 'I know we cut it out, we weren't ashamed of you, you're still there.'

On another level, it was a conceit of Craig McKay's and mine that we could tell the story again in the scenes we took out. And, indeed, we did that. You actually see the story all through, although you hadn't seen any of the scenes. It also provided an opportunity to give really good acknowledgements to many of the gifted people who work in positions that are critically important: like the guy who actually frames the shots, the sound recordist, the guy who created what, hopefully, would be a really exciting soundtrack. By stretching the movie out, we were able to pop these names on and let them be there longer than usual so that we could pay homage to the fact that many people worked hard on the movie.

INT: *You said you liked films with themes and psychological complexities. Is this what attracted you to* Silence of the Lambs?

JD: I saw the story of a woman in it. That was what appealed to me more than anything else. The idea of doing a violent picture, *per se*, didn't hold any particular appeal for me – especially violence with women as the subjects. Certainly, that is the background of the film, but the film itself is very much the heroic struggle on the part of Clarice Starling to try to save a life, and that gripped me right away.

We tried hard to swing the story very much from Clarice's point of view in order to force the audience into an even stronger identification with her than might ordinarily be the case. My cameraman, Tak Fujimoto, and I recognized that point-of-view shots are used in films often, but usually either for a particular point of emphasis, or for an extraordinary visual gag. What we decided to do here was to capitalize on the ability of subjective camera to, once again, force identification with the character. We decided to use it, not just for a particular emphasis, but to bring that kind of emphasis to everything Clarice saw: operating on the premise that every scene she's in is a scene of great importance, let's show exactly what she sees in every single scene. Aside from the 1940s film *The Lady in the Lake*, we probably made

Jodie Foster as Clarice Starling in *Silence of the Lambs* (1990)

the most use of point-of-view, in recent years anyway. We wondered if audiences might find it distracting, but we decided to commit to it anyway, because the potential was there to up the emotional ante quite a bit.

The funny thing is, it's an easy shot to set up because all you have to do is watch what Jodie Foster does in the rehearsal and what she looks at; the cameraman watches that, and then it's his turn to duplicate what she saw. It's the easiest shot to dream up because you don't actually dream it up. You just copy what the actress is doing. When you get to the editing stage, theoretically certain kinds of shots need to precede a point-of-view shot for it to flow seamlessly into the montage – usually a shot of whoever's point-of-view it is, looking very, very close to the camera so it's not at all jarring when we turn around and see what they're seeing. It's quite easy to edit in as long as you have good close-ups of whoever it is whose point-of-view you're seeing.

INT: *Why Anthony Hopkins as Hannibal Lecter?*

JD: Anthony Hopkins appears to be exceptionally intelligent; there's something about his face, something about his eyes, something about the way he expresses himself. He also appears to be deeply humanistic. He seems to be a very good person. There seems to be a tremendous depth of human feeling behind those eyes. I thought that intelligence is obviously an important ingredient for Lecter, because here's someone who's smarter than almost anybody he will ever encounter. And I felt that it was important to find someone with implications of great humanity, like Tony Hopkins has, in order to colour the character, or else he would have the potential of being an icicle, a brilliant icicle. Therefore, there wasn't much thought involved in arriving at Tony Hopkins. I've admired him tremendously over the years, and I think his characterization in *The Elephant Man* was a wonderful reference point for Dr Lecter: as good and as decent as that doctor is, Dr Lecter will prove to be the antithesis, but will also have a complexity because of all these other things which Tony possesses. Incidentally, as it turns out, Tony, as a person, is indeed as wonderful a guy as his appearance suggests.

INT: *The cell in which Dr Lecter is confined is very different from the way it is described in the book. How did that come about?*

JD: The story about the cell in *Silence of the Lambs* is fun because in trying to solve a problem we stumbled into something that, for me, is very effective in its own right: the idea of a glass-walled cell for Dr Lecter, instead of the traditional bars.

We assumed we'd have bars for his cell and we were upset about the fact that, having extended dialogue scenes, we would be stuck with the presence of bars. We were concerned about seeing both eyes of both characters at all times, and about how far apart we had to make the bars so that we could see the eyes very well, and what colour they had to be to be as unobtrusive as possible.

Anthony Hopkins as Hannibal Lecter in his cell in *Silence of the Lambs*

We started filming a number of tests: different thicknesses of bars, spaced at different intervals, painted different colours; vertical bars, horizontal bars. With horizontal bars we could see both eyes, but now we couldn't see the mouth or the nose. We were constantly frustrated; plus, on top of the technical problem of the eye/bar relationship, I started to realize that bars pulled us into a different kind of sense memory – of other movies containing other cell scenes – so it would now look like a prison movie; Lecter would be some inmate in a prison movie. It would evoke all these other scenes which we've seen throughout our movie-going lives, and it would deprive these encounters of the unique, special nature that they were entitled to by virtue of how intense the characters in the scenes were.

At one meeting after viewing yet another bunch of bars – diagonal bars, probably, that were painted pink, or something like that – somebody suddenly said, 'My God, we should just put him behind thick glass like they do rats in a laboratory, then we could see everything.' And the light bulb went on for us, and we thought, 'Yeah, why don't we do that?'

Tony worked with the glass in a wonderful way, for example, when he smells her perfume and, in fact, smells whatever scents are associated with her. It would be one thing to smell her through the bars, but Tony, at that moment, goes up on his tiptoes and sniffs through these holes way up, which turned that into a far more special moment than it would otherwise have been.

INT: *What about the problem of how much of the horror you could show without losing the audience?*

JD: We – when I say 'we' I mean the designer Kristi Zea, Tak Fujimoto, the screenwriter Ted Tally and I – we knew that we were walking a very dangerous tightrope with what we chose to visualize from the story and how, specifically, we went about visualizing it. On the one hand, we knew it was imperative that we honour the horrific nature of the book, because if you didn't, it would be a watered-down version. Also, you have to accept the fact that one reason why people find the book so powerful is that it is so horrific. On the other hand, movies don't give the viewer the same luxury that books give the reader, where you can, with your own mind's eye, picture as much as you wish of what's being described to you. And when it came to the more horrifying things that happen in the story, we didn't want to make people physically ill; we didn't want to upset them in a way that transcends the degree of 'upsettedness' we bargain for when we go to a frightening movie. We felt that this definitely had the potential for being revolting, and we didn't want to go that far.

There were endless discussions among all of us: how can we show it, yet spare the viewers having to cross a line that they would be compromised by? We worked very, very hard on it. When Dr Lecter has his encounter with

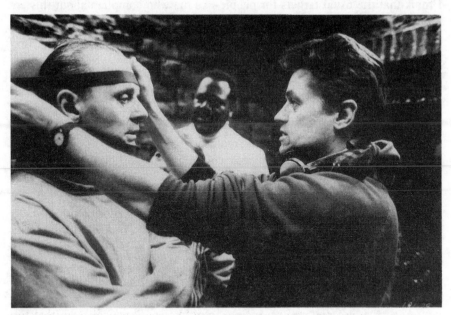

Jonathan Demme with Jodie Foster and Anthony Hopkins on location on
Silence of the Lambs

the police officers, we looked at endless possibilities of how to visualize that, and, finally, aided very much by Ted Tally's original take on it at script level – which was: to show a lot, but only for a second – we plotted our way through it.

I did make sure to shoot a little more horrifying material than probably we would be able to use, so that we could make the final decisions in the cutting room. We previewed the movie a few times and I discovered after a few previews that I was being too sensitive on behalf of the audience; in fact, the scenes that were supposed to have tremendous impact were falling short. So we started putting a bit more in, until finally we felt we'd achieved that delicate balance.

INT: *As you said about* Married to the Mob, *you have definite ideas about violence.*

JD: I think that film-makers definitely have responsibility to portray violence, first and foremost, in a way that is not thrilling and glamorizing, as many movies do – movies which I as a kid enjoyed seeing. I think it's important that when you have a scene containing violence you let people know just how awful it is, how painful and difficult it is, how unappealing it is. I try to do that as much as I can whenever there is a scene containing violence, because I think that the usual targets for people like me who complain about this are *Rambo* movies that show, in almost sexual terms, how thrilling and exciting it is to spew bullets out of your gun and see many, many people of another race writhing in exquisite agony in front of your spew. I just think that's disgusting.

As I said before, as a little boy, and even as a young man, I was very ready to be thrilled by that kind of thing in the movies. I think that the easy, cheap thrill that young men, and even older men, are able to enjoy at the sight of violence is part of the complex web of sickness that makes the male human capable of going out and performing real violence against other people including, but not limited to, women and children, and vast numbers of other people.

I think there's a good case to be made for pushing, whenever possible, for an honest portrayal of how ugly violence is. I'm still struggling with my adolescent self, who is subject to excitement at gunplay. In a lot of the movies I've done, for instance *Married to the Mob*, there's a sort of exploitative, fun use of firepower that I find so offensive – and there it is! I directed it, and I had fun directing it, and I blame the twelve-year-old that still lurks inside of me.

INT: *So how do you deal with the violence in a situation like the final confrontation between Clarice and the serial killer, Buffalo Bill?*

JD: At the final confrontation, where guns are involved, I've never heard an audience cheer for what happens at that moment in the film. I tried very hard to film it in such a way that it wouldn't provide the kind of relief that you'd get from someone biting the dust. Once again, even the idea of an essentially good person murdering an essentially bad person is not that palatable: you wish that there could be another solution to a confrontation like that.

I don't think it's something to cheer about. Although I acknowledge that audiences love to cheer at a moment such as that, I didn't think it was appropriate for the film. Also, I didn't want to relieve whatever tension the film had going at that point. I was hoping to keep the audience still bottled up a little bit, and then when they'd see the next scene where Clarice is back at the academy, maybe the feelings which might have been released by a cheer would be channelled into a more emotional place.

INT: *Up till now you've had a big critical following, but not really a large popular one. How do you feel now that* Silence of the Lambs *seems to have changed that?*

JD: Honestly, I love directing movies. I think it's exciting work; I enjoy it enormously when I do it; it's good paying work. In every way, it's something I'm just so happy I've come to as a profession. And that's 90 per cent of how I feel about me as a film-maker. If anything that I've done has had a nice review or it's been shown at a film festival, or anything like that, it's just gravy on the whole experience of being able to make movies. It's delightful, but it's a transitory pleasure. It's not something you go round thinking about. Now, with *Silence of the Lambs*, here's a movie which will be seen by many, many people. That's great because I know that at a certain point I started wondering, 'What is my problem? I can do films that are appreciated in some quarters, and so on, but either there's something that I find interesting which is getting in the way of my sharing my work with a lot of people, or there's some ingredient that I'm simply missing.' So it's great to know that, finally, you've made a movie that's seen by a lot of people.

I don't care what I get remembered for – or don't get remembered for. That's of no interest to me whatsoever. I just love making movies.

Filmography

1971   *Angels Hard as They Come*
Producer/Co-screenwriter
Director: Joe Viola

1972   *The Hot Box*
Producer/Co-screenwriter
Director: Joe Viola

Black Mama, White Mama
Co-screenwriter (with Joe Viola)
Director: Eddie Romero

as director

1974 *Caged Heat*
With Juanita Brown, Roberta Collins, Erica Gavin, Barbara Steele, Warren Miller
Screenwriter: Jonathan Demme

1975 *Crazy Mama*
With Cloris Leachman, Stuart Whitman, Jim Backus, Ann Sothern, Linda Purl
Screenwriter: Robert Thom and Jonathan Demme (uncredited)

1976 *Fighting Mad*
With Peter Fonda, Lynn Lowry, John Doucette, Scott Glenn, Harry Northup
Screenwriter: Jonathan Demme

1977 *Citizens Band (Handle with Care)*
With Paul Le Mat, Candy Clark, Bruce McGill, Ann Wedgeworth, Charles Napier,
Alex Elias, Roberts Blossom
Screenwriter: Paul Brickman

1978 *Columbo – Murder under Glass* (TV)
With Peter Falk, Louis Jourdan, Gary Goetzman

1979 *Last Embrace*
With Roy Scheider, Janet Margolin, John Glover, Charles Napier, Christopher
Walken
Screenwriter: David Shaber, from a novel by Murray Teigh Bloom

1980 *Melvin and Howard*
With Paul Le Mat, Jason Robards, Mary Steenburgen, Elizabeth Cheshire, Charles
Napier, Pamela Reed, Gloria Grahame, Bob Ridgely
Screenwriter: Bo Goldman

1982 *Who Am I This Time?* (TV)
With Christopher Walken, Susan Sarandon, Bob Ridgely
Screenwriter: Morton Neal Miller, after Kurt Vonnegut Jr

1984 *Swing Shift*
With Goldie Hawn, Christine Lahti, Kurt Russell, Fred Ward, Ed Harris, Charles
Napier, Roger Corman, Holly Hunter, Beth Henley
Screenplay: Rob Morton

Stop Making Sense
With Talking Heads

1985 *Trying Times – A Family Tree* (TV)
With David Byrne, Rosanna Arquette, Bob Ridgely, Hope Lang, John Stockwell
Screenwriters: Beth Henley, Budge Threlkeld

Alive from Off Center – Accumulation with Talking Plus Water Motor (TV)
With Trish Brown

1987 *Swimming to Cambodia*
With Spalding Gray

Something Wild
With Melanie Griffith, Jeff Daniels, Ray Liotta, Margaret Colin, Charles Napier, Jim
Roche, Bob Ridgely, Tracy Walter, Sister Carol East
Screenwriter: E. Max Frye

Haiti, Dreams of Democracy (TV)
Co-director: Joe Menell

1988   *Married to the Mob*
With Michelle Pfeiffer, Matthew Modine, Dean Stockwell, Mercedes Ruehl, Tracey
Walter, Charles Napier, Paul Lazar, Sister Carol East, Chris Issak
Screenwriters: Barry Strugati, Mark R. Burns

1990   *Silence of the Lambs*
With Jodie Foster, Anthony Hopkins, Scott Glenn, Ted Levine, Charles Napier,
Tracey Walter, Paul Lazar, Anthony Heal, Case Lemmons, Chris Issak
Screenwriter: Ted Tally, based on a novel by Thomas Harris

1991   *Cousin Bobby*
Documentary on Demme's relative, a socialist episcopalian priest

Demme has also directed the following promotional videos:
Suburban Lawns, *Gidget Goes to Hell*
Sandra Bernhard, *Everybody's Young*
United Artists Against Apartheid, *Sun City*
New Order, *The Perfect Kiss*
UB40 and Chrissie Hynde, *I've Got U Babe*
Fine Young Cannibals, *Ever Fallen in Love*
Suzanne Vega, *Solitude Standing*
Les Frères Parents, *Veye Yo*
Les Frères Parents, *Chemin Victoire*
The Feelies, *Away*
Neville Brothers, *Sister Rosa*
Les Frères Parents and Neville Brothers, *Konbit*
Neville Brothers, *Still of the Night*
KRS-1 and various artists, *H.E.A.L.*

Matters of Photogenics
Nestor Almendros

Throughout my career I have been privileged to photograph some of the most beautiful and interesting women in the world, in many countries, on two continents. Photographing actresses past their prime represents something of a problem for the cinematographer, who is forced to use diffusion filters in front of the lens to diminish the wrinkles (though in reality they don't hide much), but I have filmed most of these women at the best time of their lives. Isabelle Adjani, for example, was almost an adolescent in *The Story of Adèle H.* Her alabaster complexion had a marvellous transparency. Meryl Streep, whom I have filmed several times, is another actress with a wonderful face, whose skin has an almost marble-like quality.

I have also photographed mature stars like Catherine Deneuve, who, like good wine, has improved with the passage of time. Looking now at one of Ms Deneuve's first pictures, it is clear that when she was very young she was only a pretty girl, not the sensational beauty she is now. Without a doubt, the years have been kind, giving her style and class, turning her into a real goddess. There is a kind of woman who is at her best between the ages of thirty and forty. When I filmed her in *The Last Metro*, she was at the height of her beauty.

Photographing Simone Signoret in *Madame Rosa*, at the end of her life and career, I did not have to worry about covering wrinkles, or hiding her age, since the role did not require it. On the contrary, she had to be made to look older. This great actress took the procedure in her stride and asked that wrinkles be added to her make-up, so as to give the impression of an elderly and defeated woman. Simone Signoret was once very beautiful. Who could forget her in *Casque d'Or* or *Dédée d'Anvers*?

More recently, I have had the privilege of photographing that new French actress, the tall and beautiful Fanny Ardant. I was fortunate to film her in black and white, which is especially good for portraits. When taking close-ups in a colour picture, there is too much visual information in the back-ground, which tends to draw attention away from the face. That is why the faces of the actresses in the old black and white pictures are so vividly remembered. Even now, movie fans nostalgically recall Dietrich . . . Garbo . . . Lamarr . . . Why? Filmed in black and white, those figures looked as if they

were lit from within. When a face appeared on the screen over-exposed –
the high-key technique, which also erased imperfections – it was as if a bright
object was emerging from the screen.

But today we almost always have to work in colour. This makes good
features even more important. I photographed Brooke Shields in *The Blue
Lagoon*, when she was very young. She was only fourteen years old, really a
child, although she portrayed a sixteen-year-old. Her face comes close to
absolute perfection. But surface beauty is not everything. We could say that
Sally Fields is a woman whose beauty comes from within. In *Places in the
Heart*, she played a provincial woman, and her modesty was most appropriate
for the role. She wanted to appear almost without make-up, dressed in well-
worn clothes, as a simple American country woman – something which has
its own beauty.

At the time of writing, I am in the midst of shooting a film, *Nadine*, directed
by Robert Benton, with one of the most attractive young stars of the new
American cinema, Kim Basinger. Kim's career has just started, but she is
making her presence felt. Both her face and her figure are perfect – it is rare
for one person to have both. Her face is completely symmetrical, which is
quite unique. Her perfection might even seem excessive, almost as inhuman
as a mannequin's, a problem sometimes experienced by models (which Ms
Basinger once was). However, she is also an excellent actress, with a fiery
look, and that saves her. In *Nadine*, which is set in the 1950s, the dresses are
of bright solid colours, and the lipstick and nail polish are of a violent red,
which was the fashion at that time. This was a challenge for me, and I can't
predict how well the photography will turn out, because it is the first time I
have been faced with such a range of colours.

It is impossible to say which is the most beautiful of all these women,
because each in her own way is extraordinary: Deneuve, as a great lady, is
splendid, a classic beauty for all times; personifying the freshness of youth,
Brooke Shields is unique; Meryl Streep, whose face looks as if it has been
sculpted by Brancusi, is the most expressive and intelligent. But there is
something common to all of them, something that makes them photograph
well. The truth is that the camera lenses love some women more than others.
The mystery of being photogenic has to do with bones. A person who 'has
no bones' is very difficult to light. The great beauties of the screen such as
Garbo, Crawford and Mangano all have a well-structured face. The nose was
sufficient and well defined, not a cute little one; they had high cheekbones,
well-drawn eyebrows, splendid jaws. A good bone structure in the face gives
the light something to hold on to and allows it to create an interplay of
shadows. If the face is flat, the light has nowhere to fall.

Of course, the eyes are very important, and I believe that dark-haired
people with light-coloured eyes have a great advantage in the movies, because

of the effect of contrasts on the face. Blondes with very light eyes are difficult
to photograph, because there is a certain visual monotony. It is not by chance
that Gene Tierney and Hedy Lamarr, two women with dark hair and very
light eyes, were such a sensation on the screen. This asymmetry might also
be said to apply to Deneuve, who is a blonde with dark eyes – an eye-catching
contrast.

Most of these beautiful stars have had a fair complexion, without any tan.
The problem with suntan is that it makes the skin appear monochrome on
the screen. A face which has not been excessively exposed to the sun will
have rosy cheeks, white forehead and natural red lips; different shades of the
skin will show through. With a bronzed complexion, however, it all comes
together and appears uniform. In any case the woman with a suntan has been
over-exploited by commercial advertising, to the point where it has become
rather a vulgar image. Yet until the 1920s women used umbrellas as protection
against the sun. It is true that sometimes an actor's role requires bronzed
skin, yet having a tan has often become an obsession to the extent of defying
all logic. Male actors today are especially inclined to fall victim to the suntan
craze. Roy Scheider, an excellent actor, always has a tan because he believes
it is becoming. But when we were filming *Still of the Night*, in which he
portrayed a New York psychiatrist, that suntan was not appropriate to the
role. Robert Benton, the director, and I had to insist that he stop sunbathing
at weekends. The same thing happened with Jack Nicholson in *Heartburn*.

Certain movie stars, international celebrities, turn out to be, in person, less
interesting than you expected, and can even seem unattractive. Is there a
secret to that improved image we see on the screen? I believe that the lens
captures their inner personality. Thanks to the close-up, the camera almost
acts as a microscope, revealing their hidden beauty.

But one should remember that even the most beautiful person in the world
has some defects. The important thing is to pinpoint such flaws and try to
minimize them, so that they will not show on the screen. For example, a very
young actress (I shan't name her) whom I had to photograph had overgrown
gums. When she laughed or smiled, they were revealed in their abundance,
giving her an almost horsy look. I became aware of this before the filming
started, so I informed the director, and the actress, since a good actress is
always ready to co-operate with the director of photography. Our job is similar
to a doctor's, who diagnoses an illness and prescribes a remedy. We spot the
defects and must do our best to hide them. In fact, most actresses are aware
of their flaws, because they know themselves well, and are grateful to us for
helping them hide such imperfections. Consequently, once they know we
know, they put themselves in our hands with confidence and let us guide
them. In this case, we advised the actress not to laugh or smile openly during
the film, but merely to smile with her eyes, Mona Lisa style. Having followed

these suggestions, she appeared incredibly beautiful on film, and in no time at all was a star.

There are other ways of hiding imperfections. One is by use of corrective make-up, a technique that is not that well known to lay people. For example, an actress with whom I worked some years ago had a very low and narrow hairline, which reduced her forehead, unbalancing the face and making her jaw look very prominent. I suggested lifting the hairline about an inch by means of hair removal. This procedure had been undergone many years before by Rita Hayworth, who had a similar problem. Her image was changed with the hair-lift and from a third-rate starlet she became the 'sex symbol' of the age. Another example of camouflage through make-up, lights and angles is Marlene Dietrich. When she started in the movies she had a rather round face, like a German peasant's. It is said that when she moved to Hollywood she asked her dentist to extract some molars; this operation served to emphasize her cheekbones. She also lost weight, as she had been asked to do. One should compare the German film *The Blue Angel* of 1930 with *The Shangai Express*, filmed in America two years later. Another method of hiding an actress's flaws is to photograph only her best angles. Some people have one profile which is better than the other; that is to say, their faces are uneven, one side quite different from the other, or the nose is not straight. If this is the case, the photographer should place the main light opposite the side towards which the nose leans, making it look straight.

But let's go back to Marlene Dietrich, who knew herself so well. Marlene thought, not without reason, that her profile was inferior to the frontal view of her face, that she had a duck nose. In love scenes, which show the profiles of the man and woman looking at each other, she always managed to face the camera, and always with a light placed in such a way as to emphasize her famous cheekbones. Since the man was in profile and she was facing the camera, she had to look at him sideways, something that later became Marlene's trademark in the movies. This sideways glance developed into her famous *femme fatale* look. This is how Dietrich, very intelligently, turned a defect into an advantage. Perhaps von Sternberg was instrumental in this. Another strategy well known by men and women in the movies, especially older ones, is to smile. A smile stretches the skin and so thus lifts the face. This is why many actors and actresses smile all the time at the cameras, even where the scene calls for no such thing.

In some cases what might be considered a flaw turns out to be an advantage. Richard Gere's eyes are quite small. I realized this right away when looking through my view-finder, during the filming of *Days of Heaven*. But I decided that, far from being a drawback, they gave him a certain animal look, penetrating and alive, that has become part of his sex appeal and has contributed to

Marlene Dietrich as Lola-Lola in *The Blue Angel* (1930)

Emil Jannings and Marlene Dietrich in *The Blue Angel*

Studio portrait of Marlene Dietrich

his success. Actors with enviably big eyes often project a beefy, boring and expressionless look, a false beauty.

It is true that the movies make people look taller than they really are. The explanation is very simple: it is because of the enlargement of dimensions as the film is projected on to the screen. Since comparisons cannot easily be made, everyone looks the same height. But if the leading man happens to be shorter than his partner, we raise him on a platform to add some inches; on the whole, feet don't show, so there is no problem. Perceived height is also linked with personality: stars with a strong personality seem taller. When I filmed my second picture with Meryl Streep, as usual there was a stand-in for the actress. Stand-ins should be at least the same height and should project a similar general demeanour, to facilitate our work in lining up the shots in the actors' absence. I began to think that Meryl's stand-in was shorter than the actress, yet after measuring her we found that she was in fact slightly taller.

It is often said that people look slightly heavier on the screen, but I believe that the notion that the camera adds 10 pounds is an exaggeration. I have no doubt that in order to be photogenic an actress doesn't have to be thin. The diet craze is misconceived. Women of yesteryear, with their curvy shapes, had a very special beauty. The advertising media have done much to promote this modern preoccupation with being almost emaciated, an image which is now all but played out. In the movie *Witness*, Kelly McGillis is a slightly plump woman by movie standards. When she appears in the nude, she looks attractively like the Venus de Milo. I believe that women should have curves. But that does not mean I approve of the present tendency towards developing muscles.

Any worthwhile director of photography will work closely with the hairstylist, costume designer and make-up expert to create that elusive image of the woman whose beauty is admired by all. In any film with a substantial budget, tests are made for the hairstyles, wardrobe and make-up. During preproduction all possibilities are explored; tests are filmed, shown in a projection room, discussed and submitted to the director and producer for approval. The tests include, of course, variations of lighting. One might find out then, for example, that an actress who has a rather round face should never have both sides of her face lighted with the same intensity, since this will make it seem wider. We will illuminate half of the face and leave the other side in semi-darkness. We might discover too, if a person has a longish face, that lighting one side only will accentuate the length; so a frontal light will have to be used. We will see that, if the actor or actress has deep-set eyes, the lights should be placed low, because if they are high the shadow of the eyebrows will not let the eyes show. This was the case with an exceptional

French actor, Jean-Pierre Léaud, with whom I have filmed four pictures. Lit properly, his eyes were his greatest asset.

One of the actresses with whom I have worked had a gorgeous face and a marvellous torso and arms, but the lower part of her body was not too well shaped. The strategy was to dress her in long, dark skirts that covered her legs, and to avoid showing her body full length. Obviously, these decisions should be taken after the tests are made. It should be stressed that in our efforts to beautify the actresses, there is no magic, no mystery – just common sense and hard work.

As director of photography I have to walk away from what a woman wants us to believe and, instead, analyse her just as she is. Many women have personalities which make men think they are beautiful, without actually being so. In my profession I have to be totally objective, going to great lengths, when I am working, to become an asexual human being, analysing people in a dispassionate manner. Very often the director, full of enthusiasm for an actor or actress, is not aware of their physical shortcomings. It is my job to point them out so that something can be done to help minimize these flaws. I am paid to do this, not just to light a scene.

There is a law which may be applied to nature, as well as to the movies, and it is that no woman's face can stand the light that comes from high above. That is why in the tropics many girls of marriageable age would go out only in the late afternoon, when the sun is low and the light has a warmer tone and is less harsh, which improves their looks. The midday light forms a shadow under the eyes, which clouds the look, and another under the nose, giving the impression of a moustache. In movie sets, as well as at home, a light that comes from the top should illuminate a plant or a painting, never a face. The most flattering lights are those from lamps set at the sides – lights that are not harsh, but soft, diffused. That is why the invention of the lampshade was so important! The spotlights or track lights that became fashionable in the 1960s are a disaster, because they emphasize all the flaws on the skin. Another classic trick is that used by the character of Blanche Dubois in *A Streetcar Named Desire*: low-key lighting to camouflage imperfections. Also effective is the use of warm-coloured lampshades like rose or amber. This unifies and hides sun blemishes and ageing and may be used in real life as well as in cinema. Candlelight is very flattering too, a fact well-known even by decorators of second-rate restaurants and nightclubs.

Which actresses from the past do I wish I could have photographed? In first place is the great Marlene Dietrich. After her I would place Louise Brooks, Hedy Lamarr, Ava Gardner, Maria Felix, Gene Tierney, Joan Crawford, Silvana Mangano, Danielle Darieux, Alida Valli and Dolores del Rio. Unfortunately, when I started working in the movies, these exquisite actresses were on their way out.

And what should be said about Katharine Hepburn? She had a difficult face, a face, as Truffaut said, to which 'one had to get used'. Her kind of beauty was not revealed immediately; but, once it was, it left an indelible impression. I don't think that Marilyn Monroe was beautiful. She had quite a few physical flaws: her eyes were too far apart, the nostrils too visible and the face rather wide. It is true that her figure was attractive, but, I repeat, her face was imperfect, even rather vulgar. Without cosmetics and her intelligence and sex appeal, Marilyn would have looked like a common country American girl. My ideal woman is the Latin type, probably because I was brought up in Spain and Cuba, where the majority of women are brunettes.

Years ago in the movies beauty was mandatory, for both actresses and actors. To become a leading lady, an actress had to be a sensational beauty; acting ability came second. Later on, realism took the movies by storm and the importance of beauty declined. Now there are lots of actors and actresses who are very ordinary looking. What is more, they don't wear as much make-up as in years past, and less attention is lavished on flattering lights.

In the past, some actresses looked as if they were held together by pins. I have heard from old make-up experts that an actress in Hollywood years ago was so thoroughly worked over that she would spend more than three hours in the make-up room before appearing on the set; the make-up used was very heavy pancake, and because it had to last the whole day it was almost like a mask. Nowadays it is much lighter. Certainly there were actresses in the past who were no beauties yet became big successes in the movies – Myriam Hopkins and Bette Davis for example. But it should be noted that they did not often play women with whom men were madly in love. Mainly they portrayed bitter spinsters or villainesses.

Nowadays there are no fixed ideals of beauty. The fashion world is the same: people tend to wear what they want. There is not just one trend, but several. Brunettes, blondes, blacks or Asians, all have their chance. This is as it should be, since there is beauty in all ages and all races. As far as the male is concerned there are screen stars who embody the archetypes like Robert Redford, Burt Reynolds or Harrison Ford, with whom the public relates and with whom men would like to identify. The image of the suave, well-dressed man represented by David Niven or Frederich March is now gone. Instead, the 'macho animal' style, made popular by Clark Gable, has prevailed.

Of the female role-models of yesteryear, that of the athletic and intelligent woman created by Katharine Hepburn has survived. The shapely, curvaceous woman has disappeared, but I believe she might make a come-back. The ingenues, Mary Pickford style, have been gone since the 1930s, when Garbo, Crawford and Dietrich came into being. The vamp too has practically disappeared from the screen. The kind of woman most prized in contemporary movies is liberated and intelligent, but somewhat neurotic. Meryl Streep and Jane Fonda personify this image: an independent woman, with inner fortitude, who at the same time is sweet and feminine and capable of falling in love.

I have been most fortunate to work with Ms Streep in four pictures. It might sound obvious, but Meryl is one of the great movie actresses of this era. She can identify with any other woman and play any kind of role. In short, she is a cinematic chameleon.

A baby seizes the universe with its eyes before doing so with its hands. The movie audience comes close to the child's visual experience. Those of us who work with the camera should aim at offering the universe to the public. A great Polish writer and movie critic, Irzykowski, has said, 'The movies are a tribute to representation.' I believe this is true. Another Polish critic, a student of the movies and an obvious Catholic, once asked me if I experienced a mystical feeling when making films. This question made me smile: if I have had any strong feelings during the creative process, they have been of an erotic nature. But it is possible that the apparent incongruity of the question derived from a difference of vocabulary. I had a very rationalist upbringing, but as a very young movie-goer I experienced some very intense visual sensations which are difficult to explain. The silent German Expressionist movies by Murnau, the images by Greg Toland in *The Grapes of Wrath* and *Citizen Kane*, or those of Edouard Tisse in *Alexander Nevsky*, gave me an immense feeling of pleasure, which I would categorize as erotic and which the Catholic critic would consider mystic. This applies in other fields too; take architecture. The houses designed by Gaudí in my neighbourhood in Barcelona, with their curved façades – which I saw everyday as I passed by – gave me an almost erotic feeling. Could this be the ecstasy which St Theresa and St John of the Cross talked about and which has perhaps been described rather too simply by the Freudian school?

Of course, I prefer to photograph women, but I don't believe this has anything to do with my sexual leanings. However, if I am capable of making them look more beautiful on the screen than they are in life, this gives me a satisfaction that no doubt has erotic connotations. I remember a close-up of a great actress, Meryl Streep, the one in cold tones prior to the flashbacks in *Sophie's Choice*. Streep threw herself into the task of creating the proper image with a lot more diligence than an actor would have brought to the task. Without disturbing her, I could say to Meryl: 'This side of your face is better. Try to get the light on your cheeks. Look slightly to the left. Lift your head a hair.' And she complied with these requests, which did not prevent her from giving an exceptional performance. Male actors are usually not as interested in such demands and some of them are even quite annoyed by them. Women have more patience and greater good will.

Irzykowski has said, 'To man the most interesting revelation of matter is

Meryl Streep in *Sophie's Choice* (1982)

Meryl Streep and Kevin Kline in *Sophie's Choice*

Meryl Streep in *Still of the Night* (1981)

his own body.' This is a surprisingly accurate statement, since the first thing one sees and feels is one's own body. In my work the human body interests me enormously as a visual exercise, particularly when 'fractioned' by the camera and by editing. I love to film necks, arms, hands, legs and feet separately. It made me very happy every time Truffaut asked me to film, close to the floor, the legs of women as they were walking – something he repeated in many films. Truffaut was fascinated by feet, as I am.

I find a man's body to be as interesting as a woman's, sometimes more so, maybe because its bone structure is more visible. This may be why in antiquity the male body was the preferred subject of sculpture. Yet nowadays, in advertising and in the movies, it is women who are most often asked to appear in the nude. I have no explanation for this – I just confine myself to stating a fact. This has been true of the women in the pictures I have filmed with Eric Rohmer: Zouzou in *Love in the Afternoon*, Haydée Politoff in *La Collectionneuse*, Arielle Dombasle in *Pauline at the Beach*. Truffaut, though, was more of a prude, though in *Anne and Muriel* there were some daring moments: it may be the picture in which Truffaut went farthest in the area of sensuality. In none of the forty-five pictures I have filmed is the body of a man shown as an aesthetic–erotic object, except, to a certain extent, Richard Gere's in *Days of Heaven* and Christopher Atkins as the adolescent in *The Blue Lagoon*.

Thanks to those two movies, incidentally, I have acquired a reputation as a landscape artist. In reality nature doesn't interest me that much. After three days in the countryside I am completely bored. What really concerns me is the human being. A natural landscape is due to chance. Nature becomes interesting to me only when it reveals the work of man. Thus I was delighted to film the scenes that take place in the wheat fields in *Days of Heaven* and in the cotton fields in *Places in the Heart*. This was because, in these scenes, the landscape was not in its pure state, but had been modified by man, through agriculture. In other words, I am interested in a river only if a bridge crosses it.

There is nothing easier than to film outdoors. Any director of photography, even the most mediocre, can film good landscapes in a movie. Not many can master lighting the simple interior of a house. It is paradoxical that very often the Oscar for cinematography is given to pictures with an abundance of landscape: for example, to my own work in *Days of Heaven* and more recently to Billy Williams in *Ghandi*. Any time a film shows lots of clouds, high mountains, crowds in open spaces, the viewers exclaim, 'What beautiful photography!' The public and even the critics often confuse landscape and crowds with photography. I believe there was a lot more creative work in *Kramer versus Kramer* or in *Sophie's Choice* than in my landscape pictures.

My favourite landscape is the human face. There I find the most fascinating mountains and valleys, the clearest lakes, the thickest forests – the sum, in fact, of all landscapes. There is nothing more exciting than to light a face. No wonder the greatest master painters of the past – Caravaggio, Rembrandt, Goya – made of this simple exercise the almost unique theme of their work.

[This extract is taken from the revised edition of Nestor Almendros's *Un Homme à la camera*, by kind permission of Hatier, Littérature Générale, Paris.]

7   My Director and I
River Phoenix

Introduction   Graham Fuller

Gus Van Sant's *My Own Private Idaho* – the title taken from a B-52 song and the story, in part, from *Henry IV, Parts I* and *II* – stars River Phoenix and Keanu Reeves as street prostitutes in Portland, Oregon: one a narcoleptic, the other a modern-day Prince Hal to a gay, Falstaffian gang leader (William Richert). The movie maintains the affinity for strung-out rebels that the thirty-eight-year-old Van Sant, a Rhode Island School of Design film graduate and former adman and Roger Corman PA, had demonstrated in his two previous films. *Mala Noche*, shot with considerable verve on 16mm for $20,000 in 1985, was the story of a convenience-store manager's forlorn passion for a Mexican migrant labourer. *Drugstore Cowboy*, probably the best picture of 1989, was an agreeably grungy and bitterly funny slice of nostalgia for the low-life junkie culture of the early 1970s that sacrificed neither the jaunty skid-row lyricism nor the raw romanticism of its predecessor.

Drugstore Cowboy's star was the newly wise, swashbuckling Matt Dillon, its patron saint William Burroughs, whose story 'The Discipline of D. E.' Van Sant had filmed in 1977, one of several shorts he made prior to his first, now forgotten featurette, *Alice in Hollywood*. Van Sant's future films include an adaptation of Tom Robbins's novel *Even Cowgirls Get the Blues* and an elliptical biopic of Andy Warhol.

Just before the cast and crew of *My Own Private Idaho* left Seattle for the final days of shooting in Rome, River Phoenix interviewed his director over the course of a day as they ate, drove and ate again. It was appropriate that the conversation should take place in transit, for Van Sant's films are nothing if not investigations of uprootedness and the spiritual quest for home – 'home', of course, always connoting far more than four walls and a roof.

In a Seattle sushi bar
RIVER PHOENIX: *In general, do you have fun?*
GUS VAN SANT: In general? Do you mean when I'm not shooting?
RP: *Specifically, do you have fun if you like something that you're working on, or do you just enjoy yourself anyway?*
GVS: No, I don't actually. I have fun sometimes when I'm not working, but when I'm working I just concentrate on the work. I guess if you get good results, then you start to have fun. But if you're not getting good results, you

Gus Van Sant

say, 'Well, how can we make this better? It's not sounding or looking right.' Then somebody says, 'What do you mean by "right"?' And you say, 'Just better.' And they go, 'Well, sorry.' So in those instances you don't have too much fun, because it seems like you can't get what you want. I get frustrated.

RP: *I see you smirking very often.*

GVS: Really?

RP: *You get a sort of perpetual-bliss glaze to your eyes.*

GVS: *During* the work?

RP: *Yeah. But it's also like a creative spark at the end of takes, say. If you're getting new ideas, your eyes kind of vibrate.*

GVS: Well, part of it's like I'm the audience sitting in a theatre. I'm not really pretending I'm in a theatre, but I'm looking at the scene as I *think* it's being shot, because I'm not looking through the camera.

RP: *Didn't you once say that you kind of slip in, like a hand into a glove – the actor being the glove – and share that sensation of being in the moment?*

GVS: Yeah. Like I'm one of the characters.

RP: *So you lose objectivity sometimes?*

GVS: Yeah, so then—

RP: *So you turn to your technical crew.*

GVS: But I'm attached to them too. See, they're also like the actors. I put myself into each of those technical positions – sound, camera – so it's confusing in a way.

RP: *Do you have a fragmented personality at the end of a day?*

GVS: No, because I'm doing it intuitively. I'm not really doing it intellectually.

RP: *As far as sitting down and applying motivation and drive to your ever-changing creative world, how do you discipline yourself? Is there any sort of philosophy that keeps you in line with that discipline?*

GVS: When I see something – a film, say – that I think is a good idea, something that I might want to do, I don't really see it as a whole. I see an image that I think represents the whole film. And so then I start to work towards that image, and then I fill it all out, and it becomes very complicated, because you have to have a lot of elements to make the image come to life. And on the way, you usually lose that one image. It becomes a new thing, a thing unto itself. You keep it going along the lines that it's got a mind of its own, and then by the end you say, 'Oh yeah, I remember the first image of this particular idea. I thought it was going to be like this black-and-white, dark thing that was set in the 1950s.' And you actually end up with a very colourful, bright story set in the 1990s.

RP: *Referring to* My Own Private Idaho?

GVS: Yeah, *Idaho* is a very good example, because it *is* very bright and colourful, and it *is* set in the 1990s. And I think the original ideas were dark and shadowy, but there's not a lot of shadow in it.

Gus Van Sant on location for *My Own Private Idaho* (1991)

River Phoenix, Gus Van Sant and the crew on location for *My Own Private Idaho*

RP: *Like there is in* Mala Noche. *So you start with a 'theme seedling', and then that sprouts into its own tree and you don't really try to trim it. You let it grow and the end result is – whatever. Do you refine it? Do you try to reroute it back to what it was?*

GVS: You refine it every step of the way. Usually I'm presented with new ideas. Like, our production designer, David Brisbin, showed up and said, 'I think that red and yellow are the colours of the film.' And I might have no conception like that myself.

RP: *Right, right.*

GVS: Except, actually, I gave him a book cover that was yellow, and *that* book cover *did* inspire the look of this film. So he was actually reacting to something. But it was a new idea to me when he said 'yellow' and based the colour scheme on pornographic bookshop storefronts, which are usually yellow, and neons . . . the city colours. So directions keep changing, because everyone's interpreting things in their own way. I know that you persuaded me against using black and white. You said, 'No, no, no. It has to be colour.' I don't know why you said that.

RP: *I wanted black and white, and, for me, colour was wrong, and that's why I thought we should try for it because otherwise we might have ended up with something that really couldn't be redone, like* Stranger Than Paradise *or* Raging Bull. *But black and white is dated in a sense, and this is a timeless picture. One of the things that I really appreciate in working with you is that in that collaborative stage you have no fear of your ego being stripped or anything. You're not possessive, like some can be, but you let all these others ideas filter through without stopping them for fear of losing control, which would be a rightful fear for someone who wants it to stay as pure as possible.*

GVS: Yeah, that whole method of allowing new contributing factors to just enter in at will is the thing that I've personally worked on. Like here, for example, if you just walk around downtown, there are things thrust in your face, like, every ten seconds. And, like a documentary, the film just absorbs that, or things that happen during rehearsal. Happy accidents, as we call them. Sometimes they're not so happy, and usually people can tell when they're not working.

RP: *All these seedlings for different projects you have –* Even Cowgirls Get the Blues, *the* Andy Warhol *film – are starting to grow. Is that really exciting for you?*

GVS: Yeah, they're inspirational; they're, like, my favourite stories. *My Own Private Idaho* might be the only one of my own stories that I ever get to tell, though of course I do have a bunch of Shakespeare in the middle of it. It's the ability to actually do something about these things now that is pretty unbelievable. I was just telling Tom [Robbins] last night that the first time I met him was at a book signing in 1984, and I was standing in a long line of people with Walt Curtis, who wrote *Mala Noche*, and we were just *fans*. And

Tom was signing books and you hoped that he'd write, like 'To Gus. Best wishes Tom'. I was a film-maker and I really wanted to make *Even Cowgirls Get the Blues* into a movie. I had made one short film from a William Burroughs story, but I had no clout or power, or any money. I probably made, on average, like $100 a week doing something or other, and so I was penniless and without a portfolio. But I said to Tom, 'If I ever get the money, I want to come back to you and do the film.' He said, 'That sounds good,' and signed the book. I figured it'd never happen, but I might as well say it. So now it's a pleasure to be able to have the kind of support to do dream things like that.

RP: *Were you interested in film at art school?*

GVS: Yeah, I majored in film. I changed from painting after my first year because I thought that maybe a career in the film business was a more moneyed career than a painter's.

RP: *[laughs] A safe assumption.*

GVS: It was a safety bail-out. But, also, films were more complicated, and I'd pretty much mastered – at least in my estimation – painting. But film-making was a big mystery, and I thought to get anywhere in the business I'd have to work really hard and forget about painting for a while. And that's what I chose to do.

RP: *Did some of your paintings – particularly your more recent ones – conceptually influence Idaho?*

GVS: Yeah, because you know those paintings are of Idaho. Idaho desert is what I'm painting. The Sawtooth Mountains and a road that leads to a house that's sometimes flying in the air and crashing to the earth. So, in a way, the story of *My Own Private Idaho* is the film version of the paintings. Because the paintings are about home, and they're about love, I guess. And they're about relationships and turmoil. Something to do with my upbringing in a middle-class family. And this is, like, the generic, box-like, red-roofed, white $17,000 home, smashing into a road. And a road symbolizes the journey of life, and the horizon is the future.

RP: *Is it later that you articulate and identify the images as symbolic? Or is it something that you think out?*

GVS: No, I think that it's something I think out after the fact. I have been obsessed with my family's house and where we lived when I was around six, which was in Colorado. Because I guess that's where I first lived, you know? That's my concept of home. Then we moved away, and I probably didn't like moving away. So then the house smashing in the road is like my destruction of the house that I miss. But when I painted the paintings, I never thought, 'Oh, I missed my childhood, and now I'm showing how that childhood has been smashed in 10 million bits' – though I can interpret them that way and then be sort of surprised.

RP: *This is getting* too *close to home.*

GVS: But the road also – there's been a lot of travelling. My family moved around a lot, about five or six times while I was a child. So the road symbolizes the journey back and forth across the country: from Colorado to Illinois, to San Francisco, to Connecticut, to Oregon.

RP: *Why did you move around so much?*

GVS: My father was making it up the corporate –

RP: *Ladder of success?*

GVS: Yeah. And he made it to president.

RP: *President of what?*

GVS: Of McGregor Doniger sportswear.

RP: *Great!*

GVS: And actually that yellow thing that you wear is a McGregor. That's very symbolic, actually, but it wasn't planned that way. McGregor windbreakers were very popular in the 1950s – I should show it in the film. Yesterday you were lying in a White Stag sleeping bag, and my father was the president of White Stag. That's why we moved to Oregon. He changed his presidency from McGregor to White Stag.

RP: *Wow. So what is your father doing now?*

GVS: He's in the fashion business – he has a women's clothing company called Intuition.

RP: *But he also does your accounting, right?*

GVS: Yeah.

RP: *Should we erase that?*

GVS: No, no. You can ask me anything.

In a van travelling to location

RP: *I had a Thai dinner the other day with some women on this shoot. On this film I've been around a lot of boys, but for variety I like sitting and listening to women talk about what they do. And I mentioned it to you afterwards: 'Well, I have some gossip about some gossip for you. And not to mention names, but these two people are trying to figure you out.' And your response was, 'What? Sexually?' And that was the first thing. But more, I guess, intellectually. Or what was your—*

GVS: What makes me go?

RP: *Yeah. Trying to figure out the Van Sant mystery.*

GVS: Is that a mystery though? See, I have no concept of what—

RP: *I know, I know. Me – I'm the same way. I mean . . . um, you just live. We're all just, like, living, hanging out, doing our thing.*

GVS: But I'm fascinated by what they said.

RP: *Me too. It was* completely *like a cliché.*

GVS: You can say that about this film here.

RP: *Oh yeah. It all came back to the film. You yourself said, 'What is Gus doing this for?' Does it bother you when people try to figure you out?*

GVS: No, not at all, because I'd like to figure *myself* out actually.

RP: *Yeah, so would I like to figure myself out. So if they can give me a clue, I'm always interested to hear.*

GVS: Right. Yeah, I'm pretty much in the dark about myself – I haven't done any psychotherapy. I don't know if that would help. I don't think that there's much to be figured out. I think that one thing about me is that I've worked pretty hard since I was twelve, and I don't know why exactly. Only on my own things, you know, which first was painting.

RP: *You started when you were twelve?*

GVS: Yeah. Some time during adolescence I just buried myself in my work. Before then, I was pretty much like a normal neighbourhood kid. So the work itself became pretty important, but it's impossible to figure out what the kind of art that I do is, because its progressed. You'd have to follow the progression and say, 'Well, he made this piece because this happened to him.'

RP: *Right. But I'm surprised by the arrogance displayed by people who try to figure you out just by looking at a piece of your work.*

GVS: Well, maybe there's people in the business who have never written or directed before, so maybe it's easier to interpret their work. There's this thing where somebody was talking about this one director they had worked for – it's gossip, really, – and they were saying, 'He became obsessed with this one actress.' He would work for *ten* hours just lighting this shot where she walked through the door. It was like this sort of cuckoo obsession.

RP: *That was true. I heard about that too.*

GVS: I think it's really cool. I mean, I can become obsessed with something, you know. So far that hasn't happened in my work, but I guess it *could* happen. I tend to be pretty professional that way and catch myself if there's *any* inkling of that kind of stuff. It's like the door shuts.

RP: *Right. How do you feel about the way women are portrayed in modern-day cinema?*

GVS: It's hard for them to find themselves, really. They're not really portrayed at all, except in a man's world.

RP: *How do you feel about that? Because in this film you have this character, Carmella, who's kind of a female cliché.*

GVS: Yeah, she's one of those.

RP: *But then you want to do* Even Cowgirls Get the Blues, *which has to be one of the first books—*

GVS: Tracing the notion of a female hero.

RP: *Right, so you're doing that, so that balances this. Some people won't know that you're doing that when they see this film and I guess it's no big deal, except I've been kind of curious about that myself. I can't imagine being an actress today. If I was a woman, I wouldn't be who I am now. I wouldn't have had the chance to grow to this point. It's like a real hard road for someone to get to be like Sissy Spacek or Meryl Streep.*

GVS: Most of the time, [a film] is from a man's point of view. You know, the female characters are one-dimensional sex objects and pieces of property, and that's what Carmella is because she's seen from the point of view of the male characters in the film. It's like she's an attractive piece of flesh, you know? Like, it's pretty innocent and first-love-ish, but it doesn't really show Carmella's side of the story. In *Cowgirls*, though, you don't really get this sex-object angle, although at the same time you can get the feeling that the writer is living in a fantasy in sex-object land. It's sort of this other world, a city of women. So, it does have that quality which doesn't cleanse it completely from the point of view of the type of feminist who might think that dead men don't rape. But the whole project is a great women's film. It's a chance to make the ultimate remake of *The Women*, which is a beautiful Cukor film from the 1930s.

RP: *How do you feel about sex in film today?*

GVS: I don't see why it's such a problem, because there's a lot of death, so —

RP: *Why should sex even be rated as something as extreme as death, or something as negative?*

GVS: No, it should be more positive. But it's the mystery. You know, men are embarrassed by sex because they don't understand it. They can come to grips with death and use it as an icon. And they can use love as an icon, or sex even, but the actual involvement of that intimate moment – the sexual moment – is somehow embarrassing, because maybe we don't understand what it is.

RP: *So what do you do about it?*

GVS: Well, in my films I just try to be aware that people don't understand it. And I just try and walk in that direction and say, 'Well, this is this.' But even when we did our scene – you know, when you were in the middle of it – it was tough to do.

RP: *Well, when it came down to it, we were just doing it. We were just, like—*

GVS: You're just trying to, like—

RP: *To fuck.*

GVS: Just to do it from the point of view of the partners involved in having sex. That's the way to get around it. And if you can get there and make the camera not a voyeur but a participant you can sometimes get away with a little more. But it's still a problem because of our own perceptions of sex. I mean, *I'm* embarrassed by certain things. Being 'bad' is part of it, although it doesn't have to be that way, and I think other cultures know that. But our culture's pretty uptight.

In an airport restaurant

RP: *What else? Let's talk about favourites.*

GVS: Yeah. What does that mean?

RP: *What's your favourite car?*

GVS: My favourite car? Well, I have a 1982 BMW 528E. And usually the car I have is my favourite car.

RP: *What's your favourite holiday of the year?*

GVS: Probably Halloween.

RP: *What's your favourite brand of coffee?*

GVS: I usually buy Medaglia d'Oro espresso.

RP: *The reason why I'm asking you your favourites is because I have none. I'm always split decision. But it's so neat to be able to hear people commit, and you're the kind of guy who can pretty much just say, 'It's my favourite.' Who's your favourite pop artist?*

GVS: I guess it would have to be Warhol. He was sort of the Capra of the pop art movement. With the Warhol project that I'm working on, I'm trying to make a correlation between early 1950s to 1960s Warhol and then intercutting that with the later Warhol of the 1980s and his relationships with the younger artists, like Jean-Michel Basquiat and Keith Haring. It dawned on me that you look a lot like Warhol did when he was, say, eighteen to twenty-five. It would be a stretch, but you could pull off playing the young Warhol.

RP: *What is your favourite colour?*

GVS: Green. It's my middle name.

RP: *What's your favourite city in America?*

GVS: Portland.

RP: *Do you have a favourite relationship that you've had. Sexual? You don't have to mention any names.*

GVS: Do I have a favourite one? Yeah. The first one was the favourite one. But not always, actually.

RP: *How old were you?*

GVS: Thirty-two.

RP: *That was your first?*

GVS: It wasn't my first sexual relationship. It was the first one that was really, like—

RP: *That you loved?*

GVS: See, I worked all those other years, so I had to catch up.

RP: *Wow, wow. What is your favourite year?*

GVS: I don't know. Probably last year.

RP: *Nineteen-ninety is my favourite year, too, which just means that it was consistent and decent and OK. What is your favourite word?*

GVS: My favourite what?

RP: *Word. Phonetically speaking. Oh, I know you have one.*

GVS: *[pauses]* God, I can't think of one.

RP: *Like 'carousel' or 'jagged'?*

GVS: I like Italian words, because they're funny. We were just in Italy, and this big truck passed us, and it was called – it was a brand name – Bindi. B-i-n-d-i. Bindi. And that was like saying Hershey's chocolate. Instead of saying 'Hershey's', they say 'Bindi'.

RP: *[laughs] What's your favourite desert?*

GVS: Um, I don't have one. Chocolate cake.

RP: *What's your favourite—*

GVS: That's all. Let's just stop.

RP: *Just one more. Who's your favourite interviewer?*

GVS: River Phoenix.

RP: *Oh, that's a good answer.*

[This interview originally appeared in *Interview* magazine in March 1991 and has been reprinted by kind permission of Brant Publications.]

Knowing Is Not Enough
           Hal Hartley

I made three short films in 1991: *Theory of Achievement, Ambition* and *Surviving Desire*. Of the three, *Surviving Desire* was something of a workshop project.

I wanted to try some new things. I wanted to make a 'featurette' which didn't necessarily utilize the narrative arc I pay so much attention to when making features. I wanted to concentrate on the fact I was creating a one-hour television programme. I wanted to choreograph a dance number and film a rock-'n'-roll band live. I wanted to use a lot of dissolves.

It feels to me that shorter films can achieve a fullness of expression and execution, while still being essentially sketchy. I appreciate that immediacy. Shorter films don't insist on resolving. They don't cry out for the rhythm of conclusion. They can merely collapse, explode or disintegrate. *Surviving Desire* falls apart.

The script for *Surviving Desire* was written over the course of about a month. The quote from Dostoevsky's *The Brothers Karamazov* had been taped to the wall over my desk for a number of weeks. My friend Sarah had given it to me in a Christmas card. Every time I read it, I was struck by the amount of useful information contained in it. In fact, almost everything I needed to know in order to live a reasonably happy and useful life was there, taped to the wall above my desk.

But 'knowing is not enough'. And, of course, not knowing doesn't help much either. This dilemma fascinates me; my own capacity for ignoring the truth while simultaneously revering it above so much else.

Surviving Desire is a celebration of a man's capacity for self-delusion. Or, to go easier on our protagonist, it is the story of a man who disregards the knowledge he possesses in favour of knowing something he finds he cannot possess. Now, this is either a profound stupidity or an awesome faith. For me, love stories are always only the outside shell of some spiritual struggle.

Surviving Desire is less a love story than it is a story of love in bad faith.

Hal Hartley

9   Surviving Desire
Hal Hartley

INT. COLLEGE CLASSROOM. DAY

JUDE *is thirty-three years old and teaches literature at an up-state college. He's rambunctious, quick-witted, charming and physically powerful.*

As the credits roll, he paces in front of his freshman Lit. class, reading from The Brothers Karamazov.

The class fidget and moan and call out rude remarks. Students walk out in a huff.

JUDE *goes on reading aloud, deeply intrigued by the passage he's reciting and totally oblivious to the ruckus in the classroom.*

JUDE: (*Reading*) I believe you are sincere . . . and good at heart. If you do not attain happiness . . . always remember that you are on the right road . . . (*A book flies by his head and hits the blackboard. He pauses, looks up, then continues*) try not to leave it. Above all, avoid falsehood . . . every kind of falsehood . . . especially falseness to yourself.

STUDENT: (*Screams*) Teach us something useful!

(JUDE *ignores him and continues.*)

JUDE: Watch over your own deceitfulness . . . look into it at every hour . . . every minute.

(*Another* STUDENT *knocks over his desk and storms out of the class.*)

Avoid being scornful . . . both to others and to yourself . . . What seems bad to you within yourself . . . will grow purer . . . by the very fact of you observing it.

VARIOUS STUDENTS: This is ridiculous! We pay money for this! You're a disgrace!

(JUDE *lifts a finger, signalling something particularly interesting in the text.*)

JUDE: Avoid fear . . . though fear is only the consequence . . . of every sort of falsehood.

(*He comes over to a particular female student,* SOFIE. *She's beautiful and conscientious, although she is a little lost.* JUDE *sits at a desk across from her and continues, occasionally looking up at her, thinking, then returning to the text.*)

Never be frightened at your own faintheartedness in attaining love. And don't be frightened overmuch at your own evil actions. (*He begins pacing again.*)

I am sorry I can say nothing more consoling to you . . . For love in
action is a harsh and dreadful thing compared with love in dreams.
Love in dreams is greedy for immediate action . . . rapidly
performed . . . and so everyone can see. Men will even give their lives
if only the ordeal does not last too long but is soon over . . . with all
looking on and applauding . . . as if on a stage. But active love . . . active
love . . . is labour . . . and fortitude.
(*Finished, he pauses, considering, then turns to the class.*) Dostoevsky.
(*One particularly irate student,* TOM, *jumps right out of his seat.*)

TOM: So what was *that* all about?

JUDE: That's what we're here to discuss!

TOM: But you never discuss anything! You just ask questions! We've been
stuck on this one paragraph for a month and a half!
(JUDE *stomps up to* TOM, *shoves him down in his seat, and thrusts the book
down in front of him.*)

JUDE: It's an important paragraph. (*Points.*) Read.
(TOM, *threatened, turns reluctantly to the page and reads aloud in an entirely
flat and uninterested tone.*)

TOM: (*Reads the same passage*)
(*As* TOM *reads,* JUDE *paces. He continually comes to rest his eyes on* SOFIE.
She is earnestly trying to concentrate and keeps looking furtively towards JUDE
for some sort of clue.
JUDE *finally comes to a stop and stands gazing openly at her from across the
room.* SOFIE *lowers her gaze.*
TOM *finishes the passage at breakneck speed.* JUDE *turns and looks at him.*)

JUDE: What do you make of that?

TOM: It's good advice, man!

JUDE: (*Not certain*) Is it?

TOM: You tell me!

JUDE: (*Honestly*) I don't know.

TOM: But you're the teacher!

JUDE: I teach literature. I don't give advice.

TOM: You're wasting our time!

JUDE: I'm asking you questions.

TOM: *We're* supposed to ask the questions! *You're* supposed to give us the
answers!
(JUDE *stops, looks at* TOM, *thinks a moment, and finally looks back out the
window.*)

JUDE: Perhaps it's not as important to know the answers as it is to ask the
questions better?

SOFIE: (*Sits forward*) There, you see. He told us something.

TOM: No, he didn't! He just asked another question!

(JUDE *looks over at* SOFIE. *He watches her a moment, then lifts his book again and reads, pondering.*)

JUDE: (*Reads*) Never be frightened at your own faintheartednesses in attaining love . . .

(TOM *jumps out of his chair and comes forward, ready to fight.*)

TOM: Stop that!

JUDE: What is Father Zosima trying to tell this woman?

TOM: I'm warning you, man!

(JUDE *lowers the book and looks straight at* TOM.)

JUDE: Is it possible to appreciate this advice if we aren't faithful?

(TOM *rushes over and grabs him by the shirt, throwing him back against the blackboard.*)

TOM: Tell me something! Tell me something right now that'll help me pass the exam!

(JUDE *shoves him away and sends him crashing through a number of desks. Still concentrating, he steps forward and finds himself, again, looking at* SOFIE.)

JUDE: What do we mean when we use the word faith?

(SOFIE *and* JUDE *just hang on one another's gazes.*

TOM *flies in from the right and tackles* JUDE. *They tumble across a desk and* JUDE *throws* TOM *up against the blackboard. They wrestle. Students flee.*

JUDE *and* TOM *throw one another around the room.*

SOFIE *leaves slowly, trailing behind, concerned, watching even as her friend drags her out into the hall.*)

INT. CAMPUS CAFE. LATER THAT DAY

JUDE *bursts into the crowded and noisy café, which is filled with students and faculty members. He pauses as he enters when he sees* SOFIE *sitting at a table with* JILL, *her friend and roommate. He holds her gaze a moment – as always, enchanted. She looks down at her coffee.*

He moves on. Across the room he approaches his friend, HENRY. *The* WAITRESS *comes up and . . .*

HENRY: Two coffees please.

(*She moves off.*

JUDE *crashes into his seat and broods, staring into the street and sighing hopelessly.* HENRY *watches him a moment, then . . .*)

You can't beat up students because they don't like Dostoevsky!

(JUDE *just looks at him, considers, then looks back out at the street.*)

JUDE: Perhaps.

(*The coffee arrives. The* WAITRESS *moves off and they settle.* HENRY *fixes*

his coffee while JUDE *just sits and stares off at* SOFIE. HENRY *sees this,*
looks over, then back at JUDE.)

HENRY: Can you give me a ride into town?

JUDE: Sure.

HENRY: (*Concerned*) Are you OK?

(JUDE *looks up at him, pauses, then sighs expansively and considers his life*
with an almost carefree bewilderment. Finally, gesturing broadly with his
arms . . .)

JUDE: The air is too cold. The sun too bright. This coffee, although I
haven't had any yet, is undoubtedly too strong. I want to lie down and
evaporate.

(*He lowers his arms and looks at his coffee.*)

HENRY: You're having a crisis of faith.

JUDE: No I'm not.

HENRY: Yes you are.

JUDE: Henry, I'm an atheist.

HENRY: Maybe you only think you're an atheist.

(JUDE *just sighs and glances back over at* SOFIE. *Then . . .*)

JUDE: I'm in pain.

HENRY: All pain is desire.

JUDE: (*Turns back*) Is that criticism or advice?

HENRY: I think it's Buddhism.

(JUDE *sits back and sighs.*)

JUDE: Henry, I'm in love.

HENRY: (*Intrigued*) No. Really?

JUDE: I think so.

HENRY: How can you tell?

JUDE: Lack of concentration.

Obsessive behaviour.

Faulty reasoning.

Erratic mood swings.

HENRY: It's not like you to go running off after young women.

JUDE: I'm not running after anyone. I'm falling towards her.

HENRY: (*Catching on*) As if you can't help yourself?

JUDE: Yes. Something like that.

HENRY: (*Sits back*) I see. I've read about this type of thing.

(JUDE *lifts his volume of Dostoevsky.*)

JUDE: And then there's this . . . (*Reads.*) Love in action is a harsh and
dreadful thing compared with love in dreams . . .

HENRY: Is this active love or a dream?

JUDE: It's a dream about to become reality.

HENRY: Name the proofs of this reality.

JUDE: A thoughtful gesture.

    A delicate smile.

    A white, slender neck.

    An earnest, inquisitive, and alluring voice.

    A graceful figure and intelligent sensual eyes.

HENRY: Describe the nature of the dream.

JUDE: Intimacy.

HENRY: Name the constituent elements of intimacy.

JUDE: Kissing.

    Caressing.

    Holding.

    Slapping.

    Shouting.

    Talking.

    Waiting.

    Sleeping.

    Crying.

    Listening.

    Hoping.

    Encouraging.

    Forgiving.

    Laughing.

    Relenting.

    (HENRY *smokes, considers, then . . .*)

HENRY: In a word, verbs.

JUDE: And therefore active.

    (*Satisfied, they stand up and shake hands.*

    They sit back down.

    JUDE *tosses back his coffee in one fell swoop. He places down his cup, and*

    sits back in his chair.)

JUDE: Now I feel better. The waitresses are suddenly prettier than when I

    first came in. The ambient chatter is less irritating. The daylight isn't

    threatening me any more. It's just there. Filling the street for no

    apparent reason. A mistake, perhaps. But, in any event, I'm not afraid.

HENRY: I'm glad to hear that.

    (JUDE *signals the* WAITRESS.)

JUDE: Check, please.

    (*The* WAITRESS *moves off.*)

HENRY: How do you proceed?

JUDE: 'To live, just move forward towards those you love.'

HENRY: An intriguing theory.

JUDE: No. An empirical truth.

HENRY: But knowledge won't help you where you're going.

JUDE: What will?

HENRY: Faith.

JUDE: You mean love.

HENRY: No. Faith.

JUDE: What's the distinction between faith and love?

HENRY: Love without faith is merely infatuation.

(JUDE *smokes and looks off, pondering.*)

JUDE: Infatuation . . . Infatuation . . . Such a beautiful word.

(HENRY *reaches over and lays a hand on* JUDE*'s shoulder.*)

HENRY: My friend, you're doomed.

JUDE: Perhaps.

(*The* WAITRESS *returns with the check.* JUDE *pays.*)

Why do you have to go to town?

HENRY: I've been thrown out of school.

JUDE: No.

HENRY: Yes.

JUDE: What happened?

HENRY: I can't pay my tuition.

JUDE: What are you going to do?

HENRY: I don't know. Maybe I'll get a job.

JUDE: Well, if there's anything I can do, just ask.

HENRY: Thanks. I'll meet you in the parking lot at three.

JUDE: OK.

(*He glances over at* SOFIE.)

Well, here goes.

(*On his way out, he approaches* SOFIE *and her friend* JILL. SOFIE *looks up from writing in her notebook and watches* JUDE *approach, stop, reconsider and finally turn around and flee the café.*

SOFIE *watches him go, then returns to her writing, as* JILL *looks up and sees* JUDE *outside on the sidewalk. He stops, pauses, then turns and comes back to the window. He glances up at* SOFIE, *then meets* JILL*'s eyes. He turns and walks away.*

JILL *watches him leave. Meanwhile,* SOFIE *is writing in her notebook, composing.*)

SOFIE: Desperate. His frustration spills . . . no . . . bursts forth . . .

JILL: That's better.

SOFIE: His frustration bursts forth into audacity. He says . . . as fast as . . . he can . . . whatever . . . he feels. (*Leans backs and reads.*) He says, as fast as he can, whatever he feels. (*Looks at* JILL, *thinks, then adds.*) He feels hurt and speaks pain.

JILL: I like that. Very direct. Passionate.

SOFIE: He feels. He concludes.

JILL: He likes you.

SOFIE: Who?

JILL: Your literature professor.

> (SOFIE *realizes, considers, then . . .*)

SOFIE: Oh. Yes. I know.

JILL: Don't get mixed up with him. People will think you sleep with him to get a better grade.

SOFIE: People are disappointing.

JILL: Let me introduce you to Mark?

SOFIE: I don't want to get involved with anyone right now.

JILL: Why not?

SOFIE: Because I'm busy. I have a lot to study. And I'm enjoying it. Working hard.

JILL: But Mark is so good-looking. And he likes you.

SOFIE: He fascinates me a little.

JILL: Mark?

SOFIE: No, my teacher.

JILL: Really?

SOFIE: There's something sort of tragic about him, don't you think? His name is Jude, like in *Jude the Obscure*.

JILL: He looks half mad.

SOFIE: (*Smiles wryly*) He's in love.

JILL: Men are pathetic.

SOFIE: I think he's kind of charming. (*Thinks, then adds*) In a way. (*Looks at her writing, pauses, then confesses.*) I write about him.

JILL: What do you write about?

SOFIE: Different things. I speculate. Study him. I'm going to write a short story with him at the centre. Or someone like him. 'Him'. That's what I'll call it. 'Him'.

> (JILL *begins collecting up her things.*)

JILL: I've got to get to class. See you later.

SOFIE: I'm doing laundry tonight.

JILL: Me too.

SOFIE: Can we split the cost of the detergent?

JILL: OK.

EXT. CITY STREET. LATER THAT DAY

JUDE *drives up and parks at the kerb. He and* HENRY *step out of the car.*

HENRY: Thanks.

JUDE: Where are you going to stay?

HENRY: I have some friends who'll put me up. See you later.

(*He looks around, then walks up the street.*)

(JUDE *watches him go, then continues on across the street, but he is assaulted by* KATIE, *a scrawny middle-aged woman who is homeless and out of her mind.*)

KATIE: Marry me? Come on, marry me. Excuse me, sir, will you take my hand in marriage?

JUDE: Come on! Get outta here! Leave me alone!

KATIE: Marry me! To love and to cherish, to love and to cherish, to love and to cherish . . .

JUDE: Come on, get out of the street. You're liable to get run over.

(*He ushers her back on to the sidewalk. Passers-by watch and stare.*)

KATIE: (*At passers-by*) What are you lookin' at! Scram! Bug off! (*Then back to Jude.*) Excuse me, sir, but allow me to be your wife. Please. To love and to cherish, to love and to cherish . . .

(JUDE *tries to give her money and she slaps it out of his hand. She jumps back, horrified.*)

KATIE: I don't want your *money*!

(JUDE *picks up the money off the street, shrugs and continues on his way.*

KATIE *makes like to ignore him, but watches him out the corner of her eye.*)

To love and to cherish to love and to cherish to love and to cherish . . .

(*Then, spotting someone new.*) Hey! You! Marry me! Come on! What are you, scared!

INT. BOOKSTORE. DAY

SOFIE *works at a large and crowded bookstore. Her job is to assist people in finding things. She is stationed in the midst of the mob, being largely ignored, and knocked to and fro by the cross-currents of human traffic.*

SOFIE: Can I help someone?

Does anybody need any help?

Does anybody need any help?

Can I help someone?

Can I help someone?

Does anybody need any help?

Does anybody need any—

(*Her* BOSS *stops near her and says something we can't hear while pointing off at* JUDE. *He is sitting on a stepladder, deep in a secluded aisle, reading. He looks like he has been there for some time.*

SOFIE *approaches. She watches him read. He looks up at her. She comes closer.*)

My manager says you've either got to buy a book or leave.

JUDE (*Pauses, then*) Listen to this. (*Reads.*) Ignorance is the necessary condition of human happiness . . . We are almost entirely ignorant of

ourselves . . . absolutely of others . . . In ignorance, we find our bliss . . .
in illusions, our happiness.
(SOFIE *just watches and considers what he reads. He looks up from his book
to her. She pauses, looks around to make sure her boss is gone, then returns
to* JUDE.)
SOFIE: I write down all those questions you ask in class.
JUDE: You do?
SOFIE: (*Looks down, concentrates*) I take them home and I re-read the chapters
you've assigned. (*Looks up.*) It helps.
JUDE: What does?
SOFIE: Asking the questions.
(JUDE *slides off the ladder, watching her, then moves to a particular shelf,
pushes aside a book and retrieves a hidden cup of coffee. He takes a sip.*)
JUDE: How?
(SOFIE *steps into the next aisle and* JUDE *follows. She keeps a look out for
the boss as she speaks.*)
SOFIE: Submitting all I read in the book to that ongoing list of questions . . .
somehow . . . it shows . . . (*Concentrates, then . . .*) It shows how . . .
consistent his concerns were. Dostoevsky.
JUDE: It does, huh?
SOFIE: Before I began asking those questions over and over again of the
text . . . I was having a hard time . . . I couldn't see what he was getting
at . . . I kept hoping he'd get back to the story.
JUDE: And then what happened?
SOFIE: The questions focused my concentration. I'm getting more out of
my reading now.
(JUDE *just stands there watching her, quietly and blankly impressed. He sees
the* BOSS *across the store and ducks, touching her shoulder and hiding her
as well.*)
JUDE: I can't say I intended to teach you anything. But I'm glad it helps.
SOFIE: But they're your questions? You asked them first.
JUDE: I asked them for different reasons.
SOFIE: What reasons?
(*He straightens up and moves to the end of the aisle. She hesitates, then
follows.* JUDE *stops, turns and throws open his arms in befuddled dismay.*)
JUDE: The books seem alive. You seem alive. This book here seems alive
too. Things a book says are having an effect on you. Me? I read. I
understand. I appreciate. But still, I'm left unchanged. I can't put into
action what it is I understand.
(*He looks at her. She waits.*)
Shouldn't knowledge provide solace?
SOFIE: I don't know.

JUDE: (*Shrugs*) Perhaps I don't understand anything.

SOFIE: (*Concerned*) Do you have anywhere to go? You've been in here for hours.

(*He stops, pauses, then turns and looks at her. Finally . . .*)

JUDE: When do you get off work?

SOFIE: Eight o'clock.

JUDE: Can I drive you back to campus?

SOFIE: No thanks. I take the bus.

JUDE: Will you have a drink with me? Before you take the bus.

(SOFIE *holds his gaze a moment, then checks over her shoulder to see if it's safe. She turns back, pauses, then . . .*)

SOFIE: Only if you leave now. My boss is going to yell at me if you don't.

JUDE: (*Leaving*) OK. The bar on the corner.

SOFIE: Do you want to buy the book?

JUDE: (*Puts in back*) No. Books don't help.

EXT. CITY STREET. LATE AFTERNOON

JUDE *steps out of a deli with a cup of coffee and a muffin. He begins to place them on the sidewalk near* KATIE, *who is still involved in her endless routine. She sees him and stops.*

KATIE: What's that?

JUDE: It's coffee and a muffin!

KATIE: (*Jumps back*) And what's this supposed to mean?

JUDE: It doesn't mean anything.

KATIE: You can't get something for nothing, you know.

JUDE: No, not usually, I suppose . . .

KATIE: Just because a guy buys a girl a cup of coffee doesn't mean she's got to jump into the sack with him!

(JUDE *shakes his head and places the coffee on the sidewalk.*)

JUDE: Look, I'm putting it over here.

KATIE: Why buy the cow when you can get the milk for free?

JUDE: What?

KATIE: That's the truth about things, mister!

(*Exasperated*, JUDE *refuses to argue.*)

JUDE: It's right over here. See it. Coffee. And a muffin.

(*He walks off. She carries on with her routine. A* PASSER-BY *approaches.*)

KATIE: Marry me?

PASSER-BY: (*Stops*) Excuse me?

KATIE: Let me be your wife.

PASSER-BY: I'm sorry.

INT. BAR. NIGHT

JUDE *is standing at the bar near the large window that looks out on to the street.*
He keeps a look out for SOFIE. *The bartender,* GUS, *approaches.*)

GUS: You waiting for someone, Professor?

JUDE: Yes. A girl.

GUS: A pretty girl?

JUDE: Yes. A pretty girl.

GUS: And young too, I imagine.

JUDE: What's it to you?

GUS: You admire her intelligence.

JUDE: As a matter of fact, yes, I do.

GUS: And you're impressed with her charming combination of unassuming
conscientiousness and girlish naivety?

(JUDE *straightens up, defensive.*)

JUDE: So? What if I am?

(GUS *shrugs and picks up a newspaper.*)

GUS: (*Browsing*) The trouble with Americans is that they always want a
tragedy with a happy ending.

(*He moves off and* JUDE *turns to see* SOFIE *enter. She approaches.*)

SOFIE: Hi.

JUDE: Want a drink?

SOFIE: A beer, please. I have to make a call.

(*She moves to the phone a few feet away.*
JUDE *signals* GUS.)

JUDE: A beer.

(GUS *walks over, checking* SOFIE *out.* JUDE *slaps him.* GUS *moves off to
pour a beer. Meanwhile . . .*)

SOFIE: (*On phone*) Jill, it's me, Sofie. I won't be back for an hour or so.
Sorry. Something came up. I'll do my laundry tomorrow. I'm at a bar.
(*She hedges.*) No. With some friends. *Girl* friends.

(JUDE *hears all this. He turns away, glaring at* GUS *as he delivers the beer.*
GUS *moves off and* SOFIE *returns. They drink, settle, then . . .*)

JUDE: Do you like your job?

SOFIE: It's OK. I get a discount on my school books. It helps. Do you like
your job?

JUDE: Not really. I'm bad at it.

SOFIE: Are you bad at it because you don't like it, or do you not like it
because you're bad at it?

JUDE: You think I'm a bad teacher?

SOFIE: I have learned things in your class.

JUDE: You're a better student than I am a teacher.

SOFIE: That's because you gave me more attention than the others.

(JUDE *pauses, looking at her, briefly stunned by her straightforwardness. Then he drinks, looks away and finally returns to her.*)

JUDE: That's true. Does it bother you?

SOFIE: (*Carefully*) No.

(*They sit there watching each other for a moment. Then* JUDE *shrugs and lights a cigarette.*)

JUDE: To tell the truth. When I feel I'm teaching well . . . when I'm making something clear . . . when I feel I'm encouraging a student to think specifically and to articulate more appropriately . . . when I feel this, I'm usually thinking of you.

(*He looks at her, she looks down, and drinks.*)

Does that embarrass you?

SOFIE: (*Nods*) A little.

JUDE: When I'm reading something that excites me, for instance, I want desperately to share it with someone. It's you I want to share it with.

SOFIE: Why me?

JUDE: It's complicated.

(*She stares at her glass, concentrating.*)

SOFIE: No it's not.

JUDE: It's not?

SOFIE: It's because you think I'm pretty.

(*He just watches her as she stares at her glass. Finally she looks right at him. He pauses, then . . .*)

JUDE: Perhaps. I'm sorry. It doesn't change the fact that I care for you.

SOFIE: You hardly know me.

JUDE: That's true. I hardly know anyone. But I know what I feel. Even if I don't know why.

(*She smiles and keeps her eye on him. Finally, he smiles too. She looks away and drinks. She takes one of his cigarettes and lights it for herself.*)

SOFIE: Would you like me to tell you something about myself?

JUDE: If you want to.

(*She smokes and looks off into the lights to think, then . . .*)

SOFIE: I appreciate being taken seriously. But I'm always concerned that I'm not sufficiently serious. (*Looks at him, then bashfully lowers her eyes.*) I know that men look at me and they think I'm all right. But I think it's contemptuous to utilize that fact in order to achieve something. (*Looks up, very concerned.*) But, if I had to, I'm afraid I might. And that bothers me. (*Thinks about this, then shrugs and sips her drink.*) I'm very curious and I'm afraid of seeming gullible. So I'm argumentative more than I think I should be.

JUDE: Why did you lie and tell your roommate you were out with someone else?

(*Now it's her turn to be surprised by straightforwardness. She looks at him a moment, perfectly still, then lowers her beer to the bar. She shrugs.*)

SOFIE: If people knew we were out together, they would say I was sleeping with you in order to get a better grade.

JUDE: But we're not.

SOFIE: Not what?

JUDE: Sleeping together.

(*She simply watches him a moment, then smiles, and puts out her cigarette. She grabs her bag, slides off the bar stool, and kisses* JUDE *on the lips.*)

SOFIE: Not yet, anyway.

(*She leaves.* JUDE *watches her go, stunned.*)

EXT. STREET. EVENING

JUDE *swaggers out of the bar and skips gracefully out into the street, gradually breaking into a shuffling dance step. Two other men fall into step with him. Together they perform a musical dance number as they move up the street.*

They reach the corner and go their separate ways, walking normally.

INT. SOFIE'S APARTMENT. NIGHT

As SOFIE *enters, her roommate,* JILL, *is staring at the TV set watching MTV, and eating ice-cream. Her books are scattered about her.*

Throughout this scene the two girls continually move about, involving themselves in, alternately, watching TV, browsing through fashion mags, studying, checking themselves in the mirror, and getting more soda and ice-cream from the fridge. A sort of haphazard dance.

SOFIE: I don't like this song.

JILL: I love the video.

SOFIE: Can you turn it down? I have to study?

JILL: (*Turns it down*) That guy called again.

SOFIE: What guy?

JILL: You know the one.

SOFIE: The one you like?

JILL: With the long hair.

SOFIE: Did he ask you out?

JILL: Yes. But I said I was busy.

SOFIE: Do you think he'll call back?

JILL: Definitely.

SOFIE: (*Watching TV*) I wish I had legs like hers.

JILL: I wish my breasts were smaller.

SOFIE: (*Of mag ad*) Do you like this dress?

JILL: I like that one better.

SOFIE: I want to write a novel.

JILL: Now?
SOFIE: No. Someday.

INT. BOOKSTORE. DAY
SOFIE *is working.*
SOFIE: Can I help someone? Does anybody need any assistance? Can I help someone? Does anybody need any help? Can I help someone?
(*No one pays any attention to her, so she glances around, furtively, and moves off into a side aisle.*
JUDE *is there in an appropriately obscure section of the store, reading.*
SOFIE *comes over and kisses him.*)
JUDE: You weren't in class today.
SOFIE: I missed you.
JUDE: I missed you too. It was terrible. I didn't know what to do.
SOFIE: I overslept.
JUDE: My class is at two o'clock in the afternoon.
SOFIE: Let's not argue.
JUDE: I'm not arguing. I'm concerned. Are you eating all right?
SOFIE: Look. I'm a grown-up person.
(*This stops him. He kisses her. Then . . .*)
JUDE: Can I see you tonight?
SOFIE: Perhaps.
JUDE: What's that supposed to mean?
SOFIE: It's what *you* always say.
JUDE: Is it?
SOFIE: Yes. 'Perhaps'.
JUDE: When do I say that?
SOFIE: Well, for instance, whenever you don't want to admit that you're wrong. You always look away and say 'perhaps'.
JUDE: No I don't.
SOFIE: Yes you do.
JUDE: I always admit when I'm wrong.
SOFIE: That's not true.
JUDE: Yes it is. I cherish my flaws.
SOFIE: Ah, you see. That's another thing you always do.
JUDE: What is?
SOFIE: Whenever you're losing an argument, you always depict yourself as hopelessly incompetent – as if humbly admitting your shortcomings somehow places you above the argument in hand, therefore negating the other person's point of view entirely.
JUDE: You're pretty thorough.
SOFIE: Honestly observant.

JUDE: I'm terribly flattered.

SOFIE: I'll make a note of that.

JUDE: You haven't answered my question.

SOFIE: What question is that?

JUDE: Can I see you tonight?

SOFIE: Perhaps.

> (*She kisses him and hurries off.*)
>
> I've got to go! Call me!
>
> (*She goes back to work and he sits there, befuddled, but charmed. He looks up the aisle and sees* HENRY *leaning against a book rack, reading. He wears a tie and has a little name tag on.* JUDE *approaches.*)

JUDE: Henry?

HENRY: Oh hi, Jude.

JUDE: What are you doing here?

HENRY: I work here now.

JUDE: No kidding.

HENRY: Yeah, it's a great job. All these books. The boss doesn't like me. But I've always had a problem with authority. What are you doing here?

JUDE: I came to see Sofie.

HENRY: Ah, Sofie. Sophia. That's Greek, you know. Means 'to know'.

JUDE: I'll keep that in mind.

HENRY: It could be significant.

> (*They go out back.*)

EXT. ALLEY BEHIND STORE. DAY

JUDE *helps* HENRY *move boxes of new books.*

HENRY: But she's got a boyfriend.

JUDE: No she doesn't.

HENRY: She does. Lots of them. They're in here everyday. She flirts with them.

JUDE: She would have told me if she were involved with someone.

HENRY: Why?

JUDE: Why what?

HENRY: Why would she have told you?

JUDE: Because she would have wanted me to know. We are close, you know.

HENRY: How close?

JUDE: Close.

HENRY: Do you sleep together?

JUDE: Well, no. Not yet.

HENRY: So you're just friends.

JUDE: We're a little bit more than friends.

HENRY: You're deluding yourself, Jude.

JUDE: You don't know anything about it.

HENRY: A man will throw away all his hard-won wisdom, toss away years of acquired knowledge, all for what? A pretty face.

JUDE: Well, what has all your diligent asceticism and years of conscientious intellectual enquiry got you? Huh? A job in a second-hand book store.

HENRY: Peace of mind! (*Considers, then...*) Or at least something approximating peace of mind.

JUDE: You don't live in the real world, Henry. You live in books and ideas. You're a victim of theoretical abstraction.

HENRY: Hey, I struggle with my demons as much as you.

JUDE: But are they really demons?

HENRY: All distractions are demons.

JUDE: You know, my biggest fear is this: that all my studying, all my hard work, all my good intentions, have in fact been nothing but the building of a wall between me and life.

HENRY: Exactly. You must withdraw from life.

JUDE: No. I want to embrace life.

HENRY: To know about life, sometimes you have to step away from it.
(JUDE *lifts a book he finds and reads from it.*)

JUDE: Oh great. Listen to this. 'Yet, every now and then, there would pass a young girl, slender, fair and desirable, arousing in young men a not ignoble desire to possess her, and stirring in old men regrets for ecstasy not seized and now for ever past.'

EXT. STREET. THAT EVENING

A STREET MUSICIAN *serenades a* YOUNG WOMAN *in a window two floors above the street.*

JUDE *comes walking by and crosses the street. He enters a public telephone and starts looking for a quarter.*

INT. SOFIE'S APARTMENT. SAME TIME

SOFIE *is composing sentences and eating at the table, while* JILL *watches MTV and tries to decide what to wear.*

SOFIE: (*Writing*) He is quiet... yet opinionated. Powerful, but shy...

JILL: I need new clothes.

SOFIE: (*Writing*) Thoughtful and impetuous.

JILL: I hate this video.

SOFIE: I like the song.

JILL: The lead singer is hot.

SOFIE: He looks mean and insensitive.

JILL: Do you think I should make my hair blonde?

SOFIE: Not until summer.

JILL: I want to lose weight.

SOFIE: Was Marguerite Duras a lesbian?

JILL: God, I hope Mark calls me back.

SOFIE: (*Writing*) He is solemn despite himself. Reckless and hell-bent, but frightened of his own fearlessness.

(*The phone rings.*)

JILL: That's a paradox.

(SOFIE *moves to the phone and answers.*)

SOFIE: Hello?

(*Recognition, a quick, nervous glance over at* JILL.)

It's my mother. (*Ducks into the bathroom.*) How are you?

EXT. PAY PHONE/SOFIE'S APARTMENT. SAME TIME

JUDE *shoos away a young* PROFESSIONAL *and his* GIRLFRIEND *who are anxious for the phone. Then* . . .

JUDE: (*Into phone*) I'm excited. Too excited to sleep,

SOFIE: Where are you?

JUDE: On the street.

SOFIE: In town?

JUDE: I've been walking for hours. I had to walk. I think I'll walk all night. Why don't you come out and walk with me?

SOFIE: What's come over you?

JUDE: I can't get you out of my head. I'll drive up to campus and pick you up. We'll stay out all night.

(SOFIE *laughs, delighted, but tries to be sensible.*)

SOFIE: I can't.

JUDE: Why not?

SOFIE: I've got to study. I've got classes tomorrow.

JUDE: I wrote a poem for you.

SOFIE: A poem?

JUDE: Yeah.

SOFIE: Really?

JUDE: I was in a bar. I was possessed. Inspired beyond belief. I grabbed a napkin and scrawled it out in one huge burst of creativity. It was a beautiful poem. But I spilt my beer on it and now I can't remember how it went.

(SOFIE *peeks out through the bathroom door to check on* JILL. *She closes the door again and speaks, hushed, into the phone.*)

SOFIE: Meet me at the café in an hour.

INT. CAFÉ. NIGHT

The place is populated with the sparse remains of a busy night. Drunken young men arguing and spilling their drinks, couples kissing in corners, and waitresses wearily cleaning up.

JUDE *is at the counter having a coffee.* HENRY *stumbles up to him, drunk.*

HENRY: Jude, I've decided. I'm joining the priesthood.

JUDE: You always say that when you've had too much to drink.

HENRY: But this time I mean it!

JUDE: What about your job at the book store?

HENRY: I got fired.

JUDE: Jesus, Henry, a monastery is probably just the place for you.

HENRY: You think so?

JUDE: You're socially retarded.

HENRY: I march to the beat of a different drummer.

JUDE: Have you got any money?

HENRY: I don't need money! I've got conviction!

(JUDE *slips a twenty into Henry's coat pocket.*)

JUDE: Well, this will help sustain your conviction.

HENRY: You know, that's your problem Jude, you don't believe in anything.

JUDE: Is that a problem?

HENRY: Sure it is.

JUDE: It seems to me that it's the people who believe in things who are always the most problematic.

HENRY: How do you mean?

(JUDE *takes his coffee and moves away from the counter.*)

JUDE: People who bomb embassies usually insist that they believe in things. (*Sips his coffee and peers out into the streets for* SOFIE.) Rival terrorist organizations machine-gun women and children in supermarkets because they believe in things. (*Turns back in and lifts a newspaper off a table.*) Elected officials close down hospitals and vote for increases in the defence budget *usually* because they believe in things. (*Turns away and smokes, then . . .*) No. I'd rather not believe in things.

HENRY: But what's the alternative? Man can't live without faith.

JUDE: He can live without faith. He can't live without understanding. Faith comes after understanding.

HENRY: How do you suppose one gains understanding?

JUDE: Through experience.

HENRY: (*Poking him*) Ha! You want to achieve a spiritual end with materialistic means!

JUDE: Henry, leave me alone! You're drunk!

HENRY: You won't listen to reason!

(JUDE *sees* SOFIE *coming across the street.*)

JUDE: No! I won't listen to reason! Not tonight!

(HENRY *throws himself before him.*)

HENRY: But you must!

JUDE: (*Grabs him*) Don't try and stop me, Henry!

HENRY: You'll never survive this!

JUDE: How do you know? And besides . . . (*Turns and watches as* SOFIE *enters the café*) I don't know if I want to.

(*And then they all turn to watch as* SOFIE *enters. She's gorgeous.* JUDE *stands and slowly moves to her.*

Dissolve to:)

INT. JUDE'S APARTMENT. NIGHT

JUDE *and* SOFIE *kiss passionately and slowly part in the dim reflecting lights from the streets below. They look into one another's eyes for a moment, then* JUDE *stumbles away and falls over a table. He splashes into an armchair and sits listlessly, sighing hugely.*

SOFIE *comes over and leans down beside him.*

SOFIE: Are you OK?

JUDE: I don't know. Maybe. I'll never be the same again. But who cares. Kiss me.

(*They kiss again. As they do, he stands up, lifting her with him as he does. Then, parting, he pauses, just looking at her.*)

Why did you tell your roommate that it was your mother on the phone?

(*She rolls her eyes.*)

SOFIE: I told you why?

JUDE: But now it's different.

SOFIE: How is it different?

JUDE: It's understood that you're not here in order to get a better grade.

(*Waits, then . . .*) Isn't it?

(*She moves away and thinks.*)

SOFIE: It is between us.

JUDE: No one else matters.

(*She bites her lip, frustrated, then sighs. She waits, then . . .*)

SOFIE: I'm embarrassed.

JUDE: Of me?

(*She shakes her head to and fro, then looks at the floor and struggles for words. Finally . . .*)

SOFIE: I don't want to seem like somebody I'm not.

JUDE: To whom?

SOFIE: To myself.

(JUDE *crosses the room and sits with his elbows on his knees, flipping idly through the pages of some books scattered around.*

She watches him, waiting. Then . . .)
JUDE: You should go.
SOFIE: I don't want to.
JUDE: You don't know why you're here.
SOFIE: People often do things they don't understand. That doesn't make
    them less genuine.
    (*He looks over at her, impressed. He shrugs, agreeing.*)
JUDE: Maybe.
SOFIE: Do you want me to go?
    (*He watches her a moment, then . . .*)
JUDE: No.
SOFIE: Are you sure?
JUDE: Yes.
SOFIE: I'm going to undress.
JUDE: OK.
    (*He watches her as she stands and begins to undress. He looks on. She starts
    to take off coat, but . . .*)
SOFIE: Do you think I'm very beautiful?
JUDE: Yes.
    (*She takes off coat, then pauses . . .*)
SOFIE: If you never see me again after tonight will you be sad?
JUDE: Don't worry about it.
    (*She sits with him.*)
SOFIE: Yes, but will, you know, will you be (*Pause*) tortured by the memory
    of having been with me? Of having caressed me?
    (*She looks away.* JUDE *stares at her.*)
    Will you wonder if I'm with other men? Will you be jealous? Will you
    become obsessed? Will you carry your disappointment around with
    you for ever?
    (*He rolls his eyes and walks into the kitchen for a beer.*)
    Will you be maudlin and anti-social? Will you get into fights? Will you
    expect other women to be somehow more like me? The way I wear my
    hair? My mouth? My eyes? Will you? Will you be like that, you think?
    (JUDE *doesn't answer right away. He stares at her, captivated, as her tights
    flutter past him to the floor. Then . . .*)
JUDE: Perhaps.
SOFIE: It's the nature of things, you know: regret.
    (*The last of her clothes are tossed to the floor at his feet. He is gazing helplessly
    at her body.*)
JUDE: I'll risk it.
    (*He rises slowly from the chair, mesmermized, and moves off towards her.*)

EXT. STREET. NIGHT

HENRY *is wandering along, still drunk, when he bumps into* KATIE.

KATIE: Will you marry me?

HENRY: Marry you?

KATIE: Please.

HENRY: Why do you want to marry me?

KATIE: Why not?

HENRY: Well, I could think of a lot of reasons if I weren't so drunk.

KATIE: Why are you drunk?

HENRY: Oh, I don't know. The nights are too long.

KATIE: The nights are too long because you have no one to share them with.

HENRY: (*Pauses, impressed*) That's a very compassionate way of putting it.

KATIE: Marry me.

HENRY: But I don't know you.

KATIE: Oh, what does that matter? Does anyone ever really know anyone else?

HENRY: That's a good point. I'd go a step further and ask: does anyone ever really know *themselves*?

KATIE: Exactly!

HENRY: What's your name?

KATIE: Katie.

HENRY: (*Shakes her hand*) Glad to meet you, Katie. Henry.

KATIE: How are you, Henry?

HENRY: Wasted.

KATIE: So what do you say? Will you marry me?

HENRY: Well, I doubt if we can be married right here in the middle of the night.

KATIE: We could if we were in Reno. God, I wish we lived in Reno!

HENRY: Let's sleep on it.

(*She jumps away from him, angry.*)

KATIE: No way, mister! Why buy the cow when you can get the milk for free!

HENRY: What?

KATIE: You know what I mean!

HENRY: We don't have to sleep on it *together*.

(*Now she's worried.*)

KATIE: Why, don't you think I'm beautiful?

HENRY: Katie, you're a goddess!

KATIE: (*Sceptical*) Listen, pal, don't waste my time! There are plenty of men out there who'd die trying to marry me!

HENRY: I don't doubt it. Listen, why don't we just get engaged for the time being?

KATIE: Engaged, huh!

HENRY: Yeah. That way maybe I can find us a place to live and everything. Get set up right and proper.

KATIE: Don't you have a place to live now?

HENRY: Well, not exactly.

KATIE: What about a ring?

HENRY: Ring?

KATIE: A ring! If we're gonna get engaged you gotta give me a ring.

HENRY: Oh. Right. A ring. (*Takes a ring off his finger.*) Here. It's my college ring. I wear it on my pinky, but it'll fit on your ring finger.

KATIE: God, it's beautiful!

HENRY: It's a little big on you.

KATIE: It's just perfect, Henry. Thank you.

HENRY: It's worth it to see you smile like that, Katie.

KATIE: So, do you have a job?

(HENRY *hems and haws, then . . .*)

HENRY: A job? Well, no. Not at the moment. I've been working on my PhD.

KATIE: You're a doctor?

HENRY: Of theology. Almost.

KATIE: What will you do when you get out of school?

HENRY: I don't know. I've been in school all my life. I don't know how to do anything.

(*She steps away and folds her arms, indignant.*)

KATIE: Well, I hope you don't expect me to go out and support you.

(HENRY *throws up his hands and shouts.*)

HENRY: Already with the nagging! (*Turns away and hangs his head.*) What a tortuous path I've made for myself, shackling myself to you!

(KATIE *falls against the building and sobs.*)

KATIE: Oh, I'm so afraid I've made a mistake!

(*Now he feels guilty. So he goes on over and embraces her.*)

HENRY: Don't be so upset, Katie. All newlyweds have these little battles. We'll survive.

KATIE: You think so?

HENRY: Absolutely.

KATIE: You're a good man, Henry.

HENRY: Come on, let's go home and get some sleep.

KATIE: OK. I know a place.

HENRY: Good.

(*They walk away together, arm in arm.*)

INT. JUDE'S APARTMENT. MORNING
JUDE *is sleeping in bed.*
SOFIE *sits on the edge of the bed, wrapped in a sheet. She wipes sleep from her eyes and looks around at the apartment.*
She gets up and moves around the room, casually investigating. She looks at his books, glances at some papers on his desk and reads a postcard she finds on the window sill.
She lights a cigarette and wanders into the kitchen. She checks the fridge, but it's empty except for one can of beer and a half-eaten sandwich.
She stands in the kitchen doorway and smokes. She watches JUDE *sleep. Then she goes to her bag and takes out her notebook. She sits at his desk, uncaps her pen and pauses, thinking. Finally . . .*
SOFIE: (*Whispers, writing*) His weaknesses are endearing. His strengths
    threaten to eclipse my own self-confidence. (*Thinks, smokes, pauses,*
    then . . .) He eats out a lot.

EXT. JUDE'S BUILDING. MORNING
SOFIE *comes creeping furtively out of the building, looking around to make sure she's not seen. She gets down to the sidewalk and hurries along.*

EXT. STREET. SAME TIME
HENRY *is walking slowly up the street, tired and hungover. He straightens his coat, knocks dust off it and looks around. He is not sure where he is or how he got there. He decides on a direction and starts up the street.*
He reaches the corner and SOFIE *steps out of the side street. They both stop, recognizing each other.*
HENRY: Hey, aren't you . . .
SOFIE: (*Continues on*) No.
HENRY: But last night . . .
    (*She stops, scared.*)
SOFIE: I don't know him.
    (*And she runs off.*
    HENRY *watches her go, bewildered, then goes on his way.*)

INT. JUDE'S APARTMENT. MOMENTS LATER
JUDE *is making coffee as* HENRY *enters.*
HENRY: I just saw your girlfriend.
JUDE: Sofie?
HENRY: She claims not to know you.
JUDE: (*Depressed*) No?
HENRY: I'm afraid so.
    (JUDE *sits and hangs his head.* HENRY *places a hand on his shoulder.*)

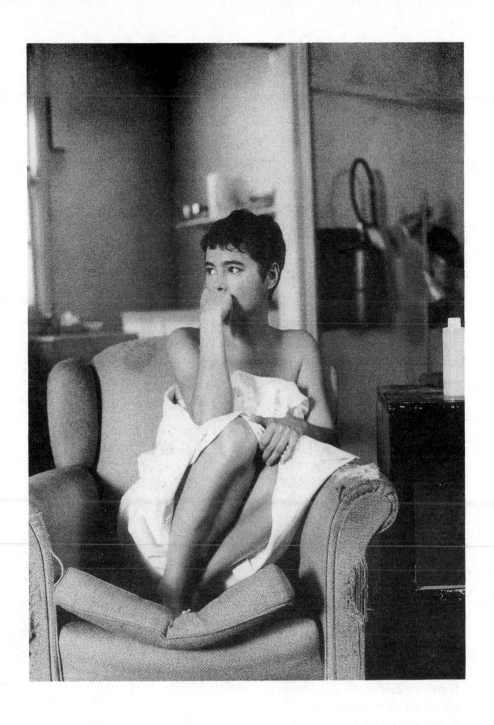

JUDE: I don't understand.

HENRY: There's nothing to understand. We're animals and Eros is a bad and fickle little godhead. (*Then, of toaster . . .*) Does this thing still work?

(JUDE *looks over at the toaster, considers, then turns back.*)

JUDE: I feel foolish.

HENRY: Today is the first day of spring.

JUDE: That's no consolation.

HENRY: Boy, I must've been hammered last night. I woke up in a strange apartment. (*Looks at his hand.*) And I've lost my college ring.

(JUDE *just looks at him, then drops his gaze to the floor again.*)

JUDE: Eat your toast and get out.

HENRY: No love is free.

JUDE: What?

HENRY: Freud said that.

JUDE: Don't start, Henry.

HENRY: I heard a fascinating statement in a movie last night.

JUDE: You don't seem to be aware of the pain I'm experiencing.

HENRY: Excuse me?

JUDE: Forget it.

HENRY: It's Biblical.

JUDE: What is?

HENRY: This statement. 'Love does not discriminate.'

JUDE: I don't follow.

HENRY: 'And the people asked him, saying, what shall we do then?'

JUDE: That's Luke.

HENRY: Chapter three, verse ten.

JUDE: So?

HENRY: 'And the apostle replies; love and cherish, unquestioningly, whoever happens to be before you. Love does not discriminate.'

JUDE: I'm no apostle, Henry.

HENRY: Take it easy, it was just something I heard in a movie.

JUDE: Listen pal, you just can't waltz in here, use my toaster and spout universal truths without qualification!

(HENRY *smells something.*)

HENRY: What's that?

JUDE: What?

HENRY: You smell that?

JUDE: Oh yeah.

HENRY: (*Sniffs*) She's left her fragrance here.

JUDE: That's it. Get out!

HENRY: What about my toast?

JUDE: Get out!

> (HENRY *gets up and storms out.*
> JUDE *sits and concentrates on Sofie's smell in the room.*
> *The toast pops up.*
> *He looks over at it, pauses, then presses it back down. He holds the button down until the toast starts burning. He wafts the smoke out into the room.*)

EXT. JUDE'S CAR. DAY
JUDE *drives to school, grim, determined, fast.*

INT. CAFÉ. DAY
JUDE *comes in, sees* SOFIE, *and moves to her.*
She is at a table, scribbling in her notebook. There is a GUY *sitting at the table with her, sipping coffee.*
JUDE *comes over and the* GUY *looks up.*
JUDE: Scram.
GUY: What?

> (JUDE *grabs him by the collar and throws him out of the way.*
> SOFIE, *looking up from under as she curls over her notebook, nearly dies of embarrassment.*
> JUDE *sits. He notices the guy's coffee and tastes it. He sits there and lights a cigarette, not even looking at* SOFIE.
> *She waits for a moment, then just shakes her head in disgust.*)

SOFIE: Why did you do that?
JUDE: I'm upset, I guess.
SOFIE: Idiot.
JUDE: Why do you deny me?

> (*She just stares him down a moment, then sighs and looks at the table. She pauses and thinks, then . . .*)

SOFIE: I don't want to get involved with anyone right now. I'm busy. Studying. I like it. Working hard. (*She looks up at him, expecting a reply, but there is none. Then . . .*) Why do you need what's between us to be seen?

JUDE: (*After a while*) I don't. I need it to be acknowledged.

> (*Frustrated, she hides her face and closes her eyes.*)

SOFIE: This is embarrassing.

> (*He sees the book open before her.*)

JUDE: What are you writing?

> (*She glares at him for a second, furious and terribly conscious of the other people sitting around. Finally, she pulls her book up and looks at what she has written.*)

SOFIE: It's part of a story.

JUDE: Can I hear it?

SOFIE: (*Reads*) He is desperate. And his frustration mounts to overflowing before giving way to his final and audacious mistake. Finally, he caves in, gives up and takes what is offered. Because he knows he can. Because he knows he wants. He lacks faith and therefore patience. The giving of himself has left him empty and old before his time.
(*She looks at him, defiantly. He nods, smokes, looks away, thinks, then . . .*)

JUDE: Interesting. But I think it should be a woman.
(*She still just watches him, but then what he has said sinks in. She looks down at the page. He waits.*)
What do you think?
(*She looks up at him again, uneasy. She returns to the page and reads.*)

SOFIE: (*Reads*) She is desperate. And her frustration mounts to overflowing before giving way to her final and audacious mistake. Finally, she caves in, gives up and takes what is offered. Because she knows she can. Because she knows she wants. She lacks faith and therefore patience. The giving of herself has left her empty and old before her time.

JUDE: I like that better.
(*She sighs and looks up at him, depressed. He watches her, softening.*)
Will I see you again?
(*She just stares at the table, then . . .*)

SOFIE: I don't know.
(*He leans over the table towards her, affectionately, wanting to comfort her. His hand reaches out to touch hers, but stops when . . .*)
Please don't.
(*He freezes. She darts a glance around at the café then lowers her eyes again. JUDE pauses, then jumps up and knocks over the table. He storms out.*)

EXT. STREET. DAY

JUDE *stalks by, then sees* KATIE *across the street. He stops, pauses, then walks over to her. She is admiring her engagement ring.*

JUDE: Excuse me, Miss.

KATIE: What do you want?

JUDE: I want you to be my wife.

KATIE: What?

JUDE: I mean it. Marry me. Please.
(*She just looks at him with a frown, then . . .*)

KATIE: Why should I marry you?

JUDE: Well, why not me?

KATIE: Listen, mister, I'm already engaged! See! This is my engagement ring!

JUDE: That's not an engagement ring. It's a college ring. And it belongs to
my friend Henry.

KATIE: Back off, pal! I don't know anyone named Henry! This is an
engagement ring! A significant emblem! A potent piece of jewellery!
And it's mine!

JUDE: I thought you wanted to get married?

(*She stares at him, then takes a few steps away, thinking hard. Finally, she
clutches her ring to her chest and looks back over her shoulder at* JUDE.)

KATIE: I just wanted somebody to ask.

INT. CLASSROOM. DAY

JUDE *stands before the class, leaning back on the blackboard, brooding. The class
waits and watches him anxiously. He looks towards the windows, thinks, shrugs off
a thought, then folds his arms across his chest and broods even more.*

SOFIE *sits scribbling on the cover of her notebook, casting dark glances up from under
at* JUDE.

Finally, JUDE *turns slowly and lifts a piece of chalk. The class sits a little forward,
as one, expectantly.* JUDE *drags the chalk across the board, writing something very
slowly while he begins to speak.*

JUDE: Fyodor Mikhailovich Dostoevsky. (*A big sigh, then . . .*) Born in
Moscow in 1821. (*Stands back and sizes up the space on the blackboard,
then goes back to work.*) His father was a drunken brute of an army
surgeon who treated his serfs horribly. So they murdered him by pouring
vodka down his throat until he gagged.

(*Students, just look at one another, wondering.*)

Fyodor had some success with his first novel. Then he was arrested
for subversion against the Tsar. After eight months in solitary
confinement, he was led before a firing squad. (*He tosses away the small
bit of chalk he has and looks around for another.*) He stood there in a
death shroud, facing an open and hastily dug grave, awaiting his
execution.

(SOFIE *is grimly scribbling on the cover of her notebook, glaring up at* JUDE'*s
back every few moments or so.*)

Then someone decided he didn't have to be shot. So for the next four
or five years he did hard labour in some cold Siberian prison. (*Takes
a step back to appraise his work thus far.*) It was there in Siberia that he
began to suffer from epilepsy.

(*A* GIRL *breaks out in tears and runs from the room.* JUDE *watches her go,
pauses, then returns to the board.*)

Finally, ten years after he had been dragged away in chains, he returned
to St Petersburg. He converted to a conservative and profoundly
religious philosophy. But, nevertheless, he was utterly destitute, an

alcoholic and a compulsive gambler. He married Anna Snitkina and wrote at least four of the greatest novels in history.
(*Finished, he lays down his chalk, ponders the phrase he has written, then steps away. The inscription reads 'Knowing is not enough.' He sits at a desk among the students and stares at the floor. The students watch him silently.* SOFIE *has stopped her scribbling and watches his back from where she sits far across the room.*
Finally JUDE *lifts his head and gazes out of the window.*)
I have nothing to say. I can't teach you anything. Class dismissed.
(*No immediate response. The class just sits there watching him.*
Dissolve to:
Moments later. JUDE *is still sitting there. The students have all gone. Only* SOFIE *is still at her desk. They sit there, saying nothing and looking at nothing.*
Dissolve to:
SOFIE *is gone now.*
Left alone, JUDE *looks up and contemplates the phrase on the blackboard:* 'Knowing is not enough.' *Dissolve to:*)

EXT. HIGHWAY. DAY
JUDE *driving, fierce and reckless.*

EXT. CITY STREET. DAY
JUDE *comes tearing around the corner and screeches to a halt. He stumbles from the car and staggers across the street, like he's been shot. But as he stumbles along, he straightens up and walks normally.*
Then he attempts to break into his little 'dance'. But it doesn't work. He tries again, but seems to forget the steps. He stops and thinks. A strange MAN *walks by, looking at* JUDE *like he's mad.*
JUDE *continues on . . .*

EXT. ANOTHER STREET. DAY
JUDE *walks wearily along. He's in an unfamiliar part of the city and the streets are deserted. He slows up . . . Begins to sway back and forth as he walks . . . He falls to his knees slowly, dramatically . . . He crawls to the edge of the sidewalk and lays himself down on his back, his head tumbling back into the street.*
He lies there, with his head near a sewer grate, listening to the water trickle by beside him. He closes his eyes. Then somebody approaches and leans down over him, placing their hands on his chest.
BRENNEN: Excuse me, mister, are you all right?
JUDE: Knowing is not enough and not knowing doesn't help.
BRENNEN: Excuse me?

(JUDE *waits, then sighs wearily. Finally, he opens his eyes and looks up at* BRENNEN, *an out-of-towner.* JUDE *waits a moment, then lays back his head and closes his eyes again.*)

JUDE: Yes. I'll be OK. Just let me rest my head here in the gutter for five or ten minutes and I'll be all right.

(BRENNEN *waits a moment longer to make sure, then moves on.* JUDE *just lies there in blissful abandonment.*

BRENNEN *returns.*)

BRENNEN: Excuse me.

JUDE: (*Looks up*) Yes?

BRENNEN: Can you tell me how to get down to the river?

(JUDE *waits a moment, thinking, then lifts his head and considers. He casts a glance up one street and then back down at another. Finally, he leans up on his elbow and points up the street, explaining and giving directions, apparently forgetting his despair.*

We can't hear what he says. We hear:)

SOFIE: (*off*) Can I help someone?
Does anybody need any help?
Does anybody need any help?
Can I help someone?

INT. BOOKSTORE. DAY

SOFIE *does her job. People push and shove themselves by in all directions around her.*

SOFIE: Can I help someone? Does anybody need any help?
Does anybody need any help?
Can I help someone?
Can I help someone?
Does anybody need any help?
Does anybody need any help?
Can I help someone . . .
(*Cut to black.*)

The End

10   Losing Touch
           In memoriam George Cukor,
           died 24 January 1983
           Tony Harrison

The contract strip taken in 1975
during the filming of an
adaptation of Maeterlinck's play
The Blue Bird.

The Blue Bird was an American–
Russian co-production starring
Elizabeth Taylor, Jane Fonda,
Ava Gardner and Oleg Popov.

Tony Harrison wrote the lyrics
for the songs in the film.

George Cukor used to send
Tony Harrison contact strips
with scribbled notes. He wrote
on the back of this strip:
frame 1 'a character' and
frame 2 'the brooding poet'.

The top picture was used by
The Times in their obituary
of George Cukor on Wednesday,
26 January 1983.

I watch a siskin swinging back and forth
on the nut-net, enjoying lunchtime sun
unusual this time of year up north
and listening to the news at five past one.

As people not in constant contact do
we'd lost touch, but I thought of you, old friend
and sent a postcard now and then. I knew
the sentence starting with your name would end
'the Hollywood director, died today'.

You're leaning forward in your black beret
from *The Times* obituary, and I'd add
the background of Pavlovsk near Leningrad
bathed in summer and good shooting light
where it was taken that July as I'm
the one you're leaning forward to address.
I had a black pen poised about to write
and have one now and think back to that time
and feel you lean towards me out of Nothingness.

I rummage for the contacts you sent then:
the one of you that's leaning from *The Times*
and below it one of me with my black pen
listening to you criticize my rhymes,
and, between a millimetre of black band
that now could be ten billion times as much
and none that show the contact of your hand.
The distance needs adjusting; just a touch!

You were about to tap my knee for emphasis.

It's me who's leaning forward now with this!

11   Making Some Light:
An Interview with Michael
Mann
Graham Fuller

Introduction   Graham Fuller

Michael Mann occupies an unusual place in the pantheon of modern American film directors, one who owes his reputation partly to his cinematic approach to television. As a writer for *Starsky and Hutch* and *Police Story*, as creator of *Vegas*, executive producer of *Miami Vice, Crime Story* and the *Drug Wars* 1 and 2 mini-series, Mann is one of the pre-eminent TV auteurs of the last fifteen years – an impresario responsible for an intensely urban, male, 'designer' (or otherwise gritty) style that reached a zenith in the slick, rock-scored investigations of Messrs Crockett and Tubbs. Mann's peers, more so than other American film-makers, are former British commercials directors like Alan Parker, Ridley Scott and Adrian Lyne, who made it big in Hollywood in the 1980s, and whose surface aesthetic at that time was the conspicuous consumerism of the Reagan era. Both compositionally and thematically, though, Mann's work has always pushed at the parameters of the TV frame – thus *Miami Vice* became increasingly (and, to NBC, eventually unacceptably) dark by the end of its five-year run in 1989, and *Crime Story* (1986–8), shifting locale from Chicago to the Nevada desert and Latin America, increasingly surreal.

A Chicagoan (born 1943) who studied at the University of Wisconsin and the London International Film School in the mid-1960s, Mann segued into films via the Emmy and DGA award-winning TV movie *The Jerico Mile* (1979), making his feature debut with an abrasive crime drama, *Thief* (1981), its bravura, dialogue-less opening sequence – in which career-criminal James Caan casually eviscerates a corporate safe – anticipating *Miami Vice*. *The Keep* (1983), a neo-Gothic subversion of the Grail legend set in Nazi-occupied Romania in 1941, was a bold failure. But, if the relentless stylization – wide, expressionistic angles, music by Tangerine Dream – seemed anachronistic to that film, it perfectly suited Mann's next.

Manhunter (1986), based on Thomas Harris's novel *Red Dragon*, is the story of a disturbed FBI man, Will Graham (William Peterson), persuaded out of retirement to track down a serial killer of young families. Featuring the first chilling screen appearance of Hannibal Lecter (Brian Cox) and tightly scripted by Mann, *Manhunter* is a cool, dispassionate descent into madness – into a world of unsettlingly bright chemical colours (the azure ocean backdrop to Graham's and his wife's lovemaking) and spatially bizarre *mise-en-scènes* (the murderer's lair with its arty props and malfunctioning TV). Given its sci-fi veneer and Graham's scary decision to empathize with his quarry in order to catch him, it's a movie that edges into hyperspace – and as such it now looks like a small, but visionary, masterpiece.

With his latest film, *Last of the Mohicans*, Mann could be said to have entered virgin forest – the realm of the studio blockbuster, although, by current standards, this $35 million colonial epic from Twentieth Century-Fox is scarcely exorbitant. It stars Daniel Day Lewis as the rugged, principled frontiersman Hawkeye (alias Natty Bumpoo, here shortened to Poe), Madeleine Stowe as an English colonel's daughter, Cora Munro, and Jodhi May as her younger sister, Alice – genteel initiates to the harsh ways of the woodsman. The Lakota activist Russell Means plays Hawkeye's Mohican 'father' and friend, Chingachgook, Eric Schweig is the latter's son, Uncas, and Wes Studi their unrelenting Huron adversary, Magua.

James Fenimore Cooper's 1826 romance, the second and most famous of the five books in the *Leather-Stocking* cycle, is set in 1757, during the French and Indian War, when the Marquis de Montcalm and his Huron allies had laid siege to the British forces at Fort William Henry on the southern tip of Lake George in upstate New York. Mann's screenplay, modelled on that written by Philip Dunne for the 1936 film directed by George Seitz, has reworked Cooper's plot so that the famous interlude in the caves at Glenn's Falls follows, rather than precedes, the Huron atrocities at the fort, while hardening the conflict between the proto-rebel Hawkeye and the reactionary British Major Heyward (Steven Waddington), who vie for the affections of Cora. One of Mann's prime concerns has been to authenticate the period, offering a version of history that is more emotionally dynamic and realistic but no less thrilling than Cooper's tale. *Last of the Mohicans* was shot – by *Manhunter*'s cinematographer Dante Spinotti – in the dense forests and waterways of the Blue Ride mountains in North Carolina where, on a Sunday afternoon in September 1991, I talked to its writer–director–producer about his most ambitious project yet.

GRAHAM FULLER: *Did you have a struggle to get Twentieth Century-Fox to finance this picture?*
MICHAEL MANN: It was not a struggle at all. Joe Roth (Fox chairman) and Roger Birnbaum (president of worldwide production) got it right away.
GF: *Was that based on reading the screenplay?*

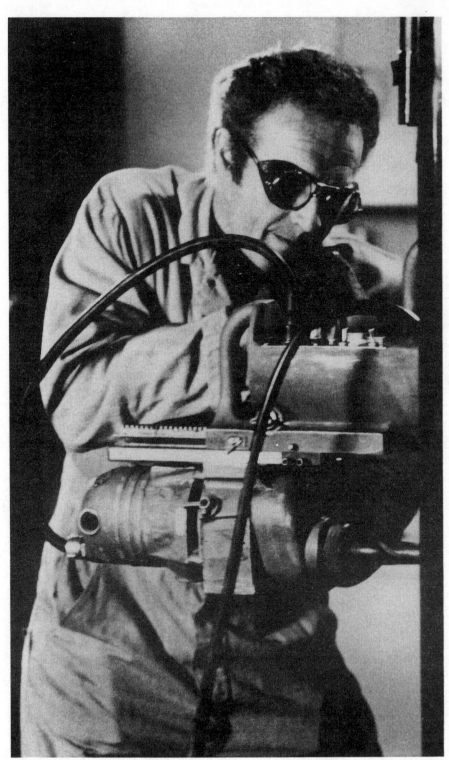

Thief: James Caan eviscerates a safe

Manhunter: William Peterson in a cool, dispassionate descent into madness

MM: No. Before it was a screenplay. I'd acquired the rights to Philip Dunne's 1936 screenplay myself, had done a story outline based on it, and walked into their offices and basically said, 'Guys, I want to do *Last of the Mohicans* and I want to do it in a vivid, realistic way.' They said, 'Yeah, great idea.'

GF: *Had you read James Fenimore Cooper's* Leather-Stocking Tales *when you were young?*

MM: Absolutely not! I probably read a classic comic-book version or something when I was young. But I've read a lot of history and this period has fascinated me for a long time. I saw the movie when I was a kid. It occurred to me recently that it may have been the first film I saw that made an impression on me. It was after the war, around 1948 or 1949, when I was four or five years old. There was a church in my neighbourhood, about a block away, and they used to show 16 mm films in the basement – and they showed the 1936 version with Randolph Scott as Hawkeye. I remember the corollary tragedy of Uncas and Alice at the end, plus the fearsomeness of Magua, and the uniqueness of the period.

I couldn't identify what was so fascinating then, but I can now – it's the combination of three discrete and very exciting cultures in the same motion picture, which happens to be a very tightly plotted war movie. One is the extremely formal culture of a reactionary European ruling class. Secondly, even Magua in the 1936 movie was an expression of a fascinating Native American, northeastern woodlands culture of Hurons and Mohawks, men with their heads shaved and with tattoos. Thirdly, the familiar image of the frontiersmen – Hawkeye, incidentally, is the progenitor of all the American Western heroes in a direct evolutionary line from *Last of the Mohicans* through *Stagecoach* to *My Darling Clementine*.

Then there's Hawkeye the character: what made him, where he came from, what kind of a man he was, what he would have thought and felt, what his rhythms would have been, being able to move through and survive in wilderness forest, how sophisticated or unsophisticated, how 'urban' his attitudes may have been, given the volatile times and incendiary ideas 'blowing in the wind'. How close was his culture on the frontier to, say, the new ideas being preached from Albany, New York, or Boston pulpits. In researching the period, I found that events in 1757 moved as fast as in 1968. And suddenly this period became as alive to me as, say, seven or eight years ago.

Ultimately, for me, it's about trying to make Hawkeye as real as if I was writing and directing a picture about a man who is alive today. The big encounter in the movie is between Hawkeye and Cora Munro, effectively a meeting of people from two different planets. It's a collision between the child of Scottish-Irish immigrants – people who were probably impoverished tenant farmers from the borderlands in the north of England – and a woman who thinks she's going to New England – almost an extension of Grosvenor

Square – only to discover that this is a vast new continent, and that attitudinal changes and ideas are sweeping across it. But the characters do not come from an upper-middle-class intelligentsia. Hawkeye comes from a grass-roots level, from Iroquois culture – as if it produced its own John Locke 200 years ago but nobody knows about it yet – and from the experiences of poor people on the frontier. It's like hearing the new music before anybody else – the man who sings the songs is Hawkeye, and the woman who hears them is Cora. Suddenly she's no longer in narrow New England, she's in a whole new world. The big challenge for me was to work that Cora–Hawkeye story into a tapestry of a full-blown war with three other conflicts going on at the same time. As it becomes a romance I hope that the audience will track with the romance and want to see it survive. This woman goes through a great change and so does Hawkeye, but for him it's a transformation from being a Mohican to becoming a frontiersman – a synthesis of the European and native cultures – which is a transformation from son to man. Chingachgook realizes this before Hawkeye does and talks to him about it at the end of the film.

GF: *Was there a point when you were writing the screenplay where you abandoned Cooper's novel?*

MM: Yes, very early on, though not at a specific point but in specific areas. For example, I based [Major] Heyward on Cooper himself, not on Cooper's character. Cooper believed in static hierarchies, a kind of political harmony of the spheres: if people and classes stay in place, there's a harmony; if they don't, there are problems. In Cooper, Hawkeye is constantly apologizing or reassuring total strangers that he's not of mixed blood!: 'Hi, I'm Hawkeye, how are you? I'm not of mixed blood.' So the whole notion of races crossing, of miscegenation, of people moving into different classes, was anathema to Cooper. I decided to take all these characteristics and stick them into Heyward. If you read the novel very carefully, the daughter, Cora, who falls in love with Uncas and dies, is a mulatto. Her father, Colonel Munro, wanted Heyward to marry Cora but Heyward preferred Alice; Munro was initially insulted and went into a two-page diatribe about the fact that her mother was an aristocratic woman. I switched it around so that it's Cora and Hawkeye who fall in love.

GF: *You've also eliminated some of the more fantastical elements from the book – the character of the psalm singer, Hawkeye dressing up as a bear, that kind of thing.*

MM: The silly stuff. In fact, the structure of the story for this film is based 50 per cent on Philip Dunne's screenplay.

GF: *Why did you use that as a source?*

MM: Because it's a terrific piece of writing. Dunne did a very interesting thing. He was writing at a time of tremendous political struggle in the United States, a country caught in a depression and at the same time seeing events in Asia and Europe. The view here was isolationist, although some people with political agendas and attitudes saw the need to take part in international struggles against the rising tide of fascism. Also, there was a heavy dose of anti-British sentiment among the isolationists, led by the *Chicago Tribune*. Dunne essentially gave Hawkeye the political attitudes of the isolationists: independent, anti-authoritarian . . . anti-British. But then at the end of the movie, in 1936, both men – Hawkeye the proto-American individualist, and Heyward – both in love with Cora, march off to war together to face a greater common enemy.

GF: *Are you trying to make any contemporary political statements yourself?*

MM: No. The project's attraction lies in making a passionate and vivid love story in a war zone. To make that period feel real means making dramatic forces out of the political forces of the time, which also fascinated me. The politics are functional to the story-telling, as is visual style. I didn't want to take 1757, this story, and turn it into some kind of two-dimensional metaphor of 1991. What I did want to do was to go the other way and take our understanding of those cultures – and I think we understand them better today than Cooper did in 1826 – and use our contemporary perspective as a tool to construct a more intense experience of realistically complex people in a complex time.

GF: *Do you perceive Hawkeye as a force of nature?*

MM: He exists within nature's systems the same way any skilled Sauk, Ottawa, Mohawk or frontiersman would at that time. First of all, he can survive just like Daniel Boone did. Daniel Boone could take a 'possibles' bag, his long rifle, lead, flint, steel and tow, and a blanket and go and survive in the wilderness forest for two years. Hawkeye could do the same thing. So could most Native Americans then. So I don't see him as a force of nature – any more than anyone who is streetwise is a force of the streets. I see him as someone who doesn't view nature as an adversary, as a European might. He understands nature's systems and flows within them like a man absolutely contemporaneous to his time. That means he knows how to read the granulation of earth inside a deer's hoof-print and can tell how long ago the deer used that path because he knows how much dew there was yesterday morning. He's probably involved with the fur trade, he's living among native peoples, some of whom had successful relations with Europeans for 150 years, who were thought of by most European powers as a nation unto their own, not as a minority, as we see Indians today. The Six Nations of the Iroquois, and specifically the Mohawks, probably controlled 65 per cent of the world's fur trade in 1757 as trappers and middlemen, and they knew what they were doing.

GF: *What I am getting at is do you see Hawkeye as a pantheistic creature, the 'green man' of mythology? Is he part of the mythos of the woodsman, like Robin Hood?*

MM: It would be nice to say yes, but it's not true. He is, to my mind, something much more earthy than that. It takes a little getting used to, but I'm trying to bring out that aspect of colonial–Indian relations in images, in how the people and backgrounds mix. I started with the idea that on the frontier, for long periods of time, people peacefully coexisted and were interdependent. Coexistence became impossible only when avarice for fur and real estate was fuelled by the periodic tidal wave of European immigration. In almost all cases, the initial contact between European settlers and Indians was peaceful, and characterized by Indian generosity in sharing agricultural techniques and food. The place was abundant.

GF: *Are you showing that?*

MM: I'm showing the coexistence. In one of the early scenes there's a militia recruitment meeting on a farm in the Mohawk Valley and the community is a mixture of colonials and Mohawks, old men, men with children, women. Implicit is the fact that they know each other, they're equally well dressed and armed, their food and games are cross-cultural, and they seem relatively affluent.

GF: *This is obviously a very different kind of film for you. Apart from* The Keep, *which is set in the Second World War, you've made a crime melodrama,* Thief, *a highly stylized serial-killer thriller,* Manhunter, *and been responsible for an entire sub-genre of intensely modern, drug-related TV police dramas. Has* Last of the Mohicans *required you to make a major adjustment in terms of your aesthetic as a film-maker?*

MM: No. It's just an accident that most of the other films I've done have been in that genre.

GF: *What about the way you're shooting* Last of the Mohicans?

MM: It's pretty much dictated by the content of the story and it's exciting to me to do something different. If I'd tried to shoot this film the way I shot *Manhunter*, I don't think I'd have done a very good job. I don't think I could anyway; I'd be bored and it certainly wouldn't serve *Last of the Mohicans*.

GF: *How did you design the look of the film?*

MM: I started with nineteenth-century landscape painters – I looked at Thomas Cole, Albert Bierstadt, chiaroscuro lighting, and a lot of eighteenth-century portraits.

GF: *Did you look at N. C. Wyeth's paintings for the Scribner's Classics edition of* Last of the Mohicans?

MM: Yes, but Wyeth was a twentieth-century illustrator – I wanted to see how artists saw the environment that we were actually going to shoot in, because it didn't exist any more and didn't by the time Wyeth was working. It's been said that they didn't need roads in parts of Pennsylvania because the trees were so huge and the canopies so dense, which is characteristic of ancient forests, that the floors were clear of brush. It was dark underneath, but you could drive a coach straight through. And we've found that here on location.

GF: *Did you storyboard the film at all?*

MM: Just for a couple of sequences involving the opening and the Glenn's Falls cave, where there were a lot of complex elements. But I did a lot of very detailed work in plan, not storyboards. It's been mandatory on this picture. Nothing that had to be supplied for a scene could be rented or bought. We've made it all – from designing and manufacturing the breechcloths of six different Indian peoples to building French and English ordnance. The Hurons had had a lot of trade with the French and they were influenced by eighteenth-century French fabric design. The Abenakis were converted to Catholicism by the Jesuits, so there's Christian imagery blended with Abenaki in their tattooing and ritual mutilation. Again, we picked up stuff from paintings and made projections. The logistics of where things would happen in the fort, on the battlefield, were also interesting. I tend to design stuff like that with a floor plan, not storyboards. Usually I've designed how I'm going to shoot something, how I'm going to block it, based on how it looked the last time I was there. But when you're out in nature it only looks that way for about five minutes – you go back and a cloud came in, the sun's not there, and it's pissing with rain. What was suddenly staggeringly beautiful is *nothing*, so after a while you think – get me on to a city street under a sodium vapour lamp!

GF: *I noticed in the screenplay that you've written the fight sequences with great intricacy. How do you replicate those movements blow by blow – have you got an army of fight choreographers on stand-by?*

MM: Not really. We did a lot of research and there's been a big training programme on this film. Daniel Day Lewis and some of the others trained down in Alabama with David Webster. Daniel is very impressive. Starting with contemporary weapons and working his way back to black powder, he became a staggering shot. After a day and a half, he was knocking everything down with a .45. There are a lot of aspects to that training that are designed to give him the skills he needs to *feel* like Hawkeye – as well being able to perform them. But the real value transcends anything physical and really feeds back into something attitudinal.

GF: *A lot of that will have come out unconsciously in the acting.*

MM: Yeah – in carriage and body language. In terms of fighting with knives and tomahawks, we don't know how people fought. But we know that everybody below commissioned officers abandoned swords altogether and fought with tomahawks. If two groups were facing each other, once they'd fired off a couple of musket volleys, they'd have to engage in hand-to-hand combat, which is butchery with edged weapons. We figured out that a tomahawk is like a section of a sabre with an added mass at the back end pushing the cutting edge, and unlike a sabre, it's not going to get caught up in trees in the forest. So we used eighteenth-century fighting manuals to train everybody and a small inventory of parries and blows.

GF: *I think people naturally assume that because the Indians look so ferocious, and because of the way the Hurons are depicted massacring the women and children outside Fort William Henry in the novel, they were savages.*

MM: Well, the massacre was a savage event, but it was promoted by the French, or at least they were complicit in it. And the times were savage, certainly in terms of what happened and happens to native peoples who get colonized. That's not to excuse it, it's to know it for what it was. But there was nothing savage or culturally primitive about the northeast woodlands Indians. You can talk about the development of the European political system, yet the Iroquoian confederacy existed 200 years before 1757, as a bi-cameral parliamentary kind of democracy. Their social attitudes and value system were democratic and, on issues like child raising and divorce, strikingly modern. The Mohawks had positioned themselves commerically as almost a merchant-class between the English fur traders and the tribes further west, as well as being hunters and trappers of fur themselves. They had a corn agriculture and lived in cabins before the Europeans got here. So I don't think there was anything primitive or savage about them. One of the hardest things for this movie to communicate is how cultures, mores and values are relative to each other. For instance, it would not have been considered cruel or unjust to torture to death someone who had been captured. Conveying that cultural relativity and placing us ethno-centrically inside an Indian culture, through Hawkeye, is one of the hardest challenges of this picutre for me. Maybe it's a subtlety, but it's shot from *inside* Mohican culture, and that affects how Hawkeye comes on to Cora and certain pragmatic decisions he makes that necessarily cause him to abandon her, even though it is heart-breaking for him.

GF: *Ford's* Drums along the Mohawk *was set in the Revolutionary War, Vidor did the Rogers Rangers' film* Northwest Passage, *and Bruce Beresford's new film,* Black Robe, *is set in the 1630s. But, apart from the three earlier versions of* Last of the Mohicans, *there have really been very few films based on the Anglo-French war in the colonies and the Indian allegiances.*

MM: And really it was the first world war, because the English and French were fighting in Europe, in India and in North America. But there's been a lot of interest in the last year. *Granta* did a 'History' issue which contained a piece by Simon Scharma about the death of General Wolfe, who defeated Montcalm at Quebec.

GF: *Reading your screenplay, I wondered if you'd sold Montcalm down the river. You have him and Magua effectively plotting the Fort Henry massacre.*

MM: I don't have time in the screenplay to lay out why he did what he did, but his aide-de-camp Bougainville kept a diary, which gives a brilliant day-by-day account of what happened. Montcalm's plan was to hit Fort William Henry about six weeks earlier than he did, take it, then Fort Edward on the Hudson, and advance down to Albany. What happened was that there was so much black marketeering going on among the French in Quebec that the supplies were constantly disappearing and the treasuries were being stolen – just the usual human shit! It delayed him for about six weeks and that cost him that year and eventually the war, because by the time he destroyed Fort William Henry all his Indian allies had to canoe back to where they came from before the Great Lakes froze over. So, the taking of Fort William Henry was a Pyrrhic victory, and I think the reason he offered the English very favourable terms of surrender was to accelerate his calendar, but it wasn't enough.

GF: *Is your film concerned at all with the passing of the Indian cultures?*

MM: Yes. It comes up from two older men at the end of the film. The Sachem (the Huron ancient) says, 'More white men come with the dawning of each day. And night enters our future with them . . . I have been to Versailles. I have seen his cities. His numbers are endless. Our council has asked the question since I was a boy: what is the Huron to do?' Most of the Indians had no idea how many Europeans there were. Because there were 25,000 Mohawk, they assumed that maybe England had a population of 25,000 – they couldn't conceive of the numbers of peoples. Some, like the Sachem, had been there and had come back, and he understood that European immigration and power were destructive forces and that they were coming their way. And he has no answer to the problem of what is to be done. He poses a question. Chingachgook answers it in the last scene in the movie when he says to Hawkeye, 'The frontier moves with the sun and pushes the red man of these wilderness forests with it. Until one day there will be nowhere left . . . there will be no more frontier. Then our race will be no more or be not us. The frontier is for my white son and his woman. And one day there will be no more frontier, then men like you will go, too, and new people will come to work and struggle and some will make their light . . .' That's the way it goes. Parents give to children, children to their children. It's a one-way street. The only enduring value is making some 'light'. He is recognizing the forces of human history, sometimes tragic, sometimes impressive.

Michael Mann on location for *Last of the Mohicans*

Daniel Day Lewis as Hawkeye – the synthesis of European and native cultures

The Community: coexistence and interdependence

Cora (Madeleine Stowe) – about to enter a new world

The escape

Love in a war zone

The 'first world war'

Filmography

1 Bright Dreams, Hard Knocks

JOHN BOORMAN is the director of, among others, *Point Blank, Excalibur* and *Hope and Glory*.

2 The Burning Question: Absolute Freedom?

ARTHUR PENN is the director of, among others, *Bonnie and Clyde, Night Moves* and *Sly Fox*.

SAMUEL FULLER is the director of, among others, *Pickup on South Street, The Big Red One* and *White Dog*.

JANE CAMPION is the director of, among others, *Two Friends, Sweetie* and *An Angel at My Table*.

COSTA-GAVRAS is the director of, among others, *Z, Missing* and *Music Box*.

KZYSZTOF KIEŚLOWSKI is the director of, among others, *Camera Buff, Decalogue* and *The Double Life of Veronique*.

CLAUDE MILLER is the director of, among others, *The Best Way to Walk, Deadly Pursuit* and *La Petite Voleuse*.

FRANCESCO ROSI is the director of, among others, *Salvatore Giuliano, Three Brothers* and *To Forget Palermo*.

KEVIN REYNOLDS is the director of, among others, *Fandango, Beast of War* and *Robin Hood, Prince of Thieves*.

DENYS ARCAND is the director of, among others, *La Maudite Galette, The Decline of the American Empire* and *Jesus of Montreal*.

ISTVAN SZABO is the director of, among others, *Mephisto, Colonel Redl* and *Meeting Venus*.

KEN RUSSELL is the director of, among others, *Women in Love, Crimes of Passion* and *Whore*.

SYDNEY POLLACK is the director of, among others, *They Shoot Horses Don't They? Out of Africa* and *Havana*.

MIKE FIGGIS is the director of, among others, *Stormy Monday, Internal Affairs* and *Liebestraum*.

LOUIS MALLE is the director of, among others, *Le Voleur, Atlantic City* and *Au revoir les enfants*.

ETTORE SCOLA is the director of, among others, *A Special Day, Nights at Varenne* and *The Family*.

VINCENT WARD is the director of, among others, *Vigil, The Navigator* and *Map of the Human Heart*.

PAUL VERHOEVEN is the director of, among others, *The Fourth Man, Robocop* and *Basic Instinct*.

MICHAEL VERHOEVEN is the director of, among others, *White Rose* and *The Nasty Girl*.

DAVID BYRNE is the director of, among others, *True Stories* and *Ilé Aiyé* (The House of Life), as well as videos for the band Talking Heads.

ZHANG YIMOU was the director of photography of *Yellow Earth*, and is the director of *Red Sorghum*, *Ju Dou* and *Raise the Red Lantern*.

GUS VAN SANT is the director of, among others, *Mala Noche, Drugstore Cowboy* and *My Own Private Idaho*.

RICHARD LOWENSTEIN is the director of, among others, *Strikebound, Dogs in Space* and *Say a Little Prayer*.

PAOLO and VITTORIO TAVIANI are the directors of, among others, *Padre, Padrone, The Night of San Lorenzo*, and *Night Sun*.

TERRY GILLIAM is the director of, among others, *Time Bandits, Brazil* and *The Fisher King*.

3 Film Fiction: More Factual than Facts

SAMUEL FULLER is the director of, among others, *Pickup on South Street, The Big Red One* and *White Dog*.

4 The Early Life of a Screenwriter

EMERIC PRESSBURGER, together with Michael Powell, wrote, directed and produced *A Canterbury Tale, A Matter of Life and Death* and *The Red Shoes*.

KEVIN MACDONALD is the writer of the short film *Dr Reitzer's Fragment*, directed by his brother Andrew Macdonald.

5 Demme on Demme

DAVID THOMPSON has programmed films at London's Electric Cinema and for BBC Television, and recently produced documentaries on Roberto Rossellini and Peter Greenaway. He was co-editor of *Scorsese on Scorsese*.

SASKIA BARON was the film editor on *City Limits* magazine and TV editor on the *Independent*. At the BBC she worked on *The Late Show*, producing documentaries on Jonathan Demme and The Holocaust in the Cinema.

6 Matters of Photogenics

NESTOR ALMENDROS was the director of photography of, among others, *Claire's Knee, Days of Heaven* and *Billy Bathgate*. He is also the director of *Bad Conduct*.

7 My Director and I

RIVER PHOENIX has appeared in, among others, *Running on Empty, A Night in the Life of Jimmy Reardon* and *Dogfight*.

GUS VAN SANT is the director of, among others, *Mala Noche, Drugstore Cowboy* and *My Own Private Idaho*.

9 Surviving Desire

HAL HARTLEY is the director of, among others, *The Unbelievable Truth, Trust* and *Simple Men*.

10   Losing Touch

TONY HARRISON is one of Britain's most distinguished poets. He is the author of
'V', and the Gulf War poem 'A Cold Coming'. His theatre work includes *Phaedra
Britannica*, *The Mysteries* and *The Trackers of Oxyrhynchus*.

11   Making Some Light

MICHAEL MANN is the director of, among others, *Thief*, *The Keep* and *Manhunter*.
He was the creator of the television series *Miami Vice* and *Crime Story*.

GRAHAM FULLER is the executive editor of *Interview* magazine. He is also the editor
of the forthcoming *Potter on Potter*.